UNBLIND

FAITH

Unblind Faith

A New Approach for the
twenty-first Century

By

Michael J. Langford

PARAPRESS

Also by Michael J. Langford:
A Liberal Theology for the Twenty-First Century,
Ashgate, Aldershot, 2001
The de Vere Papers [novel], Parapress, 2008

©Michael J. Langford 2010
ISBN 978-1-898594-87-1

First published by SCM Press Ltd, London, 1982

Second revised edition published in the UK, 2010;
2nd printing in larger format with minor corrections, 2011, by
PARAPRESS
The Basement
9 Frant Road
Tunbridge Wells
Kent TN2 5SD UK

British Library Cataloguing in Publication Data
A catalogue record of this book is available from the British Library.

Cover design by Mousemat Design Limited
www.mousematdesign.com

Typeset in Garamond by Helm Information
www.helm-information.co.uk

Print management by Sutherland Eve Production
guyeve@theeves.fsnet.co.uk

Printed and bound in Great Britain by
Berforts Group Ltd, Stevenage, SG1 2BH
www.berforts.co.uk

Contents

Part Two: Problems for the Christian Faith

The common elements in religious experience
The negative arguments for faith
The witness of personal experience

Theory and practice
Prayer and magic
Three stages of growth
Can prayer make a difference?
Prayer and petitionary prayer
Work and prayer
Two senses of vocation
A range of acceptable lifestyles
The challenge and excitement of a Christian life

Preface

There is a continuing need for an introduction to the Christian faith that pays serious attention to its intellectual content without becoming too technical. This applies equally to serious inquirers, to adults or those in their late teens who are preparing for church membership or confirmation, and to those who want some kind of 'refresher course' that appeals to the head as well as to the heart. Jesus, we may recall, said that we must love with the mind, as well as with heart and soul and strength. Therefore, although there can be no question of proving the truth of Christianity by purely rational methods, the faith can be, and should be, presented in a way that is attractive to the thinking person. This book attempts to provide an aid to those who are seeking a thoughtful presentation of the Christian faith.

Although based on a series of talks given in an Anglican church, there is nothing here that is specifically Anglican except, perhaps, for some of the emphases. Therefore it might be helpful for a more general audience. There are some passages that may cause disagreement (especially concerning the nature of the church, the authority of the Bible and the way in which the doctrine of the atonement – or redemption – is explained), but these may be used as opportunities for discussion, even when there are objections to my point of view. I also hope that this book will be read by non-Christians (both members of other faiths and those with no faith) who want an introduction to Christianity with a rational emphasis. For such readers I would point out that, except for Chapter 14, the main purpose of this book is not that of showing that the Christian faith is true, but that of showing what it is.

This book first appeared in 1982 and, in this revised edition, a number of corrections and additions have been made. Also, the opening paragraphs of Chapter 1 and parts of Chapters 3, 12 and 13 have been substantially rewritten. Finally, inclusive language has now been used throughout the text.

Although this book is aimed at a general audience, every now and then an issue cries out for some comments of a more scholarly kind – for example about the meaning of 'original sin' – and for the most part these have been placed in the notes and references.

This second printing of the second edition incorporates a few minor corrections and the rewriting of two sentences:

1. On p. 38, note 9, second paragraph, instead of 'Here the Church of England recommended ...' I have put 'Several members of the Commission recommended ...' which is more accurate; and

2. On p. 172 in the middle of the page, the passage in parentheses now runs "although we may worry about hunting when it is for pleasure rather than for need". This avoids a double negative.

Part One: The Essentials of the Christian Faith

1. Faith and Reason

Christianity and the religions of the world

Why should a reflective person be a Christian rather than, say, a Buddhist or a Muslim or, indeed, a secular humanist who follows an ethical path but not a religious one? Before I present a case for Christianity it is important to stress that the position I am going to recommend does not depend on seeing all the other great religions of the world as wrong or useless, nor on seeing all secular humanists as simply misguided. On the contrary, while in the past it was common to find followers of one religion condemning all the other religions, many of us now live in a more tolerant world in which, even though we may have our own preferred way of life, we see value in other ways. In brief, while I shall claim that Christianity has something of extraordinary value to offer both other faiths and the secular humanist, this need not involve a denial of the riches that these other traditions contain.

The change in attitude can be illustrated by comparing two very different kinds of missionary. One kind is exemplified by the person who goes to a foreign land in order to convert its people to a new religion, without taking the trouble to study and understand the religion or religions that are already there. Another kind is exemplified by the Jesuit, Matteo Ricci (1552–1610), the missionary to China who spent much of his time studying the Chinese classics and becoming an acknowledged scholar, especially of the Confucian tradition. He concluded that while Christianity had something precious to offer to the Chinese, this did not mean a denial of the many spiritual insights that were already there. On the contrary, it was more a matter of

Christianity fulfilling and enriching those spiritual insights than of denigrating them. His open approach resulted in friendships with a number of highly educated Chinese of his time, some of whom became Christians. After his death, more conservative Jesuit leaders insisted on making a sharp contrast between what they saw as the truth of Christianity and the falsehood of all other faiths. Much disappointed, many of Ricci's converts went back to Confucianism, and the influence of Christianity diminished. This incident provides a powerful comment on the difference between an open, or 'liberal' kind of Christianity, and more conservative forms.[1]

The actual history of Ricci is more complicated than this brief account suggests,[2] and between the open missionary that Ricci represents and what might be termed 'conservative' approaches, there are, in fact, many intermediate positions. Nevertheless, it is not always appreciated that Ricci was following an ancient tradition in which many missionaries (including St Patrick) have sought to build links between the spirituality that was already present within a culture and the special insights that come with Christianity. In this book I shall try to present an open kind of Christianity that has something in common with the approach taken by Ricci, and in Chapter 13 I shall return to the relationship of the Christian faith to some of the other great religions of the world.

Blind faith

The truth is often discovered to be a middle ground between two extremes, both of which are false and dangerous. One must not make a dogma out of this, as if the truth were necessarily the middle position, for sometimes what may look like an extreme position may turn out to be true. However, there is much to be said for an initial sympathy with the middle way and with this as a starting point I shall argue that Christian faith should be seen as a kind of middle way between 'blind faith' on the one hand and a 'purely rational faith' on the other.

Let us look first at blind faith. By this I mean an absolute, unconditional, and unexamined trust in some person who is believed to represent God, or in some body of teaching about God. Usually this blind faith goes hand in hand with absolute obedience to what is believed to be the will of God, as interpreted by a book or a by a human authority. This is to describe blind faith in its religious form, but it has also a secular counterpart such as absolute, unconditional and unexamined trust in a political party, or a leader, or a set of duties set down by custom or by the state.

It needs little reflection to show that this kind of unconditional trust is a mistake and, indeed, part of the very nature of blind faith consists precisely in its denial of the right to start such reflection, for the very idea of reflection on a belief or practice suggests that some kind of justification should be sought for it.

One way of indicating the mistaken nature of blind faith is to look at some of its results. We may recall the fanatical followers of the religious leader, Jim Jones, who, in 1978, not only took cyanide themselves but fed it to their children at Jonestown in Guyana; or the fanatical mobs which shout for a religious leader, and which seem to be incapable of rational reflection; or the brainwashing of new converts in some of the fringe sects; and so on. Unfortunately the history of Christianity and many other religions is sprinkled with the dire consequences of blind faith and it is the horror of this spectacle that helps in large measure to explain the rejection of all religion by many thoughtful people. While I believe that this total rejection is a mistake, it is understandable, for when religion is judged by such examples, the genuinely good person is under a moral obligation to reject it.

A second and deeper ground for rejecting blind faith comes from further reflection on the question posed at the very beginning of this book. Here I am, let us say, an adult Christian. What would I be if I had been brought up as a Buddhist in Burma, or as an atheistic Marxist in Stalinist Russia? I would probably be a Buddhist or Marxist. Does this prove that people simply believe what they have been told and that reason has nothing to do with belief? No, this is too severe, because some people do abandon or change their childhood beliefs and so others must be capable of acts of reflection that have led them to confirm their early beliefs, though usually with certain modifications. But the very existence of the great variety of possible beliefs must force us to ask ourselves: "Why this faith rather than that one?" If blind faith were acceptable, then it would be proper for one person to have blind faith in Christianity and another in Marxism and so on. But such a suggestion is absurd, for even if it is the case that the great religions have a common core, there are many issues about which people disagree profoundly and not everyone can be right. There is only one rational response to this situation and that is that blind faith is never justified.

Reflection such as the above leads me to suspect that blind faith is not only a mistake, but it is essentially dangerous and potentially evil. If one happens to be following a good master with a blind faith, this is only by chance and there is a despotic element in the relationship which the good master does not want and that prevents personal growth. Much more likely is blind faith in a master who likes this kind of devotion and then both the relationships and the actual commands will probably end up as evil.

At this point, the reader who is sensitive to the Christian tradition might well say: "Hold it. Surely there is something noble and beautiful about absolute and unconditional faith, despite these negative examples. What about Jesus's call to single-mindedness,[3] and what about that total faith that sustains religious people when they are faced with persecution, or apparently impossible burdens, or death?" But a crucial distinction must be made here. Absolute faith that something is true, or that someone is to be obeyed, is one thing. This is the blind faith that asks for no reason, but which simply sees the faith as its own justification. Quite another thing is a faith that has been grounded in something other than faith itself, in other words a faith that one has some kind of reason for holding and which one then holds to in the face of enormous pressure.

The misunderstanding here arises because the idea of 'unconditional' faith is ambiguous. When the unconditional element refers to the acceptance of something as true or someone as an absolute leader, then there is a dangerous irrationality. When the unconditional element refers to the way in which people 'stick to their guns' in a time of trial, this is not a case of irrationality but of courage. In the former case, one is resisting the onslaught of reason, in the latter, the onslaught of weariness or pain or temptation. The former is blind faith, the latter is heroic faith.

A purely rational faith?

Let us look next at the religious position which is at the opposite extreme to blind faith, that of a purely rational faith. What I mean by this is the view that faith is fundamentally a rational matter and that the essentials of the faith can either be proved by a rational process, or at the very least rendered as highly probable as some of our scientific beliefs. Few contemporary Christians take such an extreme position, but some have views that tend in this direction.

What should be said about this rational approach to faith? The first point to make is that, according to Jesus, a living faith has to involve the heart and soul and strength, as well as the mind (Mark 12, 30). Therefore, it cannot be a *purely* rational matter. With regards to the claim that the fundamentals of the faith can be proved, my criticisms are less severe than in the case of blind faith for I hold that there are rational grounds of a kind for Christianity, and that no doctrine should be believed without some rational support. We might recall here the advice given in the first epistle of Peter: "Always be prepared to make a defence to any one who calls you to account for the hope that is in you ..."[4] Some translations speak of giving a 'reason' for the hope that is in you. However, the claim that we can *prove* the essentials of the faith in any ordinary sense of the word, for example, in the way in which scientists seek to prove things, is a mistake.

The principal argument against seeking a strict proof in matters of faith will become clearer in the next chapter when we discuss the meaning of the word 'God'. The essential point is this. If God is the reality of the kind claimed in the Christian tradition (and also in the Jewish, Islamic and some other traditions), then he cannot be comprehended within any system of knowledge. In additional to this philosophical point about systems of thought being unable fully to comprehend the very source of all things, including thought, there is an argument from experience. God is the name given to the one whose presence evokes awe and amazement and either silence or the sort of utterance that we find on the tongue of Isaiah or Job.[5] In all ages men and woman have had these overpowering experiences that have led them to believe they were in the presence of God. In sum, for at least two reasons the search for a rational *proof* of divine reality is misguided.

Another way of putting the same point goes as follows. Reason itself can see its own limitations and that when we use the word 'proof' we use it in a particular context. Within natural science we may properly say that we have proved some things when we have carried out certain procedures, although not with the kind of certainty that applies to mathematical proofs. For example, as a result of systematic tests and observations we can say that we have *proved* that water contains hydrogen and oxygen. But in this kind of procedure we are always explaining one part of the universe by its relation to other parts. However, when we try to explain the universe *as a whole,* or when, even more puzzlingly, we talk about a Being who is not part of the universe at all, then the procedures that are appropriate to natural science are inappropriate. It does not follow in the least that questions about God are absurd or irrational, but it does follow that they are not scientific questions, and that the very notion of proof as we normally use it (in science or mathematics or law) is inapplicable.

Unblind faith

So far I have argued against two extreme positions: blind faith, which I hold to be irrational, dangerous and even demonic; and a purely rational faith, which I hold to be impossible given the kind of reality that Christians claim God to be. I want next to explain further what I mean by the middle way, the way that I propose to call 'unblind faith', and to argue that it constitutes the only acceptable approach to belief for the thoughtful Christian.

In the first place, we must remember that we are thinking about faith, not simply belief, and a realization of what this involves can help to reinforce the understanding that a purely rational faith is not only a mistake, but an impossibility. Whereas many of our beliefs do not affect us in our way of life (for example, most of our beliefs about the past, or about scientific claims which we think to be true but which we have not yet been able to prove), *faith* – at least when it is taken seriously – always affects our way of life. With faith, in addition to belief that something is the case, there is a commitment that some people describe as an *existential* commitment because of how it changes the very way in which we exist as persons. For example, loyal workers for a political party do not only believe that their party's programme is true in some abstract way, they have faith in it. Similarly, people do not only believe in the virtues of their close friends, they trust them; similarly too, Christians not only believe that God is a reality, they have faith in him. The point is sometimes expressed in this way: Christians do not only believe *that* God is real, they believe *in* God, for faith is a belief *in* something or someone. It follows again that this cannot be a purely rational matter because not only the mind but also the heart and will are involved, and the heart and will lead people to adopt certain attitudes and certain practices that can radically change how we live.

The foregoing argument can be put in another way. When people are first introduced to a religion there is often a tendency to begin with the particular *beliefs* that are typically found within that religion. However, it would often be more informative to begin with the *practices*, or ways of life, that are typically found in followers of a religion, or of what in the eastern religions is often called a 'Way', or *Dao*. Some writers have expressed this point so powerfully that 'beliefs' are rendered almost unimportant, which I hold to be a mistake – but I do accept that practices have a certain priority, especially when children are being introduced to a faith. When, in much of this book, I seek to explain and defend basic Christian *beliefs*, this important point should be born in mind. Christianity, at its heart, is a way of life in which people try to become disciples of Jesus of Nazareth; followers of the way in which he lived. This does not render beliefs unimportant, but they are secondary.

It is for this reason that I have sympathy with Terry Eagleton's objection to much contemporary atheism on the grounds that it wrongly sees Christianity as an attempt "to explain the world" (which is the job of the scientist) rather than as an attempt to confront the world and to live in it effectively. He likens this mistaken understanding of Christianity to someone who looked at ballet as "a botched attempt to run for a bus",[6] in other words, with a basic failure to see what it is about. Similarly, in Buddhism, the first 'noble truth' is not concerned with explaining suffering, but is simply the recognition that there *is* suffering – and then follows a series of suggestions as to how to deal with it. It does not follow that Christians should not try to develop a philosophy in which there is a measure of understanding, but this does not mean a *scientific* knowledge of the world, otherwise we confuse the genuine difference between science and religion.

Notwithstanding this emphasis on practice, when we come to *beliefs*, since we are considering an unblind faith, there must be grounds for them of a kind that appeal to our reason. These grounds cannot amount to proof, for the reasons that I have given, and they must be appropriate to the kind of reality with which we are concerned, namely God. What these grounds are will become clearer as this book proceeds, but we have a clue in the words of St Paul when he describes how one day we shall *know*, but for now we must be content with puzzling reflections in a mirror, or in the language of the King James Bible, "now we see in a glass darkly; but then face to face".[7] That is to say, we must build as best we can on the intimations and glimpses of a higher reality that we are able to have.

Faith and doubt

There are many who search for a faith, but who experience grave doubts not only about secondary matters but about the very existence of God. The question then arises, can one have faith in God while experiencing such doubts? Christians have answered this question in different ways, but my own convictions are as follows. In the short run the answer is certainly yes. We are never asked to smother our intellectual curiosity and therefore, almost inevitably, Christians will have periods of doubt or uncertainty, but if they continue to try to lead the Christian life and generally to live through this period *as if* they were convinced of the reality of God, then this is a continuation of the life of faith. This involves no dishonesty, unless one claims a certainty that one does not possess. Once again, an example from a non-religious faith can illuminate the matter. If I promise to follow the leader of an expedition into the unknown and to trust this person when there is a crisis, I am not promising never to have doubts, I am promising to follow in spite of any doubts that may arise along the way. Similarly, thoughtful Christians know that they are likely to have periods of doubt in which acts of will and determination will have to carry them through.

But what if the doubts persist for weeks or months; can there still be a viable Christian faith? There can be no simple answer here, for each person's story is different. Undoubtedly, there can come a point where honesty should compel the searcher to say: "I am no longer a Christian, I am an agnostic," but there are many kinds of persistent doubt where this step is not called for. By way of example, let us consider the case of a group of Christian friends who have long periods of doubt about the reality of God, but who remain convinced that there is a real possibility that God exists, so that, from an intellectual point of view, Christianity is – for them – what has been called a 'living option'.[8] Also, they remain attracted to the Christian way of life, finding themselves drawn to it on account of its moral appeal and the sense which it begins to make of the world. In the light of all of this, they decide to live in accordance with the Christian model as they see it, and attempt both to live and to pray in the way that Jesus taught. In my judgment, these men and women can call themselves Christians and can continue to affirm the first Christian creed, "Jesus is Lord",[9] with complete honesty, even though there might be a question as to whether they should be active in the ordained ministry. I suspect that this situation is far more typical of the Christian man or woman than is generally realized, and it is important to see it as a legitimate variation on the theme of Christian faith.

Unblind faith and the New Testament

In order to strengthen our grasp of the meaning of unblind faith, I want to show how the description of faith that I have given accords with the way in which faith is represented in the New Testament.

If there were a person to whom blind obedience should be given, then surely this would be to God or, for the Christian, to his only Son, Jesus Christ. However, the philosophy of God and of humankind that I shall outline in the next chapters suggests that the last thing that God wants is a blind obedience, even to himself, for this would be a denial of the *human* response that he wants to draw from us. It is utterly congruous with this suggestion to see that Jesus, while calling people to follow him, avoided giving his teaching in the form of absolute truths, but rather used suggestive stories and poetic phrases. Also, when asked a direct question, he nearly always asked a question in return. As with Socrates, he seems to have felt that if we would know a truth, that is really *know* it as opposed merely to being able to give a correct answer which we could not go on to explain, then we must discover it for ourselves. Good teachers can sometimes help to draw this truth out from us, but they cannot simply give it to us.

With this in mind, let us return to the example of the doubt-filled Christians given in the last section, but place them in the time of Jesus's earthly ministry. They are attracted to all that Jesus stands for and want to follow him. They are happy to call him 'Lord' despite their doubts about the reality of God, for they wish to risk being his disciples and to enthrone in their own lives the values that Jesus teaches. Let us suppose that after the death of Jesus, although not among the five hundred who claimed to have seen the risen Jesus,[10] they continues as disciples, being baptized as they pronounce the first creed, and that they subsequently die for their faith. Most of us would describe these lives as both Christian and triumphant because the most important element in faith is the faithfulness that is shown in the way we live and to the person we follow. Beliefs about the nature of God or the status of Jesus are secondary. But if this is the root of faith in the New Testament, doubts in themselves need not prevent us from being and from calling ourselves Christians.

This understanding of the nature of faith should explain the use of the term 'Christian agnostic', which is puzzling to many people, but which has been used by a number of deeply committed Christians in order to describe their point of view.[11] Strictly speaking, the word 'agnostic' simply means 'one who does not know' and since Christians claim to believe, rather than to know, there is no reason why a Christian cannot be 'agnostic' about the reality of God. In popular usage, of course, the word refers to someone who neither knows nor believes and, in order not to cause confusion, I shall normally use the word in this sense. However, the use of the term 'Christian agnostic' does serve a useful purpose. It reminds us, first, that Christians do not claim *knowledge* of God in this life; second, that doubt is not the opposite of faith. The opposite of faith is faithlessness.

Hebrew and Greek

Within the early church, some disciples had a Hebrew and some a Greek background. This is important because it indicates the comprehensiveness of the church, both in its first years and in our own time. Christians are united in their love and devotion to Jesus, but they do not all have the same world-view in all respects, nor the same approach to faith. Because the Hebrew and Greek represent types of person that we still find, I shall outline the difference in their approaches. In doing this I shall be forced to oversimplify the issues grossly and I shall have to lump all Hebrews and all Greeks together in a way that cannot do justice to the individuals that actually made up those communities. Nevertheless, this review of the difference between typical Hebrew and typical Greek can serve two useful purposes for us. It can help us to understand how Christian philosophy developed as a response to both traditions and it can help us to appreciate the fact that the church holds within itself a great variety of people and views.

Whereas Christians with a Hebrew background thought of God as the one who had delivered the Jews from Egypt and saw Christ as the long-expected Messiah foretold by the great prophets, some Christians with a Greek background started with an idea of God that was much less personal. God is the ultimate reality that lies behind the world that we can see, or the supreme principle by which all things can be explained.

We have already seen how careful we must be if we refer to God as providing some kind of 'explanation' for the world. Religions do not – or at least should not – provide rivals to '*scientific* explanations' about how the world is organized. Instead, they offer ways of living, or philosophies of life, that give responses to certain fundamental questions that are not, strictly speaking, scientific questions at all, such as 'what is the meaning of life?'[12] Nevertheless, the great religions of the world not only offer some account of how we ought to live; typically, they offer a kind of 'explanation' for why there is a universe at all. They also try to integrate the different aspects of our lives and our experiences.

Within Greek thought of particular influence on Christianity was the thinking of Plato, and this was familiar to many of the first Christians who came from a Greek cultural tradition. Ultimate reality, for Plato, was the Good, the True and the Beautiful, and these three were united in the 'One': that supreme reality by which alone we can make sense of the multiplicity of our experiences. It followed that whoever followed or sought after what is good, or true, or beautiful, was in some sense seeking after God. Moreover, when Jesus is called the 'Word' in St John's gospel (John 1, 14), the actual term that is used is *logos*, which is Greek not only for 'word' but also for 'reason'. This was highly suggestive and attractive to those with a Platonic education, for they could then see Jesus as the expression, or model in human form, of the perfectly good and true and beautiful.

Christian teaching about God is the result of a complex blending of the Hebrew and Greek cultures. Some Christians find this an embarrassment for Christianity and so one sometimes hears preachers calling for us to purify our faith by removing the Greek influence and returning to the strictly Biblical view. I take the opposite stand and hold that the blending of Hebrew and Greek views was one of the things that enriched Christian teaching and enabled it to conquer both the hearts and the minds of all kinds of people in the ancient world, including many of the most intellectually gifted. The Christian God is the God of the Old Testament *and* the Father of Jesus *and* the supreme principle by which alone humankind can hope to begin to understand all things. This does not make for an easy or simple philosophy, but why should we think that the truth is easy or simple? There may indeed be a kind of 'simplicity', or singleness of vision that the truly good can reach, but very often the request to make everything simple is a cowardly request; a demand for an easy answer whether or not it is the true answer. I believe in Christianity because I believe that it is true, but the truth is something that we can reach only, if at all, by hard work. In one sense Christian faith is simple; it is that trust which enables one to say "Jesus is Lord". But when we are ask what our faith teaches us about the nature of God, or humankind, or Jesus, then we have no right to demand that we have simple answers. We must follow the argument and the evidence where they lead. When Jesus said that we should become like little children, I suggest that he was referring to the innocence and to the boundless imagination that many children have. Surely he was not asking us to smother our intellectual curiosity?

Let us see the import of all this for the idea of an unblind faith. A blind faith might express a genuine search for what is good and beautiful, but it cannot possibly express a search for what is true. A purely rational faith might express a search for what is true, but it cannot by itself express a striving for what is good and beautiful. Thus, if we seek a faith that is adequate for our vision of God, it must be an 'unblind' faith, of the kind that I have attempted to describe.

Finally, let us return to the problem that faces those people who are seeking God, but who feel that they have not found him and that they have no faith. Pascal said that one would not be seeking God unless one had already found him. From what has been said about God as the Good and the True and the Beautiful, we can now see why, in a sense, this must be true. Furthermore, we have the Biblical promise that those who truly seek God will eventually find him, a promise that is powerfully expressed in Mendelssohn's oratorio, *Elijah*: "If with all your hearts ye truly seek me, ye shall ever surely find me."[13]

Notes

1 The word 'liberal' is used in many ways, but here I refer to the *Oxford English Dictionary's* definition 'free from narrow prejudice; open-minded, candid' – which it gives as a usage (e.g. in Edward Gibbon) since 1781. The claim that 'liberal' means something like 'woolly' is usually made by those who disagree with a liberal position.

2 Ricci supported a return to (his interpretation of) an older Confucian tradition, in opposition to the kind of Neo-Confucianism that was popular at his time. This led him to dispute the views of many contemporary Confucians, but by an appeal to a source that they too acknowledged. Part of his appeal to the scholars of his time was

the way in which this helped him to distance his views from those of contemporary Daoists and Buddhists – both of which traditions were often felt, by the Confucian scholars, to be at odds with the Confucian tradition. (For a sympathetic but critical examination of Ricci's handling of the classics see the introduction by Douglas Lancashire and Peter Hu Kum-chen, to their translation of Ricci's *The True Meaning of the Lord of Heaven*, Hong Kong 1985, pp. 48ff.) Among later Christians, reactions to Ricci's approach have varied greatly. Many, including some Protestants, thoroughly approved his accommodating style, others felt that he was deliberately underplaying some central aspects of Christianity in order to make his appeal more popular. For example, his public writings avoided discussion of the crucifixion. In his defence, it should be stressed that he saw his writings (especially his important *The True Meaning of the Lord of Heaven*), as primarily a kind of preparation, or 'pre-evangelistic' work for the understanding of the gospel, and in his private faith and his teaching to converts, the crucifixion did have a central place.

3 E.g. Matt. 5, 8; Luke 9, 26.

4 1 Peter 3, 15. The Bible translations are from the Revised Standard Version except where otherwise indicated.

5 Isa. 6, 5; Job 42, 2–6.

6 Terry Eagleton, *Reason, Faith, and Revolution*, Yale University Press 2009, p. 50.

7 I Cor. 13, 12.

8 See the essay by William James, *The Will to Believe*, 1897 (and many later editions). James is sometimes said to have claimed that belief was basically a matter of choice – but in fact he limited rational choices to those within the *range* of 'living options' for which there was some kind of evidence.

9 See Acts 19, 5; I Cor. 12, 3 and chapter 9, Level A. *Christ is Lord*.

10 I Cor. 15, 3–8.

11 E.g. Leslie D. Weatherhead, *The Christian Agnostic*, Hodder and Stoughton, Abingdon 1965. An earlier example of a Christian who appreciated the place of doubt in an honest approach to the Christian faith was Sebastian Castellio in a book whose title begins '*The Art of Doubting*' (*De Arte Dubitandi*, 1563).

12 The traditional Christian response to this question goes: To find true happiness within a loving relationship with God and other people. Clearly, this is not a scientific answer.

13 Jer. 29, 13 (translation from the Oratorio).

2. The Idea of God

What do we mean by 'God'?

If one is trying to understand the Christian idea of God, the first question to ask is not "Does God exist?", but "What do we mean by the word 'God'?" All sorts of people use the word 'God' in many different religions and, although there are connections between the different uses of the word, it is by no means obvious that all people mean the same thing. Sometimes when I hear atheists say they do not believe in God, I find out on further enquiry that they have such a peculiar idea of God that I am tempted to say that I do not believe in God either, that is *in their sense of the word*. Since there are these different ideas about God and since some people deny that the word has any meaning at all, there is no point in trying to decide whether God is a reality until we have begun to understand what we mean by the term. In this chapter, I shall try to lay the foundations for such an understanding, based on the conviction that within the tradition that is common to Judaism, Christianity and Islam the word 'God' does have a coherent meaning that, to a certain degree, can be brought out and explained. The word also has some common ground with the use of the term in many other religions, but this is not a topic I propose to take up here, except to say that, in many non-Abrahamic religions, 'God' stands for an ultimate principle that may not have any personal characteristics.

I stress that the explanation can only be 'to a certain degree' because, when we reflect on the matter, there must seem to be a sort of absurdity in the attempt to write about the idea of God even in a long book, let alone in a short chapter. How could one define or describe God? The very attempt suggests that one is treating God as a thing within the universe rather than as its source, and therefore that one just does not understand the idea. Nevertheless, some things can be said which begin to remove false conceptions of God and other things can be said which may evoke or call forth an understanding of God, even though he cannot be defined in any straightforward way.

It is useful to note that many of our other fundamental concepts cannot easily be defined either. For example, consider our use of the words space, time, consciousness, freedom, life, understanding, happiness and beauty, to list but a few. We need all these words and, if we abandoned them because of the fact that they cannot be defined in a straightforward way, as can words such as table, red and mammal, then we would simply have to introduce new words to play their roles. So it appears that none of our fundamental concepts can be defined in a simple way, even though we can learn how to understand them and to use them. Therefore, the peculiar difficulty that we face in trying to deal with the word 'God' is no ground by itself for rejecting the idea of God, for such difficulties are typical of fundamental concepts.

Many philosophers say that if you want to understand the meaning of a word, you should begin by seeing how it is *used*, either in a collection of writings or in a body of discourse. This leads to my first suggestion about how to search for an understanding of the idea of God. We can begin with an historical approach in which we observe how the word 'God' is used and, at the same time, has undergone change, within a tradition of sacred writings. In particular, within the Bible, we can observe the stages by which the idea of God has grown when an old tradition has been stretched in order to make room for a new vision. This process can be observed when we examine the sacred writings of many of the great world religions. Next, this historical approach must be combined with reflection on our own experience.

I am not suggesting that this is the way in which we first learned to use or understand the idea of God, for in many cases this may have happened the other way round (that is, beginning with our personal experiences), but that this is a good way of approaching the problem as we reflect on it now.

I have already pointed out that the Christian faith has origins in both Hebrew and Greek thought and, with this in mind, let us proceed by looking at the historical development of the idea of God within these two traditions.

The Hebrew background

There are many ways of reading the Old Testament. If we read it as straight history, we find a fascinating story, but also a terrible one that is not at all edifying in many places and which often presents sub-Christian ideas about God. Also, we come across some passages that must strain our credulity if we have any historical sense. On the other hand, if we read the Old Testament as pure myth, although we are provided with many powerful symbols, we lose a sense of realism and vitality. A third approach and, I shall later argue, the best one, is to read it as a mixture of history and myth in which we can observe a *development* in the human understanding of God. For example – if we take this historical approach – when we read the book of Joshua we do not learn that God wanted the Hebrews to slaughter the women and children of Jericho and Ai, but that the Hebrews at that time *believed that God so willed*.[1] Thus the history reveals not only what the Jews did, but what they believed about God. Similarly, the myths reveal how they thought about God at a certain point in time. Approached in this way, the Old Testament begins to make new sense; a drama unfolds in which we see new ideas about God emerging and we need no longer be embarrassed by the early, primitive ideas. This emergence can be described in terms of three stages, though this suggests a tidier scheme than the reader of the Old Testament will actually find, for the three stages constantly overlap.

During the first stage, we observe the emergence of the *one* God from the many tribal gods of the ancient world. This happens gradually, for, between polytheism (belief in many gods) and monotheism (belief in one God), there is usually an intermediate belief called 'henotheism', meaning a belief in many gods, one of whom is superior to any of the others. Gradually the superiority of this chief god is advanced until he becomes different *in kind* from the other gods and then we begin to slide over into monotheism. Examples of this intermediate belief can be found in many places in the Old Testament. One is where the Hebrew God is angry because he has been described as a god of the hills, but not as a god of the plains, so that it is not wise to fight Jews in hilly country.[2] Another is where the psalmist says, "Blessed is the nation whose God [*elohim*] is the Lord [*yahweh*]".[3] The Hebrew word *elohim*, it should be explained, is used in some places to mean 'god' in the sense of one of the gentile gods and in others to mean the one God. In essence then the psalmist is saying our God is the Lord, your god is not.

The emergence of the idea of *one* God was of enormous importance and influence. Some think that it resulted from contact with the Egyptian monotheism of the pharaoh Ikhnaton, who probably lived at about the same time as Moses; others that it the result of a personal revelation to the patriarchs; and still others as a logical development, as the world was increasingly seen to be *one* world, with the same laws pertaining everywhere. Perhaps it was a mixture of all three of these influences. In any case, the point is that there is change and, I suggest, progress with respect to the idea of God, both intellectually, since a unified approach to the world becomes necessary, and morally, because all humankind is comprehended under the same creative care.

During the second stage, we observe the emergence of the idea that God is not only powerful, but righteous. This can be seen most clearly in the development of the notion of holiness. At first, this is a reference to the danger – one might say contagion – likely to be suffered when one gets close to the awesome God. The purity demanded before any approach is a ritual purity. Shoes must be taken off on the holy mountain, various washings must take place, not for reasons of hygiene, but for ritual cleanliness. All sorts of other taboos must be observed lest one be instantly destroyed. In most cases these taboos have nothing to do with morality as we know it. For example, consider the case of Uzzah who touched the ark in order to stop it falling and was instantly struck dead.[4] The rational approach to this passage is similar to that in which God is said to have ordered the slaughter of women and children, in that we see what people believed about God, not what God actually commanded. I shall take up this point again in chapter 12. What probably happened is that Uzzah died of a heart attack when he realized that he had broken a taboo, but the account illustrates perfectly how people of the time thought about God's holiness.

We can watch this old notion of holiness gradually giving way to the claim that God is righteous, in the sense of caring for how we treat our neighbour and the stranger at the gate. There is certainly a suggestion of this moral dimension to the concern of God in the second half of the Ten Commandments, which might go back to the time of Moses, but the implications of this seem hardly to have been seen until we come to the great prophets, like Micah, who gave us this magnificent passage around 700 BCE: "What does the Lord require of you but to do justice, and to love kindness, and to walk humbly with your God."[5] Other prophets of the time make explicit reference to God's concern with how we treat others, especially the poor, and Isaiah actually identifies God's holiness with this kind of righteous concern.[6]

The emergence of the third stage in this development of the idea of God makes for compelling reading, as indeed do the other stages if we are sensitive to the drama that is unfolding in the Old Testament. In this last stage, we see the stern and righteous God becoming also the loving and merciful God. We can find suggestions of this in the author of the later chapters of Isaiah and in Jeremiah, but it is most obvious in the prophet Hosea. The central theme in this prophet is the loving-kindness (*hesed*) of God and he illustrates this by acting out a parable in front of his listeners. He marries a faithless prostitute, thereby symbolizing how God is prepared to love and care for Israel, even though she has been faithless and wanton. Here we are beginning to get close to the idea of God that enables Jesus to call him *Abba*, Father.

The Greek background

We have seen that the Hebrew background to the Christian idea of God was not one of a single and unchanging idea, but rather a story of rival views of God, with certain dominant themes emerging to produce a more or less orthodox doctrine of God by the time of Jesus. The Greek background is even more diverse: some Greeks believed in a personal God or gods, some were atheists, a small but influential minority had a philosophical notion of God as a supreme principle. Such was the importance of this last group for later thought that we must now examine its beliefs more carefully.

As we saw in the first chapter, one theme within Greek philosophy was the search for a unifying principle by which all could be explained. This search lies behind the apparently bizarre claims of some of the early philosophers, such as "all is water" or "all is fire". The crucial thing here is that they were able to ask questions about everything, or the 'all', which in itself shows an advance in view parallel to the Hebrew discovery of the one God who ruled over all. One of these early philosophers suggested that "all is mind".[7] He did not mean that everything was made out of mind, but something closer to the idea expressed in a sentence such as this: "Everything that there is makes some kind of sense and has an explanation that thought can grasp – in principle, everything is intelligible." It was not very difficult to go from this to the idea that a supreme intellect, or Mind, lay behind all things. This in fact became the position of some of the great philosophers and some of them called this mind *theos*, the Greek word for 'God'. However, this God was not a creator, nor even a maker who had somehow fashioned the world out of some kind of primeval matter. This act of making was left to a demigod, while God himself was left in a splendid isolation, not directly in contact with anything (for they thought that this would demean God), but drawing all things to him and enlightening all things. Plato used the material sun as a simile for this God. The sun does not know us, but it illuminates us, and stands both for the highest and most beautiful thing that there is and for that which allows us to see. Aristotle, too, had God as the pinnacle of his heavenly hierarchy, but so distant that he could not know us, though we could contemplate him. The idea of friendship with God he regarded as absurd.

Why, it may well be asked, were ideas such as these so crucial for the development of Christianity? The principal answer is this. If Christianity were to win out in the ancient world, it had to satisfy the basic longings and searchings of all people. It was not enough to provide an active personal God, or even a personal saviour. God had also to satisfy humankind's intellectual striving. This didn't mean that they could actually hope to comprehend God, but that he had to be the Mind behind the created order, in whom all things had an ultimate explanation and whom, in the end, we could hope both to love with our hearts and grasp with our minds. Therefore Christianity took from the Greeks the idea that God is Mind, though it rejected the view that this Mind is impersonal and cannot be known in friendship.

This many-sided human striving is as true today as in the world of the first Christians and helps to explain the complex character of the word 'spiritual'. Our search for forgiveness, love and friendship is part of our spiritual nature; so too are our questioning and searching minds. Indeed the true scientist, historian and philosopher are just as much evidence that humanity has a spiritual dimension as are the poet, the artist, the saint and the lover.

Anthropomorphism

Let us now move on from the historical background to the Christian idea of God to the development of the idea of God in our own individual minds. There cannot be a total change in approach here, for my individual awareness has developed in the context of a knowledge of Christianity, and I am likely to interpret any private experience in the light of the religion I know. Nevertheless, there is a change of emphasis as we look at how the idea of God forms in a particular individual.

First of all, in so far as a personal God is conceived at all in childhood, he is almost certain to be conceived as a kindly old man. When children are taught to go beyond such nursery ideas and learn that God is everywhere and perfect and eternal, and that 'she' could be just as suitably used in referring to God as 'he',[8] many aspects of the human model still remain. This building of God in the human image is called 'anthropomorphism' and, to some degree, it is inescapable for the Christian (or Jew or Muslim) if people are to talk about God at all. The very claim that God is personal, or that he is Mind, reflects our understanding of the human person and human mind. Again, words like 'love' and 'father' when applied to God get their initial meaning from human experience.

It is easy to see why many people attack any religion that talks of a personal God and that uses words like 'love' and 'father'. All we are doing, it is alleged, is building the sort of God we would like out of our ideal picture of humans.

To this attack, the Christian who holds an unblind faith has a reply that it is important to be able to make and to understand. It goes like this. Certainly there is a danger here, and lots of people describe God and think of him far too much in terms of a human model, but it does not follow that we cannot use human terms such as 'father' at all, provided that we realise that we are using *analogies*. The important thing here is the Christian belief that God chose to make humankind in his image,[9] and therefore that at our best we really can reflect something of the nature of God. Thus, when we see in a human life or in a human family the emergence of self-conscious awareness, freedom, creativity, love, and the other aspects of humankind that belong to us as humans (as the kind of creature that God intended), then we see what was always intended to be a reflection of the creative power that made us. So in one sense anthropomorphism is bad, as it is a self-centred likening of God to a super-human; in another sense it is inevitable and, within certain limits, perfectly legitimate. Just as great artists leave a kind of 'stamp' or indication of their character within the works they produce, so something of the character of God can be sensed in all the things he has made, and most especially, in those beings who participate, even to a small extent, in his providential care for the world. We can recall that Adam was given the task of *tending* the mythical garden of Eden. What we have to remember is that what we see in human persons can only be an *image* of God, a puzzling reflection in a glass,[10] though Christians believe that there is one particular image that does properly reflect the nature of God in so far as a being in space and time can do so, namely Jesus of Nazareth.

Revelation and the numinous

So far, I have indicated two of the ways in which the idea of God is built up, one historical, the other through our experience of human life. However, neither of these ways by itself tells us how we can have an idea of God that is not ultimately of our own making. What needs to be added is the notion of revelation, that is, of the claim that it is not simply a matter of human beings searching around in their understanding, but of God reaching down to us and in some way *showing* himself, or revealing himself to us. This is the third part of the answer to the question of how we come to have an idea of God, and it lies behind the other two, for in order for them to make sense, we have to believe that God has revealed himself to men and women in the past and that he reveals himself now through men and women whom we meet.

The sceptical response to this is to ask how we know that God has revealed himself and that it is not just a case of our unconscious mind playing tricks, or of our jumping to the wrong interpretation of some quite normal and earthly experience. The Christian reply to this is that, strictly speaking, we cannot *know* that it is God who shows himself and we cannot fully satisfy the kind of demand for proof or strong evidence that the sceptic is probably asking for, because this demand is itself loaded. It usually expects us to be able to give the sort of proof or evidence that would be appropriate for showing that a physical thing exists, not for showing that there is a spiritual source for the whole physical order. But Christians can offer rational grounds for their belief *of an appropriate kind* and, as I have promised, I shall turn to these in chapter 14.

If we return to the claim that God shows himself to us in certain ways, then there is one particular kind of experience that I want to stress and this is often called the sense of the numinous. It is impossible to describe this experience accurately, but fortunately many people have had some glimmering of it in their own lives and they will be able to recognise what I am attempting to describe. Sometimes it arises in the context of the awareness of great natural beauty, sometimes it arises quite unexpectedly for no reason that we can see, but when it comes it is an overwhelming sense of being in the presence of a being that is other than ourselves and that is at the same time awesome and fascinating. There is a sense of the uncanny and mysterious that frightens, but at the same time a sense of beauty and awe that attracts and captivates us. Many writers have tried to describe this experience, but all admit to the near total inadequacy of our words.[11]

There is no doubt that these numinous experiences occur and that they occur to all sorts of different people in all the great religions of the world, although they are interpreted in different ways. My point is that it is this kind of experience that has helped to give force and shape to the ideas of God in all the great monotheistic religions and that has helped the ordinary worshipper to understand what is meant by the divine. God is not just an abstract idea, nor even simply a personal being that is believed to have spoken to our ancestors, but he is to some degree encountered by ordinary worshippers in the glimpses they have had of the numinous. For them, too, he is a terrifying but beautiful reality in whose presence they have been.

Of course not all people have had an experience of the numinous, even in the form of a hint or suggestion of a mysterious presence, and for them it is that much harder to give force to the idea of God. The following illustration may help to explain the sense of the numinous to those who have not experienced it for themselves. In certain psychological states, often induced by drugs, physical objects take on an incredible immediacy. People seem to be aware of their texture and colour as if for the first time, with an amazing vividness and intimacy. In a similar way, those who have experienced the numinous tend to say that they have encountered the living presence of the divine, with an immediacy that is overpowering and that is at the same time both fearful and wonderful.

The religious person puts into a broader context experiences that many of those who call themselves atheists or agnostics admit to having felt, especially in the context of awesome beauty. Here we may recall a powerful passage by William Wordsworth:

> And I have felt
> A presence that disturbs me with the joy
> Of elevated thoughts; a sense sublime
> Of something far more deeply interfused,
> Whose dwelling is the light of setting suns,
> And the round ocean and the living air,
> And the blue sky, and in the mind of man;
> A motion and a spirit, that impels
> All thinking things, all objects of all thought,
> And rolls through all things.[12]

Faith and the idea of God

We have now reviewed the principal ingredients of the Christian idea of God and this is enough to show why there cannot be a simple definition of God. In traditional Christianity, God is said to be 'simple', but this is primarily a reference to the fact that he is not made up of parts, like a physical object. 'Simple' here is contrasted with 'composite', not with 'complex'. On the other hand, our understanding of God arises through many strands of past Christian experience and through many varieties of our own experience. There is the historical saga of the discovery of the one God who is both righteous and loving; there is the intellectual search for the Mind that orders all things; there is the experience of what is good and noble in human beings; there is the awesome experience of the numinous. All of these elements are brought together within the Christian idea of God, of the one who is said to be the source and ground of the physical universe, but not a part if it; a spiritual reality that has no location in space or time and yet who watches over and enters into all space and all time. Most of all, the Christian would say, a being who is the source of what is most strange and wonderful about humankind, our minds and our love, and these two things above all else point to the being that planned their emergence in humankind. So God can be called *Love*, reflecting the insight of the Hebrews, or he can be called *Mind*, reflecting the insight of the Greeks. The other two names that are most appropriate come directly from the Bible; the Old Testament name for God, 'I am who I am',[13] sometimes translated as 'He who is', and the New Testament word used by Jesus, *Abba*, the Aramaic for Father.[14]

At this point it may be illuminating to refer to the problem that faced Chinese missionaries when they wanted to translate 'God' into Chinese, for example, in their translations of the Bible. After much internal debate the Roman Catholic Church adopted the term *tianzhu* (literally 'ruler of heaven') while the Protestant churches tended to use either *shiandi* (literally 'emperor of the highest') or *shen* (the general word for a god or a spiritual entity). It was recognized that all of these words were problematic, either because of their political overtones or because of the way the word was already used in sacred writings – but with different senses. Two other words might have been used if they had not implied something totally impersonal, namely *li* and *dao*, both of which can be used to mean an 'ultimate principle'.[15] In the light of the difficulties, some missionaries suggested inventing a totally new word in order to convey what the Bible meant by God,[16] but this would have the result of magnifying the gulf between Western and Chinese spirituality – the very thing that missionaries who followed the spirit of Ricci wanted to avoid. There is no easy solution to this dilemma, but it can be hoped that the more one of these terms is used in the context of Christian worship and the use of the Bible, the more it will tend to gather the intended meaning.

The whole issue can be put this way. There is a sense in which God does not have a 'name' at all, that is in the way that individual animals or persons in the created order have names, because he is the unique creator of all that is; as Christians theologians have put it – not a 'maker' – but a Creator 'out of nothing'.[17] However, we need some way of referring or pointing to God, especially in the context of his calling to us, and the two words that we have been given, in the Old and New Testaments, namely 'He who is' and 'Father', straddle the usual distinction between a 'name' and a 'description' that applies to things within the world.

Why has it been necessary to stress the difficulty of talking about God and to provide what some Christians may find a very academic discussion of the nature of God? Because without some grasp of the full richness of the idea of God, mature Christians will inevitably grow out of their faith and find that their God is too small. Perhaps most of those who reject their faith, or who just let it fade away, have rejected not the Christian God, but some caricature of it that they had long since grown out of.

Some of the questions that people ask Christians or ask themselves indicate this failure to let the idea of God grow. For example, the questions "Where is God?" and "Who made God?" cannot be answered, not because Christianity demands a blind faith, but because the questions themselves betray a misunderstanding of the idea of God. The proper reply is to show why these questions are in fact 'question-begging', because they already imply atheism. If God could be located, or if his being depended on something else, he could not correspond to the Christian idea of God.

Another example of a common question that is based – at least in large part – on a misunderstanding of the nature of God goes: "Why does God allow suffering?" and I shall explore this matter in chapter 10. Yet another goes: "Why worship this God?" When this means "Why should we go to church or sing hymns?", this is a perfectly reasonable question to ask and I shall turn to it in chapter 7. However, the question is often much broader in scope and questions the very notion of worship, as if God could be interested in human flattery. In this form, the question is another example of an inadequate awareness of the idea of God, for true worship is totally unlike the flattery offered to a human monarch. Worship is the word we use to express the only possible response to God when we begin to see him as he is. Plato thought that the physical sun was the best symbol for his God, because it was that splendid and beautiful fire that invited us to contemplate with joy the still greater beauty of God. The Christian idea of God owes much to Plato, for Christians, too, feel drawn to gaze, not only at the sheer beauty of the things that God has made, but, if they can, at the absolute beauty of God himself. This is the true context of adoration and of worship.

Notes

1 Josh. 6, 21; 8, 1–2, 24–8. This is a claim that was powerfully (and at the time, controversially) made by the Quaker preacher, Hannah Barnard, towards the end of the eighteenth century.
2 I Kings 20.
3 Ps. 33, 12.
4 II Sam. 6, 6–7.
5 Micah 6, 8.
6 Isa. 5, 16.
7 Anaxagoras, born about 500 BCE.
8 Despite the attempt to use gender-neutral language, it is difficult not to

use 'he' when referring to God, largely because of the traditional use of 'Father' in prayer. Strictly speaking, however, 'Mother' would be equally appropriate, and some saints, including Julian of Norwich, refer to Christ as our 'mother', in order to express their insight that God, while personal, is no more male than female.

9   Gen. 1, 27.

10   I Cor. 13, 10.

11   See R. Otto, *The Idea of the Holy*, Oxford University Press, 1923 (and many later editions).

12   Wordsworth, *Tintern Abbey*.

13   Exodus 3, 14.

14   Mark 14, 36; *cf.* Rom. 8, 15 and Gal. 4, 6.

15   *Dao* can also mean a 'way'.

16   For the history of this debate see Ralph R. Covell, *Confucius, The Buddha, and Christ*, Orbis, New York 1986, pp. 61–2, 87–90, 102.

17   According to traditional Christian theology, even space and time are the products of the creative source of all things.

3. The Story of Humankind

What is it to be human?

More light will be shed on the idea of God during the course of this book because the fundamental ideas that we use come to be understood through their relationships with other ideas. Therefore, as we explore ideas such as those of humanity and of Christ, we shall also be adding to our understanding of the idea of God.

"What is man?" the psalmist asked[1] and in different ways just about every thinking person has asked the same question. We must note that the question asked by the psalmist is not primarily a scientific question, but a value question, and what some philosophers would call a 'metaphysical' question. There is, of course, a scientific question: "What is man?" (or, as we would now put it: "What is it to be a human being?"), that can be answered, at least in part, by modern biology and zoology. The human species is an organism with certain characteristics, physiologically related to certain other organisms. I have no quarrel with such a reply to the scientific question, including its reliance on a Darwinian theory of evolution, but it does not help us very much with the psalmist's concern that was asking, in a kind of shorthand, questions such as "What is the meaning and purpose of humanity?", "Where does our species fit into the great scheme of things?" and "What ought human beings to be striving for?"

At this point the secular humanist will very likely say that these questions have no meaning and that to demand answers is to beg the question of whether or not humanity has some kind of purpose. There is some point to this complaint, but it must be realized that the secular humanist's rejection of these ancient questions is just as much the taking of a stand as the religious person's insistence that these questions should be asked. Part of what it *means* to have belief in God is precisely to believe that questions like "Why does anything exist?" and "What is the meaning of life?" are real questions that have possible answers, while a large part of what it means to be a secular humanist, is the denial that these are real questions. Thus the complaint does not produce a new argument against Christian philosophy, it is rather a further affirmation of the disagreement.

The traditional story of humanity

The literature and poetry of the Christian tradition give an answer to the question "What is man?" in the form of a story. Let us look at this story and then see how far it can stand up to reflective consideration in the twentieth century.

The traditional story begins with Adam and we must remember from the beginning that 'Adam' has three meanings in Hebrew, which are cunningly interwoven into the Genesis story and of which the original readers would all have been aware. 'Adam' can be the name of an individual like 'John', it is a collective term meaning 'humankind' and (in a derivative form) it is a word that can mean 'earth' or 'ground' out of which Adam was made.

In a beautiful tale, we hear that Adam and Eve were created in innocence and in the image of God. However, they were not satisfied with this state and wished to be equal with God.[2] This led them to their first act of disobedience and through this, a fall from the perfection that they had been given. Then began the wanderings and sufferings. But God had mercy and, in order to bring humans back and eventually to restore them, he began to call forth a special people who would act as his messenger and, in due course, as a light to the other nations. Moreover, when the time was right, God could enter into the history of this people in a new and unique way. So a faithful group is gathered. The Noah story is part of this process; the story of Abraham (who became the great symbol of faith in God's promise) another part. Eventually, under the leadership of Moses, a whole tribe is brought out of captivity and invited to enter into a special relationship or covenant with God. Humankind must keep God's law, especially its summary known as the Ten Commandments and, on his side, God will watch over and protect the tribe of Israel.

Then begins a new saga of wanderings and a new drama, for the people still fail to be faithful, except in a few instances. God's servants, the prophets, call the faithful back to God and give new insights into what God requires, but Israel stays rebellious even after the punishment of exile in Babylon, followed by yet another act of forgiveness when Israel returns to the promised land. Then comes the climax. After careful preparation, the image of God himself, the true Messiah, comes to live among the chosen people, not only offering forgiveness, but the possibility of life in communion with him. But, yet again, the majority of those who hear Jesus refuse God's grace and 'the Son of man' is rejected and crucified. However, out of the faithfulness of Jesus and his followers, a new Israel is born, which carries on the message of Jesus and represents him in the world.

All this is the essential story of humankind so far, but it has still to be completed. The meaning and purpose of life, according to this story, is for us to discover or rediscover both goodness and joy in union with God and in the communion of saints. When the time is ripe, this will finally be achieved, at least for all the faithful, and the human story, so far as this earth is concerned, will come to an end. Jesus will come again and all the redeemed will enter into eternal life.

Humankind and evolution

Such, in brief, is the traditional Christian story of our species. It can be found in the Bible, in Milton, and in many other writings. We must now ask ourselves how far this story can be accepted in the light of intelligent reflection and an unblind faith. I suggest that in the light of what we now know about humans from biology, anthropology and history, we can reinterpret the traditional story in a way that preserves its essential insights into our nature. Here is the story as I think that it can be retold, making use of the theory of evolution. This new story should not be seen as an alternative to the first story, but rather as an addition to or commentary on it.

God, from the beginning of creation, purposed to make humankind. He intended to make a creature that could *voluntarily* respond to him and love him, that would be *responsible* for brothers and sisters, and for animals, and that would imitate his own creativity. But he would not, and I shall try to show *could* not, create such a creature in an instant. Humans, if they are to correspond at all with our experience of them, must have an historical dimension. For example, each adult man and woman has a personal history in which he or she has actively participated in the achievement of character.

If my character were simply 'put there' as part of me, in an instant act of creation, it would not be *my* character, for which I have some responsibility. If we realize that this historical dimension is essential to humankind, then there is a mistake in thinking that human beings *could* be created in an instant of time, because process is part of our nature. Further, just as we think of the individual person as evolving in the womb, it is much more natural to think of the human race as evolving through stages.

However, the evolution of humankind, which the Christian can see as the unfolding of a divine plan, does not proceed in a simple curve. There are stages that represent radical innovations, even if some kind of evolutionary explanation can be given for the change. For example, from the primeval sludge came life, in the sense of self-reproducing organic bodies. Whether or not scientists will one day be able to reproduce this step I do not know, but if they do so, it will not affect the essential point that I am making. The important thing is that with life we have a new *level* of being, a new kind of entity that requires new words and new categories of thought to describe. It is not simply that life is more complex (in a way it may be less complex than some non-living compounds), it is complex in a new *kind* of way.

But this is only the beginning. After life came the evolution of sensitive life, that is of animals that are conscious of and react to their environment through a complex nervous system. Next came self-conscious life and with it reflective thought, freedom of action, creative genius and sacrificial love. At each of these stages in evolution we find a new *level* of being that demands new words and new categories of thought. For example, *thought*, in itself, cannot be described, let alone explained, except in terms of mind, that is at the level of self-conscious awareness. A biologist's account of electrical energy in the brain may describe what accompanies thought, or what is the physical manifestation of thought (or possibly what causes thought), but there are serious problems with the idea that thought can simply be reduced to descriptions of neurological activity.

Great care must be taken here not to misunderstand what is essential to the Christian position. Some philosophers use the word 'physicalism' for the claim that thought *is* a certain kind of neurological activity. However, not all 'physicalists' are also 'reductionists' (meaning people who claim that all language about thought can simply be reduced or translated into language about neurons, or that thought can be fully explained or predicted by scientific laws). Donald

Davidson provides a recent example of an important philosopher who took a non-reductionist, physicalist position. My personal view is that this kind of position is not incompatible with either a Christian doctrine of humankind, or of immortality, provided that the latter is expressed in terms of the resurrection of a body. In general, the Christian position is much more 'materialistic' than is often realized. The language of believers often suggests a kind of Platonic view, in which human beings are essentially spiritual souls, encased in physical bodies. However, orthodox Christian teaching is quite different. It is that essentially (as in Hebrew thought), we are *animated bodies*. This issue will be revisited in chapters 8 and 11.

As we think of the different levels at which creatures exist, we should note that the possible existence of intermediate levels is not ruled out. For example, some have argued that evolution is incompatible with Christianity because at some stage evolution demands semi-humans. But the Christian should be agnostic, in the strict sense of the term, on the subject of whether or not there were once such creatures. It is possible that there was a mutation jump to the first self-conscious human mating pair, in which case there would not have to have been any semi-humans, but it is not necessary for Christians to insist that this must have been the case, and my personal belief is that it represents a most unlikely scenario. Why does it matter if there were intermediate beings at some stage, perhaps creatures that had occasional glimmerings of self-consciousness? In other words, there is a difference of level between consciousness and self-consciousness, but there could be beings that lived partly at one level and partly at the other.

In fact, Christian nervousness on this issue is largely based on the dogma that human beings have souls, but that animals do not, or, if they do, souls of a quite different kind. But although an absolute divide between humans and other animals is official doctrine in some churches, it is quite unnecessary for basic Christian doctrine. I shall take up the question of the nature of the human soul again in chapter 8.

To return to the stages of evolution; if we stress the emergence of new levels, from matter to life to consciousness to self-consciousness, then far from evolution being an embarrassment for Christian faith, it can be seen as an aid. Not only is there compatibility between science and religion, the idea of emergence illuminates the *spiritual struggle* that is an essential element in human life.

In order to see this, consider the following analogy. At some point in the evolution of life on this planet, there was a movement from the sea to the land. What probably happened is that some fish began to drag themselves onto the land and to spend part of their time there, either to avoid predators or to take advantage of food on the shoreline. No doubt these creatures were pretty uncomfortable out of the sea for they were in the process of emerging from one domain to another. The hybrid creature, half in the domain of sea and half in that of land, provides a metaphor for the state of humankind as it emerges from the animal world to the human world. In other words, the truly human level is not a given, it has to be *achieved* as one chooses to try to live on the higher level. Evolution has produced a being with a nervous system that is capable of developing self-consciousness, freedom, love, etc., but all of these things have to be worked for as the new level emerges. In this struggle, the existence of intermediate positions, that is of those who are half animal and half human, is the order of the day, not the exception, but of course this is not the same as the semi-human we have just considered. The semi-human would have physiological conditions that prevented more than occasional glimpses of the human level, whereas the 'half-human' (as I am using the term) is the creature who could be fully human, but who has failed in the spiritual struggle, or at least, partially failed.

I could easily be misunderstood here. I am not saying that the animal level, that is the conscious but not self-conscious level, is bad. On the contrary, the Christian regards all the levels of creation as intrinsically good. The point is that the truly human or spiritual level is a higher level and one that all human beings are called to reach by a process that involves struggle (and, as we shall see, grace). Evil only enters the scene when some glimpse of the new level is seen and then rejected. Animals as such cannot be evil, only those with the capacity freely to choose a higher level of being. However, we may be agnostic on the question of whether some of the higher animals, other than humans, can begin to transcend the strictly animal level. Once again, Christianity is not bound to a doctrine of an absolute division.

There is another way in which my stress on human character as an 'achievement' might lead to misunderstanding. Becoming a human being, in the way that a young baby (and arguably at least, a foetus)[3] is a human being is not an 'achievement'; it is an endowment, or from a Christian perspective, a 'gift'. The fact that an *individual* human being does not have rationality, or a moral character that has been built up over a period of time (as with the very young or some of the very disabled) is not a ground for denying humanness. Both rationality and moral character are typical aspects of the mature individual, but the definition of being a human being should be – in my view – membership of the human species. For this reason, we need to treat with respect those vulnerable members of our species who lack some or all of the typical human characteristics. To put this another way: rationality and moral character are typical characteristics of the human species – not criteria for judging whether or not x is a human being.

Nevertheless, I do claim that what might be called 'full personhood' for the individual can only be achieved in an historical process in which a new level of being emerges through a process that necessarily involves a kind of struggle. In this context we do not find the doctrine of evolution a rival to the doctrine that God created us, but rather an illuminating comment both on the process by which our species came into being, and on the process by which an individual gains full maturity.

Original Sin

While modern biology and anthropology pose no challenge to the basic doctrine of the creation of humankind in God's image, they do challenge the traditional doctrine of original sin as it has been expounded in the Western churches. This must be faced squarely and, in my judgement, the outcome of serious reflection is not that the ancient doctrine must be abandoned, but that it must be reinterpreted (as, indeed, it has been by a number of Western theologians from the time of Abelard in the twelfth century).[4]

The classical doctrine, as commonly expounded, included the following elements: (1) there was an historical fall when the individuals, Adam and Eve, were disobedient; (2) as a result, all humans beings are now born into a state of sin; (3) for this reason they inherit both moral weakness and a kind of moral guilt (*culpa*) at their birth which can only be dissolved by baptism (and this is part of the reason for infant baptism); (4) the fall has profoundly affected human sexuality, so that the lust which men and women have for each other is itself a sign of sin. Ideally, the procreation of children should be without this lust and more extreme elements in the church have sometimes claimed that the perfect Christian should abstain from all sexual activity. This is part of the background for the doctrine of the ever-virginity of Mary, taught in some churches, which claims that Mary continued as a virgin for *all* her married life.[5] This doctrine must not be confused with the doctrine of the virgin birth that refers strictly to the birth of Jesus alone. Hence, too, the 1954 encyclical in the Roman Catholic Church which insists that the celibate state is intrinsically higher than the married state.[6]

It is doubtful whether some elements of this traditional view can stand up to rational criticism, especially the historical fall (given the fact that the Genesis story was written in symbolic form, not as history); the notion of inborn guilt[7] (when our ordinary morality insists that we must participate willingly in any act for which we can be held responsible) and the puritan doctrine of sex,[8] which most churches have rejected in the twentieth century.

It is important to appreciate how the doctrine of 'original guilt' – *originalis culpa* – was based, in large part, on a misleading translation of St Paul's Greek. Jerome's enormously influential Latin version of Romans 5, 12 included the claim that we all sin *in* Adam – "in whom all have sinned" (*in quo omnes peccaverunt*) – whereas the more natural reading of the Greek suggests something like "we all sin like Adam". The scholarly Anglican bishop, Jeremy Taylor, 1613–1667, discussed this mistranslation and argued that the traditional doctrine of 'original guilt' is not, in fact, Biblical – although he endorsed the account of moral weakness that I have expressed. On this basis, he criticized the cruelty of the Calvinist doctrine that God condemns people to hell for sins for which they are not responsible.[9]

Most contemporary Christians feel that there is something true and important in the old doctrine of original sin if it is stated properly, so that element (2) is explained more carefully, and the other elements are reinterpreted or discarded. The following points need to be stressed as true and important:

(i) There is a universal, or near universal, fact of moral failure. The chief reason for this failure is that we start life with an animal egoism, which, although not sinful in itself, invites all humans to prefer selfish satisfaction to a response to the good. This animal egoism, I have tried to show, is the necessary *starting point* for *human* development.

(ii) This moral failure is due not only to our individual weaknesses, but also to social pressures that invite and encourage our failure, pressures that come from a sort of collective force of human evil that is there before we are born. In my view, the principal reason why Christians should continue to refer to 'original sin' and the 'fall', despite the misunderstandings the terms tends to cause, is because it brings out this truth that 'sin' is not only a matter of wrong *action*, but is a *state* of being – a state of moral weakness that is both individual and social. When Christians refer to the 'fallen' nature of man, this is the truth that is enshrined in the myth of the fall.

(iii) While we cannot inherit guilt, we can inherit responsibilities of a kind (not only to honour our parents, but also to right some of the wrongs for which our parents or our culture have been responsible).

Here are three important truths, and I shall argue in Chapter 13 that part of the trouble with Marxism is its failure to understand them. In a somewhat confused way, the doctrine of original sin has always stood for these ideas, but they have been mixed up with a primitive version of human solidarity (in which we can punish the children for the sins of the father and mother). An unblind faith must reject this view of solidarity, although it represents an idea that is historically understandable, for it looks back to the days before Jeremiah[10] when societies tended to believe in collective guilt as part of their way of thinking. In this revised form, original sin is perfectly compatible with evolution and with the other insights into the nature of humankind that have been provided by contemporary science. At the same time, any notion of 'original guilt', meaning a kind of moral condemnation that could be applied to infants, must be rejected.

The story of the individual person and the story of humankind

The view that humans are by nature creatures in process and that moral and spiritual qualities have to be achieved rather than given, can be illustrated and supported by observing the similarity of the story of the individual person and the story of humankind.

One aspect of the analogy is the purely biological one. We have learned that the human embryo and foetus in its mother's womb goes through many of the stages that humankind has passed through as a species. For example, there is a fish-like stage that gradually gives way to a terrestrial-like stage. It has always seemed odd to me that anti-evolutionists don't have any problem with the evolution of individuals in the womb, while they object to the evolution of humankind in history. This is particularly odd in view of the fact that we are not perfectly formed, for example, our backs and knees tend to be too weak for upright posture and for the typical, physical demands of a long, active life, but this imperfection is completely explicable in terms of evolutionary theory.

However, there is another aspect to this analogy which is even more interesting and that is between the struggle of individuals and that of humankind in order to become (properly) human. The story of humankind is one of a struggle to survive and then to flourish. We discover that we can only survive as a species through social co-operation and the increasing use of our intelligence. The struggle is against the hardships of nature and the danger of fellow-humans and also against the selfish or egotistical side of our nature, which struggles with our capacity to cooperate and to love. As we have seen, human egoism is not *initially* evil, it is simply part of our animal nature and perhaps essential for our survival, but it becomes a source of evil when the private good, or rather the private apparent good, is preferred to the social good. This is the context for the moral and spiritual struggle of humankind, the result of which can be the emergence of something not formerly seen on this planet, namely moral character.

The point I am making here is that the last few sentences can apply equally to the story of humankind and to the story of the individual man or woman. In Biblical language, the flesh fights against the spirit,[11] but the flesh is not evil in itself, it is only evil when chosen instead of spirit. Hence the word could become flesh.[12]

Thus the analogy between the story of individual persons and the story of humankind helps to indicate what we are and where we are going. Finally then, what can be said of the end of individual persons or of humanity?

The word 'end' in English has two meanings. It can mean 'end' in the sense of 'final stage', just as a station may be at the end of the line. Here 'end' corresponds to the Greek word *eschatos*. It can also mean 'end' in the sense of 'purpose', just as we might say that the end of the railway was to make safer passage between two cities. Here 'end' corresponds to the Greek word *telos*. In a Christian philosophy, there must be an end for humanity in both senses, but the second sense, that of *telos*, is the most crucial, for the Christian sees the whole creation as the product of a Mind that has a purpose for us. I shall take up the question of this final end or purpose in Chapter 8.

Notes

1   Ps. 8, 4.

2   Gen. 3, 5.

3   The point at which, within gestational life, it is proper to treat an embryo as a human person is highly controversial. If it is insisted that 'ensoulment' comes at a particular moment, there is a good case for saying that conception – which marks the start of a new genetic entity (or entities) – is the most logical marker (even though, within the Jewish tradition, many support viability). However, some thinkers worry about this language of 'ensoulment' at a particular moment. My personal view is 'to give the benefit of doubt' to the embryo, and to argue that any destruction of an embryo needs strong and unusual reasons – somewhat akin to rare cases of justifiable homicide. However, the issue of what legal enforcement of this view is appropriate is very difficult, and here there is – in my view – a case for a more 'liberal' policy.

4   Abelard argued that although we could inherit the consequences of Adam's sin (such as the loss of immortality) we could not actually inherit the *guilt*, until we had in some degree co-operated with evil.

5   The New Testament has several references to Jesus's brothers and sisters and many Christians have thought that these were children of Mary and Joseph, born after Jesus (e.g. Mark 6, 3 and Gal. 1, 19). The Roman Catholic view is that these were half-brothers and sisters of Jesus, born to Joseph by his first wife, and the Greek does not rule out this interpretation. However, the chief reason for the Roman Catholic view (which seems to go against the most natural reading of the Greek and the implications of Matt. 1, 25) is the concern to exalt Mary. I agree with those who claim that if Mary had natural children after the birth of Jesus, this in no way diminishes her stature. Hence, while the doctrine of the virgin birth is Biblical (even though some liberal Christians do not think it is important), I am doubtful as to whether the 'ever-virginity' of Mary should be taught as official doctrine. I much prefer to see Mary as a model for Christian marriage.

6   The encyclical *Sacra Virginitatis* of 1954.

7   The only way in which it could be meaningful to speak of individual guilt in a baby is if we accept reincarnation (a belief that some Christians have held – prior to redemption in Christ – but that is denied in orthodox teaching). Doctrines of collective guilt run into grave moral objections. See, for example, H. D. Lewis, *Morals and Revelation*, Allen and Unwin, 1951, ch. 5.

8   'Puritan' views of sex vary considerably, but I have in mind the extreme

view (held by some, but not all of those who are called Puritans)
that sexual passion, even between married partners, should not be
enjoyed.

9   This important point needs some academic background if it is not to be
misunderstood. Jeremy Taylor is one of several seventeenth century
scholars who insist on going back to the original Greek, for example,
in *Unum Necessarium*, 1655 and *Deus Justificatus*, 1656. When he
discusses his rejection of the traditional teaching on 'original sin' it
is clear that it is 'original guilt' that he is attacking, and in one of
his letters he specifically says that he is not rejecting 'original sin',
but that "which it is supposed to be" (*Works*, 1828 ed. IX, p. 368,
cf. 1–25 and 93ff.). As in my account, he stresses the weakness of
human nature, especially when we consider its social aspect, which
he likens to a fleet of ships colliding in a storm, and he stresses how
– in descendants of Adam and Eve – "sin was easy and ready at the
door" (*Ibid.* pp. 316–7). (Jeremy Taylor must not be confused with
the free-church minister, John Taylor, who, in 1740, published an
influential book attacking the idea of original sin which was much
criticized by John Wesley.) A little later we find the same analysis of
the Greek text in the writings of the Quaker, Robert Barclay. While
Abelard had argued on the basis of the logic of 'guilt' Taylor and
Barclay argue on the basis of both logic and the actual teaching of
the Bible.

On the issue of original guilt, see also the report of 'The
Commission on Christian Doctrine' appointed by the Archbishops
of Canterbury and York (1922), *Doctrine in the Church of
England*, SPCK, London, 1938, pp. 63–4. Several members of the
Commission recommended a doctrine of original sin that is similar
to the view generally held in the Greek Orthodox Church (which
never had to rely on the misleading translation in the Latin Bible),
seeing a fundamental truth in the doctrine, while distancing this
from any notion of inborn guilt (*culpa* or *reatus*). On this matter, see
Archpriest Alexander Golubov, *Rags of Mortality*, available on the website of the Orthodox Research Institute. Here there is still reference
to an inherited stain, but one that is distinguished from guilt.

Aquinas's teaching on original sin (in his *Summa Theologiae*
1a2ae Qs 81–3) has several strands. On the positive side he uses the
expression *peccatum originale*, which, in my view, is less suggestive of
the notion of blame than *culpa originalis*. Also, in some passages he
is sensitive to the problem of attributing guilt to infants. However,
he still insists that the child can inherit sin, and gives the example
of sharing the disgrace of a forebear's crime (81, 1 *ad* 5). However,
sharing disgrace (*ignominia*) is very different from sharing fault (*culpa*

or *mens rea*), which, in the subsequent discussion, is assumed to be present in the child prior to baptism (e.g. 81, 3 *ad* 2, where the key word is *reatu*). He also stresses the moral weakness of human beings who are subject to the 'tinder of sin' (81, 3 *ad* 2), and this is in line with my own stress on the weakness of the human condition in the context of a kind of communal solidarity. More negatively, not only does Aquinas insist that original sin is physically inherited as a result of Adam's sin, but that the stain comes through the male semen – not from the woman – for, if only Eve had sinned, there would not have been a transmission of original sin to Adam's offspring. Following Aristotle, Aquinas thought that the mother was basically an incubator, providing the 'bodily material' but not the 'seminal source' of our natures (81, 4 *ad* 3; 5 *ad* 2.) In this way, Aquinas was able to say that Jesus did not have original sin because (if one accepts a literal virgin birth) he was, biologically, a child of Mary but not of Joseph. In chapter 5 I shall suggest a different way of handling the issue of original sin in relation of Jesus's humanity. Aquinas was writing before the official sanctioning of the doctrine that, as a result of the 'immaculate conception', Mary was born without original sin. However, since, on Aquinas's view, the inheritance of original sin only comes through the semen, this does not materially affect his teaching.

Following Aquinas, Catholic teaching has insisted on original *guilt*, for example in the Decrees of the Council of Trent, session 5 of 17/06/1546, which speaks of *reatum originalis peccati*, and in the papal bull *Ineffabilis Deus*, 1854, which defines and declares the doctrine of the Immaculate Conception of Mary and includes the statement *omnes homines* [Jesus and Mary excepted] *nasci originali culpa infectos*. Traditional Lutheran and Calvinist teachings have usually followed the same pattern. However, more recent statements of doctrine often do not mention this aspect of official teaching, for example, the *Catechism of the Catholic Church* (Chapman, London 1994) has a section on original sin which makes no reference to the guilt of infants, although (rightly in my view) it stresses the moral weakness of the human condition. There have been some recent attempts to distance official teaching in most Western churches from inherited guilt by claiming that *culpa* or *reatus* did not mean 'guilt' in the modern sense. However, I think that such attempts fail to appreciate the clear meaning of the doctrine in many ancient sources, including Augustine. It is better, I suggest, to admit that, for the most part, the Western churches, unlike the Greek Orthodox Church, got this matter wrong.

The foregoing account of original sin raises problems with

respect to some of the 39 Articles, especially 9 and 13, and it is interesting to find Jeremy Taylor writing at length to interpret them in a non-Calvinist way (e.g. *Ibid.* IX, pp. 107 ff.). Although such interpretations may be possible, I think it would be much better to rewrite the offending Articles.

The relationship of original sin to original guilt can be further understood in the light of the distinction between 'shame cultures' and 'guilt cultures' that has been made by many scholars. (For example, see E. R. Dodds, *The Greeks and the Irrational*, University of California Press, 1951, ch. 2) During the archaic period of Greece, before about 500 BCE, the human concern was much more a matter of shame and honour than of individual responsibility and choice. In the later classical period, there is a switch towards a greater sense of inner, private responsibility and, with it, of what we would now recognize as personal 'guilt'. At the same time the gods, including Zeus, become recognizable moral agents rather than arbitrary dispensers of good and evil. Parallel changes can be seen in Hebrew and many other cultures. The change is not absolute, for vestiges of shame culture persisted, and still persist, in many places. The belief in 'original guilt' can be partially understood when it is seen as a relic of a shame culture in which a kind of 'pollution' can indeed be inherited from one person or family to another. (See Dodds, pp. 35 and 155–6.) I would argue that the Christian doctrine of sin goes hand in hand with a recognition of personal responsibility that emerges within a culture that thinks much more in terms of guilt than of shame.

There is clearly a degree of tension between the emphasis on personal responsibility and the emphasis -- frequently made in this book -- on our interdependency on other people. We are 'relational beings' and neither the idea of a church or of a 'communion of saints' makes sense if we look only at the individuality of persons. This is, I suggest, one of many places where we need to find a balance, or 'creative tension', for example, between freedom and grace or justice and mercy. Nevertheless my view is that within this balance the acceptance of 'inherited guilt' (and the allied notion of 'collective punishment') ought to be abandoned.

10   Jer. 31, 29–30; *cf.* Ex. 20, 5.
11   Gal. 5, 17.
12   John 1, 14; *cf.* II Cor. 5, 16.

4. Jesus is Lord

Jesus and God

The Christian will often hear a preacher say 'Jesus is God', or will be expected to sing hymns which refer to Jesus as 'Lord God Almighty'.[1] It may surprise some readers to hear that most Christian writers avoid these expressions because they give a misleading picture of Christian doctrine. The idea of God, in itself, is of a being that transcends space and time, so that it could not be correct to say, *without qualification*, 'Jesus is God'. This would suggest that one could equally say 'God is Jesus' and that is certainly not Christian doctrine. Therefore, the official doctrine has tended to qualify claims about the divinity of Jesus and say 'Jesus is the son of God', or 'Jesus is the second person of the Trinity', or 'Jesus is the Word of God', as described by St John.[2] The phrase which I prefer is that of St Paul when he describes Jesus as 'the image (*eikon*) of the invisible God'.[3] This way of using language may seem too cautious for some readers, but I believe that important principles are at stake – so that personally I much prefer to say "Jesus is divine" than "Jesus is God".

Why have Christians made such claims about divinity and what do they mean? It is especially important to answer these questions when we hear well-disposed critics of Christianity say: "Why can't we just say that Jesus was a very good man, or one of the prophets, or even the greatest of the prophets?" I shall try to answer this question from the point of view of a Christian philosophy. This philosophy may not be one hundred per cent orthodox, but is certainly a *Christian* view rather than a Humanist or Unitarian view, and it is also one that I believe can be held with complete integrity by one who seeks an unblind faith. It is also compatible with either a Protestant or a Catholic emphasis. The first half of my answer involves an examination of the Biblical account of the life of Jesus, and the second half, which is equally necessary, involves seeing the Christian doctrine of Christ within the context of an overall philosophy of God and humankind.

Jesus in the New Testament

In chapter 12 I shall tackle the question of the accuracy of the Bible, but for the time being let us work on the assumption that the New Testament, even if inaccurate in some matters of detail, does give a generally true picture of the life and character of Jesus and, in particular, of the stories that he told (which were the things most likely to be remembered with accuracy).

It is clear that Jesus saw his coming as a climax in the history of Israel. His parables claim that now is the crucial moment, the time of the coming of the bridegroom, of the gathering of the harvest, of the finding of treasure, of the drawing in of the net and so on. One parable is of particular interest in this connection, namely the parable of the vineyard as it occurs in the twelfth chapter of Mark. All of Jesus's hearers would know that he was retelling the story of Israel, for the vineyard was a common symbol for the chosen people and Jewish coins sometimes used bunches of grapes to symbolize their country, just as some Canadian coins use a maple leaf. When the harvest is ready, the Lord of the vineyard sends his servants to collect the fruits, but the servants are rejected by the tenants and some are killed. Again, every hearer would have seen the point, for the prophets were commonly referred to as the 'Lord's servants' – the messengers who came to Israel in every age calling for good deeds, the fruits of obedience. Then the parable goes on: "He had still one other, a beloved son; finally he sent him to them, saying, 'They will respect my son'. But those tenants said to one another, 'This is the heir; come, let us kill him, and the inheritance will be ours.'"

It is clear from this, and from the other parables, that Jesus did not see himself merely as one of the prophets, but as something more. His own preference for a title seems to have been the phrase 'son of man', but he also accepted Peter's suggestion that he was the Christ, the son of the living God.[4] 'Christ' in Greek is the same word as 'Messiah' in Hebrew and means 'the anointed one'. It is evident that Jesus accepted this title and also that he interpreted it in a different way from many Jews, notably the zealots, who were looking for a political Messiah. His decision to ride a donkey into Jerusalem rather than a horse might have been a deliberate sign to the zealots of the nature of his Messiahship and his frequent use of the suffering servant theme from the prophet Isaiah reinforced this. The Messiah had come to rule, but in hearts and minds, and his path was one of suffering and humiliation.

There are many further indications that Jesus saw himself as something more than just another prophet. There was his claim to be able to forgive sins, which shocked many of his listeners,[5] and his claim to be able to revise the law that God gave to Moses, especially his rejection of the old law, "An eye for an eye and a tooth for a tooth."[6] In passing we should note that when Jesus tells us, in his revision of the law, to turn the other cheek, he is referring to insults; he is not necessarily insisting on an extreme form of pacifism. Another critical passage is when the disciples of John come to ask whether he is the expected one, and Jesus replies: "Go and tell John what you hear and see."[7] In the context it is clear that Jesus is referring to the signs that accompany the coming Messiah.

Some writers would add the miracle stories as vital testimony to the nature of Jesus, but from the point of view of the unblind faith that this book is seeking to describe, I think that this is a mistake. This is not because I do not accept some of the miracle stories, but because (a) they are among the most disputed passages of the New Testament, and at this stage I want to base the Christian claim about Jesus on a foundation that does not depend on historical passages that can easily be challenged; (b) even if accepted, the miracles do not prove Christian claims about Jesus, for it may be the case that many holy people have performed miracles; and (c) Jesus himself seems to have played down the use of his miracles as evidence.[8]

Nor, at this point, do I wish to make use of the series of 'I am' statements recorded in St John's gospel, such as "Before Abraham was, I am."[9] The reason for this is that it is difficult to be sure how far these statements refer to the actual sayings of Jesus and how far they reflect a meditation by the author of the gospel on the meaning of the life of Jesus. I must not be misunderstood here. I am not saying that Jesus did not say these things; I am saying that for the seeker of an unblind faith they cannot be used as *primary evidence* for the nature of Jesus. I tend to think he may have said these things *because* I believe, on other grounds, that Jesus is the image of God. In a similar way, rather than believing that Jesus was the Messiah *because* of the miracles, I think that some of the miracles may have happened *because* I believe that Jesus was the Messiah. This is a more rational approach than the one that uses these sayings or miracles as primary evidence when they are open to such obvious difficulties.

Jesus and prophecy

It is clear that, according to the most ancient tradition in the New Testament, Jesus saw himself as the Messiah and as more than a prophet. But this is not enough for a Christian philosophy, for it must be asked, "Could Jesus have been wrong in his assessment of his own mission?" and "If Jesus were more than a prophet, what exactly was he?" In order to respond to these questions, we have to look beyond the New Testament, for the New Testament picture itself is being challenged. In this section, I shall begin to build up a Christian philosophy of the nature of Jesus by looking at the Old Testament context of the life of Jesus, for he claimed to fulfil its prophecies.

We must note that 'prophecy' can mean two things. One we can call 'crystal-ball gazing' and refers to an attempt to see the future in a kind of vision of what *is* there to be seen; as if in the middle of reading a novel we were to glance at the last page to see the future that is laid out. The other kind of prophecy is a matter of proclaiming the meaning of things as they are now, sometimes with the implications for the probable future. The great prophets of the Old Testament were primarily prophets in the latter sense, that is, they were 'spokespersons' or 'forthtellers' rather than 'foretellers'. No doubt there are elements of the first kind of prophecy in some of their utterances,[10] but in general thoughtful people are very nervous about this kind of prediction, partly because the notion that the future is fixed in detail seems to conflict with our ideas of freedom and responsibility and partly because it lends itself to unprofitable speculation, for example, about exactly when the world will end. When this kind of 'foretelling' prophecy is found we can think of it either as the indication of a probable outcome, or more radically, as a relic from a more primitive outlook that should be discarded.

We should note here that when Jesus prophesied the destruction of the Temple at Jerusalem,[11] this too can be seen as a prophecy of the 'forthtelling' kind. He was not 'crystal-ball gazing', but seeing the natural outcome of the contemporary tension between the Romans and the Jews and, in particular, the probable result of the growth of the zealot party. His prophecy was a kind of political realism. It was not a case of "This is what is laid down in the future", but "This is how things are going to turn out if people continue with their present policies." It was the same kind of realism that led Jesus to predict his betrayal and death. Towards the end of his ministry it became clear to Jesus that Judas would be the betrayer, but not because Judas was destined from before his birth to betray Jesus.

The great Old Testament prophets had something of the same sensitivity to the meaning of events and the character of God that Jesus displayed. They saw that the Jews had been chosen, not for their own sakes, but to be 'a light to the nations'.[12] Gradually, therefore, the Jews had to be taught their role and the true nature of God. Again and again God had rescued Israel, sent messengers and tried to draw the people to himself. So the prophets, as they began to understand the character of God, looked forward to a time when God would complete the process he had begun when he had called Israel. They saw this as happening through a new deliverer, the Messiah, who would unfold God's plan. When we ask what this Messiah would be like, we see the dramatic insight of these later prophets, especially in the writings of Isaiah. These prophets began to understand the inevitability of suffering by the good and something of its redeeming quality when experienced in the right way and for the right end. So the coming Messiah was not to be a conqueror, like Joshua, but a suffering servant. Indeed, the implication is that this is the role for the whole of Israel, if they are to fulfil God's purpose for them. So we find in Isaiah, Jeremiah, Hosea, the author of Job and in several psalms, a new sensitivity to human life and human needs and a new vision of the nature of God's love.

This is the context in which we must understand Jesus's claim to fulfil the prophets, and the Christian claim that he died and rose again 'according to the scriptures'.

Jesus as logos

So far we have explored how Jesus saw himself and the prophetic tradition that he claimed to fulfil. To these insights, a Christian philosophy must add a universal context in which we see the role of Jesus in terms of world history and the meaning of all life. In this way, Christians can explain why they take the Bible as central for the meaning of life, rather than the scriptures of other religious traditions – even though many of these other scriptures may hold great insights, and have much value for all of us.

The Christian philosophy goes as follows. God is the father of all humankind and he seeks human fulfilment by encouraging us to love both other people and himself. To this end, he speaks to us in many ways, of which the sayings of the prophets are but one. Whenever God expresses himself through the presentation of what is good, true, or beautiful, we can speak of his 'word' to humankind. Once again, we are relying here on a human analogy because we communicate with each other most typically in words. However, while the expression 'God's word' can refer to any of a thousand ways in which God speaks to humankind, there is a specially appropriate sense of 'Word' that refers to what Christians believe is the climax of God's revelation, or showing of himself, within the history of his relationship with the Jews. In this relationship – as it is portrayed in the Bible – we see God reaching down to humankind, stage by stage extending his love and compassion. But there is a logical climax to this process (using 'logical' to mean a consistency with a general pattern), for all of God's acts of love point to the possibility of an ultimate act of love in which God *identifies* with humanity, so far as it is possible for an eternal being to do so. Thus St Paul says, "God was in Christ reconciling the world to himself"[13] and others have said, "We see in Jesus, in time, the character of God in eternity."

This way of looking at things, which sees Jesus as more than a prophet because he is the embodiment of an act of identification, involves going beyond the purely Biblical context, for it relates to our experience of life as a whole. Each day, we see love and hatred and their effects and we see how the highest form of love between human persons involves an act of identification. In this act, sometimes we have to go literally 'where he was' in order to reach our friend, just as the good Samaritan had to go physically to the man in need, and it always involves a mental and spiritual identification with the friend or neighbour. This identification may involve physical suffering and it always involves spiritual suffering as we share another's burden (or spiritual joy as we share another's happiness). It is this human experience of love, with its logical climax in acts of identification, that adds enormous significance to St John's assertion: "And the word became flesh, and dwelt among us ..."[14] Here the Biblical tradition of God's love reaching down to humankind and the universal human experience of love come together. God expresses his love and shows us his Word in the most complete way possible within the conditions of this world.

The initiative of God

It must now be evident why it is so hard for Christians to say precisely who Jesus was or is, and why, when we speak of the nature of Jesus, we are bound to claim that we are dealing with a great mystery. A 'mystery' in the proper sense of the word is not a superstition, it is rather a word we use when human experience confronts us with mind-boggling questions that we find ourselves compelled to ask, but which we are aware that we are incapable of answering adequately. Modern physics is full of such questions, and so is religion. From the point of view of an unblind faith, there are no grounds here for accepting the irrational, but there are grounds for making do with only partial answers (or, for example, in physics, with alternative models). Faith, Aquinas insisted, may sometimes lead us to go 'beyond' reason, but not 'against' it.[15] What faith affirms may sometimes be 'non-rational', but not 'irrational'. The latter suggests the acceptance of a contradiction in the way things actually are, rather than in our limited view of them.

With respect to the nature of Jesus, the mystery arises because the indications that we have explored in this chapter suggest a person who is truly a man (otherwise he cannot *identify* with humankind), but who is also, in some extraordinary way, a unique revelation of God. One theme that brings together this dual aspect of the nature of Jesus is that of the *initiative* of God in Jesus, an initiative that is indicated in all three of the contexts we have explored (Old Testament, New Testament and daily experience). If Jesus were simply a very good man, as is the belief of many non-Christians who have a profound respect for him, then what happens to this initiative? Perhaps it is not lost altogether, but essentially it is the same sort of initiative as can be seen when God is in contact with any prophet or saint. For example, on a humanistic interpretation, what happens to the Christmas story? It is still beautiful, but it only has significance because of what Jesus *became*, it cannot in itself be any more significant than the birth of any other baby boy or girl (though I certainly don't want to belittle the significance of that). But for the Christian, the story has an enormous additional meaning, even if some of the details, such as the virginity of Mary, are pious myths rather than historical fact. On such matters we may be agnostic and Christian at the same time. The point is that here God takes a new and awesome step in the drama of his approach to humankind; he chooses to become as human, that we might become as God. He came to share our humanity that we might share his divinity. As Athanasius put it, powerfully even though a little misleadingly, "God made himself man, that man might become God."[16]

No doubt such language is mysterious, but I have argued that it is not *totally* baffling, because we have glimpses of what it means through our own experience. We know what it is to share with others, to take part in their joys and sufferings and in a sense to choose to be 'one' with them. Similarly, God chose to be 'one' with us and hence the mystery of Christ. Some of the ways in which Christians have attempted to describe this mystery will be examined in the next two chapters.

Jesus is Lord

The first Christians did not have a worked out formula for the nature of Jesus, but they had a creed, an extremely short creed that is frequently referred to in the Acts of the Apostles,[17] namely "Jesus is Lord", or "Christ is Lord". Christians tend to speak of 'Jesus' when they are thinking of the person whom they follow and 'Christ' when they think of his role, or the meaning of his life. To assert this creed, plus genuine repentance, was all that was required of the first Christians at their baptism. This creed put on one side all sorts of complex questions about exactly how Jesus is related to God, but it affirmed that believers accepted Jesus as their Lord, as the one they had to follow in order to find the true meaning of life. Jesus stood for the good, the true and the beautiful, and thus pointed humanity towards God.

In chapter 9, when we look at the essentials and the non-essentials of the Christian faith, I shall recommend a return to the use of this simple creed for many occasions. A person who doubts just about everything in traditional Christian theology, but who can say "Jesus is Lord" with conviction, is a Christian in a real sense. Such people may not yet have developed a Christian philosophy, they may even have doubts about the reality of God, but this commitment puts them inside the circle of faith. This is the chief thing that binds all Christians together in one family over whom Christ is Lord.

Notes

1   For example, in the hymn 'In the Bleak Mid-Winter', verse 2.
2   John 1, 1.
3   Col. 1, 15; *cf.* Heb. 1, 3.
4   Matt. 16, 16. The term 'son of man' was used in the popular literature of Jesus's time (for example in *The Similitudes of Enoch*), to indicate one of the Messiah's titles.
5   Mark 2, 5–7.
6   Matt. 5, 38-9 *cf.* Ex. 21, 24.
7   Matt. 11, 4.
8   John 10, 38; *cf.* Matt, 8, 4. On many occasions Jesus asked those whom he had healed not to spread the news abroad. Especially in St John's gospel, the message seems to be that those who are of the light will be attracted to the light for its own sake, and not – at least primarily – for the signs that accompany the light.
9   John 8, 58.
10 E.g. I Kings 22, 17.
11 Mark 13, 2; *cf.* Matt. 23, 37–8.
12 Isa. 42, 6.
13 II Cor. 5, 19.
14 John 1, 14.
15 E.g. Aquinas, *Summa Contra Gentiles*, I, ch. 7.
16 *De incarnatione verbi*, 54 (PG volume 25, 192B), *cf.* Gal, 4, 4–7.
17 E.g. Acts 2, 38; 10, 48.

5. Jesus is Saviour

Jesus and Superman

Gradually the central role of Jesus in a Christian view of the world is emerging. First we had to build an idea of a loving God who is seeking to reach down to humankind and call us to union with himself and our fellow human beings. Then we had to understand the essential nature of humanity and the emergence of a spiritual nature as we attempt to reach up to God. Then we come to Jesus, who is a kind of bridge figure, who binds together within himself the principles of God and of humanity.

One way of drawing out the significance of Jesus for the Christian is to contrast him with 'Superman' or with many of the other heroes that the young, and the not so young, are being presented with. Heroes like Superman are basically irrelevant to our lives, not because they are imaginary, but because they share few, if any, of our human problems. In an emergency they can catch bullets with their teeth, or fly away, or call upon super-human strength, or magic. In contrast, the heroes of great literature share our human condition and we can be inspired by them even when they are imaginary. This applies even to fantasies like Tolkien's trilogy of the ring, where Boromir is tempted and falls and where even Gandalf has to fight the temptation to take and use the ring of power.

This illustrates the importance of the claim that Jesus was tempted, or tested, in all points like ourselves[1] and that he would not call angels to his aid[2] and indeed *could* not if he were to accept the full implications of taking on the human condition.[3] Thus he can inspire us because his life is relevant. He shared our condition and yet, we believe, lived in total obedience to the good, without sin. He had no special advantage in this respect and the old teaching that he alone (except perhaps for Enoch and Mary) was born without original sin is misleading, because it can be taken to suggest that he did, after all, have a special 'advantage'. As explored in chapter 3, when properly described, original sin is an aspect of the human condition in a 'fallen' world in which, in addition to the temptation to personal egoism, there is a kind of human solidarity through which we can easily become involved in a collective selfishness. However, this does not mean that we *must* sin, by some absolute inevitability. The perfect person will be tempted (among other reasons because, like Jesus, all of us have the passions or drives that come with a human body), but with God's help it is possible not to sin.

One of the reasons why Christians claim that – unlike Superman – Jesus is able to redeem us, is precisely because of this sharing in our condition. That is why he is called not only lord, but saviour. This is in part a play on the name 'Jesus', which literally means 'saviour' in the Hebrew, but it also refers to the claim that with his help we can be saved from sin and from the final death that is its result. The meaning of this claim will be explored in the rest of this chapter.

Although Christians insist that Jesus shared our humanity, in order to avoid misunderstanding, they avoid saying that he too had 'original sin'. The basic Christian position here is difficult to express in a few sentences, but I shall attempt to do just that. In chapter 3 we saw how the Christian doctrine of original sin has been consistently misunderstood and misdescribed, except within the Orthodox tradition. The Bible does not teach a doctrine of original *guilt*, but does suggest that virtually all men and women are, from childhood, actual sinners, because they have been unable to resist either the pressures of an inborn ego or the social pressures that surround us from birth. Also, the Bible uses the word 'sin' not only to refer to wrongful acts, but to the sinful or fallen *state* that people are in. Although Jesus shared our human nature, neither of these situations applies to him. He was (according to the Christian tradition) totally free from actual sin, and his character was free from any corrupting vices – remembering that vices arise, not from having temptations, but from yielding to them. Thus, even though I want to stress how Jesus shared our humanity, I do not want to say anything that might imply that he too was dragged down by the condition of 'original sin'. This is one of many places where the attempt to do justice to the situation makes it difficult to find language that will not be misleading. I would summarize the situation by saying that Jesus shared our nature, but not our *fallen* nature. I would add that part of what we *mean* when we refer to the divine nature of Jesus, is that although he shared the feelings that come with temptation, his character was such that he would not yield to temptation.[4]

Sin and guilt

Both the Hebrew and the Greek words translated as 'sin' convey a series of ideas, but the central one is of 'falling short of the mark', like an arrow that fails to reach its target. Thus sin, in its primary sense, is the voluntary choice of something less than the good. It refers both to many of the acts and to the condition of all, or almost all, men and women once they have reached years of discretion. Because of the pressure of our culture and of our fellows, sin has a frightening element of predictability about it. Nevertheless, I stress again that it is a voluntary matter, otherwise we can make no sense of God's judgement and of our responsibility. If, at any moment, a person *cannot* choose the good, or at least the lesser evil, perhaps because of a chemically or physically damaged brain, then the question of sin – at least in its straightforward sense – cannot arise. What is inevitable and predictable, given the myriad occasions and the nature of the forces as work, is that sooner or later almost all people will sin.

The effect of sin is the destruction of what is truly human, if by 'human' we mean what we can become when we respond to the good, the true and the beautiful. It distorts or destroys the process of emergence from the animal level. Humans do not then return to the animal level, for this in itself is natural and sinless, but sink to a level below it. Paradoxically, our own egoism then gets us caught up in a selfishness that destroys the possibility of anything beyond a superficial happiness, for true happiness depends on relationships of love with others that cannot coexist with selfishness. Worse still, this selfishness becomes a sort of disease that feeds on itself as one sin leads on to another.

Guilt is the appropriate sentiment for someone who knows that they have sinned. Contrary to what some psychologists say, there is nothing essentially neurotic about guilt; the problems with guilt, as typically experienced, are (i) that many people feel guilty about the wrong things and (ii) that there is often no way of lifting a burden that can drag us down. With respect to the first of these problems we can take the example of many Victorian boys and girls who were taught to feel guilty about their adolescent sexual dreams and fantasies, which were mostly perfectly natural and were either sinless, or sinful in a very low degree. At the very same time, they were not generally taught to feel guilty about the intense suffering caused when they bullied an unpopular classmate. But here, I maintain, feelings of guilt would be highly appropriate. With respect to the second problem, part of the essence of Christianity is the discovery of a wholesome way of shedding the burden, through forgiveness and reconciliation. In sum, many of us may have neurotic guilt feelings but it is not the guilt itself that is neurotic, it is the lack of judgment about where and when we should feel it and the absence of an appropriate way of shedding the burden.

One other aspect of sin must be stressed here. We are not only responsible for our voluntary actions; in the long run we are also responsible for many sides of our character. Even in the fourth century BCE Aristotle saw that this must be so if we are to give an adequate account of the moral life, for otherwise we could simply blame many of our bad actions on our temper or moodiness. Similarly, good actions are typically the result of *virtue*, consequences of a character that has been achieved.[5] No doubt some aspects of our character are purely genetic and Aristotle calls these 'natural dispositions' (in contrast with the 'acquired dispositions' which constitute real virtue),[6] but by the way we choose to act now we form habits that gradually develop into our genuine virtues and vices. If adults have bad tempers, they are at least partially to blame.

Atonement

One of the great insights of the Christian faith is the recognition that, in the face of sin, self-help is not enough. Human effort is certainly demanded, but by itself it often leads to despair. Indeed, in an odd way, the very struggle to improve the self tends to turn in upon itself and intensify the concern with *myself*. Further, when there is some success in the struggle, pride in this success tends to follow.

However, some people, both Christian and non-Christian, can and do transcend this vicious circle of egoism and achieve a level of selflessness. This is part of our human experience and we see it happen whenever people love. I am not primarily talking about 'falling in love' in a romantic way, though this too is a beautiful thing that often includes love in its richest sense, but love for one's friends and, if relationships are as they should be, love for parent or child. We are all capable of this love and when we experience it we are in some degree drawn out of our selfish centres and others become as central and important in our eyes as we are ourselves.

The origins of this capacity to love are probably there in the evolutionary process. For a species to survive, it often became necessary that members should sacrifice themselves for others. For example, we can see in nature how a mother bird may deliberately sacrifice herself when a bear climbs the tree towards the nest where the fledglings lie. Thus the cynical suggestion that humans *can* only act selfishly (for example, for the sake of gaining heaven, or being well thought of, or appeasing our consciences) is a mistake. Along with many other animals, we have evolved with both ego drives and species drives and the latter look to the good of the group, or at least to the good of one's kin. The development of morality depends upon building on this species drive that is already there within us. But, just as in general the emergence of the human order involves a *new level* of being, so here, in human moral life, a quality of love can emerge that can go beyond the species drive. The poetry of love, including the thirteenth chapter of I Corinthians is abundant evidence of this.

Thus love is the answer to sin and guilt and to the selfishness that underlies them. It is important to see that the Christian doctrine of forgiveness and atonement (in which we become 'at one' with God and fellow human beings) is based on this universal human experience of love, but it is raised to a universal teaching about human salvation and based on a spectacular outpouring of God's love. The Christian claim is that in Christ we find the universal symbol for how humanity can discover its true end and, moreover, that in Christ there occurred in history a divine action that transformed the situation caused by sin. The prodigal son can return home as a son because the father has reached out to meet him.

The symbolic meaning of Christ's work is not hard to see. St Paul put it like this: "As in Adam all die, even so in Christ shall all be made alive."[7] Adam symbolizes raw humanity, that is human beings struggling to emerge from the animal level, but failing to achieve their potential. Christ represents the new humanity, the new creation, the image of what we can be and shall be. But when we seek to go beyond the symbolism and ask: "How does this divine initiative actually help us?", what can we say? Although we cannot fully understand the mystery of Christ's work, we are not asked blindly to accept it as a fact. Once again we can strive for an unblind faith and in the next two sections I shall show how we can begin to grasp the significance of what Jesus did. Additional material will be provided in chapter

14 when, in the discussion of caricatures of Christian teaching, four theories of the atonement will be reviewed.

The power of love

The first way in which we can begin to understand the work of Christ is to appreciate the power of example and the way in which a demonstration of love can draw out a response that would not otherwise have been possible. So, looking at the results of the life of Jesus, St John said, "We love, because he first loved us"[8] and this effect seems to have been anticipated by Jesus himself when he said, "I, when I am lifted up from the earth, will draw all men to myself."[9]

Here is one of the many places where there is harmony between the teaching of the Bible and our contemporary experience of human life. For example, A does an injury to B out of anger or malice, but quite unexpectedly B does not retaliate but offers a creative solution to the quarrel. At this point A faces a new opportunity. The hand of friendship may be rejected, or (and most of us have seen this happen) it may be accepted, and then, out of the quarrel can emerge peace and reconciliation.

In the above example, it matters that the person showing love actually demonstrates it in a particular event or set of events. Similarly, if someone is to know the love of God with all the power that actual examples can have, then there has to be an actual event or set of events in which we see the love of God. This, Christians believe, is part of the meaning of the cross. In one sense, the cross transcends time, for it demonstrates an eternal principle, that is of the lengths to which God's love will go; but for our sake this love had also to be acted out in an historical event. Because of this event, we can respond in a way which would not otherwise have been possible, for the demonstration of love calls forth a response of love. Henceforth, we can serve Jesus as Lord not for our own ends, not even for the sake of heaven[10] (the search for which can easily be a long-run variety of selfishness), but purely as a response to God's love. When we love, we do not need an additional motive, the other becomes for us an end in himself or herself.

In stressing the power of the example of Jesus, we must not look at the cross in isolation from the rest of his life. If we do, there tends to follow a morbid concentration on blood and sacrifice and a magical theory of the atonement in which an angry God is somehow appeased by the offer of a sacrificial lamb. There is, indeed, great symbolic power in this notion of the sacrificial lamb, but in the hands of many fundamentalist preachers it is taken so literally that we end up with absurdity, as if blood in itself had any power, or as if the righteousness of Christ could be transferred to us in a quasi-mechanical exchange. To believe in the atoning power of the work of Christ does not involve having to accept dubious theories that do violence to our rationality and our morality. God did indeed achieve reconciliation, not by magic, but through an extension of the power of love that we see all around us.

When we emphasize the cross in the context of a whole life, then we see that the particular manner of Jesus's death is secondary. The essential thing is that, in being faithful to his identification with humanity, it was inevitable that sooner or later he would be violently rejected. We may recall that Plato had prophesied, in the true sense of prophecy that we have referred to, that a truly good person would eventually be put to death.[11] Jesus had to live as a man, not as a Superman or as an angel dressed up as a man, and he had to live through this act of identification to the end.

Some radical Christians would go even further than I have here and suggest that even if Jesus died of measles, or some other disease that happened to be humanity's enemy at the time, it would have made no difference, for this too would have been the acceptance of the human condition with no strings attached. Others claim that the symbolic power of the crucifixion is such that providence steered the inevitable death to take this form. Readers can reflect on this suggestion for themselves, but my own view is that both the symbolic and the psychological power of Jesus's life are increased by the nature of his death.

One further reflection on the power of love is appropriate at this point. In human relationships, one of the most powerful forces is the acceptance of people as they are. For example, in true friendship, we love the friend as he or she is and not as we think that person ought to be. The result is that one does not have to act a part in the presence of one's true friends, as if one were in danger of losing their affection. Again, one of the most powerful elements in the stability of family life, at its best, is the fact that children feel a loving acceptance, not for the gifts or virtues that the parents would like to see, but simply for themselves. Similarly, those who are seeking God can find an incredible sense of relief and joy in the realization that God loves them as they are. As Jesus put it, he came to call the sinners, not the righteous.[12] Thus one Christian writer has expressed the heart of the Christian message as the call to "accept that we are accepted".[13] The same note is sounded in the hymn "Just as I am, without one plea ... O Lamb of God, I come."

Life 'in Christ'

When we consider the achievement of Christ, the power of the example of Jesus does not exhaust the meaning of his life when seen as an historical event. Another crucial result of his coming is the opening up of a new kind of participation or union with others 'in Christ'.

For some readers this will seem a very strange idea, so let us begin its exploration outside the Bible and then return there, in order to see how yet again the Christian view is one that completes or fulfils something found in everyday experience.

Suppose that we ask how far our true nature lies in our private individuality and how far it lies in a merger with a group or whole. On this issue, a traditional Christian philosophy steers a middle course. The purely individualistic life is incomplete and lonely and yet the opposite extreme, where there is to be a merging of ourselves with a whole in which we altogether lose our individuality, also seems to be a mistake, even though it is the express goal of some religions which speak of our souls being absorbed into the great Soul, like a drop into the ocean.[14] If such is to be the final end of every person, what is the purpose of the creative activity that brings forth such variety, and the wonder and beauty of individual characters? Thus a compromise is suggested. True human living involves transcending our egotistical view of the individual person and seeing our very life as being bound up with the lives of others, with whom we share joy and sadness, but in a relationship in which there is still an 'I' and a 'you'.

This is the place to bring in the proper use of the word 'mysticism'. In popular usage, this word often refers to anything mysterious or odd, but properly used, it refers to an important and specific type of experience that is found in all the great religions, the experience described as union with God. Whatever we make of experiences of this kind, they are in one sense facts, at the psychological level. As I have pointed out in the case of the experience of the numinous, which has something in common with the experience of union, one of the grounds for taking religion seriously is the fact that different people in many times, places and cultures, have described very similar experiences. Sometimes the account is of a person becoming literally one with God, in a kind of organic union. In other accounts, the description suggests that there is a joy caused by a close relationship with God in which there is still a self that is distinct from God's being. For mystics who use the second kind of language, an analogy for union with God is often sought in the union of two human lovers, as in the *Song of Solomon*. How we should interpret these accounts is a fascinating and difficult question, but all that I want to do here is to re-emphasize that there is a general human experience of life in communion, in which our true selves are found only in the context of a fellowship in which the very core of our being is transformed through our relationship with God and with others.

We can now turn to the Biblical expression of this kind of human experience. It is strongly emphasized in the teaching of Jesus. For example, consider his statement: "Unless a grain of wheat falls into the earth and dies, it remains alone; but if it dies, it bears much fruit. He who loves his life loses it ... "[15] This expresses the theme briefly and brilliantly, for it is precisely the solitary state, the remaining 'alone' that is the cause of the real death of the person. We should also recall the last conversations between Jesus and the disciples as recounted in St John's gospel. Even if these are meditations on Jesus's life rather than his actual words, it is reasonable to assume that they reflect what the author had learned from Jesus. Of particular interest is the passage "You will know that I am in my father, and you in me, and I in you", followed by "I am the vine, you are the branches."[16] To these sayings we must add the recurring theme of St Paul's letters concerning life 'in Christ'. This is the new level of being that he and the other Christians had come to experience and which was symbolized in baptism, which indicated that one died, lived and rose again, with Christ and 'in Christ'.[17]

The principal reason for the shallowness of so much contemporary church life and for the boredom that accompanies so many church services and meetings is that this life 'in Christ' is not the living experience of the ordinary churchgoer. It is either unknown, or merely an interesting *idea*. But for those who can recapture the living experience, we have here the principal clue to understanding how Jesus's coming, in a unique historical event, can open up a path to salvation. Just because he became human, we can enter into a new kind of union with him in which the whole level of our being is raised. "No man is an island"[18] in so far as they have discovered what being a person is really about. This discovery, as I have shown, is indicated in our daily experience of love and friendship and it is spotlighted and brought to fulfilment in the mystical experience of the saints in all the great religions. The work of Christ takes on a new dimension of meaning when we see it in this context, for what he did was to open up to all of us the possibility of a new life in union with him.

Notes

1   Heb. 4, 15.
2   Matt. 26, 53.
3   *cf.* Phil. 2, 5–8.
4   We saw in chapter 3 (note 9) that according to a Western tradition, Jesus did not share our original sin because this – it was believed – only passed through the male seed. In consequence, belief in a literal virgin birth implied that this condition was not present in Jesus. Even if one believes in the virgin birth as an actual event, this raises difficulties, because we now know that half of our physical inheritance comes from the mother, and the difficulties are compounded if one has doubts about the literal truth of the virgin birth. I prefer to locate Jesus's sinless nature differently, and in a way that – in my view – is less in tension with any special moral 'advantage' given by the circumstances of his birth, which can distance his nature from ours. Any coherent doctrine of the Trinity has to claim that the Son existed before the birth of Jesus, and this pre-existence is also the clear teaching of the New Testament. Therefore, despite the claim that Jesus shared our nature, he was different from us in respect of having a kind of character (*cf.* the Greek *karakter* in Heb. 1, 3) prior to birth, whereas, as I have stressed, for us, character is an *achievement* within the temporal process of earthly life. In his human life, Jesus felt all the pressures of human temptation, but he already had the moral character to withstand them. This is part of the very *meaning* of the claim that he is divine. This suggestion may provide at least the beginning of a fuller understanding of the issues. A more adequate treatment would need to contrast aspects of a 'human character' – that could be a kind of 'achievement', built up during the early life of Jesus – and a 'divine character', including a moral strength that would always be able to withstand temptation.
5   *Nichomachean Ethics*, 1113b–1115a.
6   *Ibid*, 6, 13, 1144b. Genuine virtues, or 'acquired dispositions' are

termed *hexeis*.

7   I Cor. 15, 22 (RV).

8   I John 4, 9.

9   John 12, 32.

10 See the hymn "My God I love thee; not because I hope for heaven thereby", attributed to Francis Xavier. Also, ch. 8 note 2.

11 Plato, *Republic* 361, 364; *cf. Apology* 28a.

12 Mark 2, 17.

13 P. Tillich, *The Courage to Be*, Fontana, 1962, ch. 6.

14 In chapter 13 we shall note how this language of total absorption is not always to be taken literally.

15 John 12, 24–5.

16 John 14, 20; 15, 5.

17 Rom, 6, 3–5.

18 John Donne, *The Bell*, in *Devotions upon emergent occasions*.

6. Father, Son and Holy Spirit

Reason and paradox

For many thoughtful Christians, the doctrine of the Trinity represents the most baffling part of the Church's teaching. In this chapter, my purpose is not to make the idea of the Trinity clear and simple, for that would be as absurd as trying to give a simple yet adequate account of the nature of God. My purpose is: (a) to indicate that the doctrine is not there for the sake of bafflement, but represents human attempts to grapple with some fundamental aspects of experience; and (b) to give an initial insight into the meaning of the doctrine.

A rational approach to humanity's fundamental questions does not always demand that we be able to understand all things, but that we stretch our rational faculties as far as we can and that we only accept paradoxes when they seem to be forced upon us by the need to be faithful to different aspects of experience. We recall that we are looking for an unblind faith, one that is neither blind acceptance nor a demand that we be able to comprehend all things. To put this another way; there is one kind of paradox that we should be prepared to entertain, namely one that is not a contradiction as such, but one which we believe *appears* as a contradiction because of our limited viewpoint and which arises out of our attempts to explain things that our minds can only begin to grasp. As stressed in chapter 4, modern physics provides many examples of this, some with regard to the origins of the universe, some that arise when objects approach the speed of light, some that arise in the discussion of black holes, and so on. In the light of the paradoxes that physics has to produce at this stage of its growth, we have no grounds for objecting in principle when religious thought faces paradoxes in its search for answers to some of our most fundamental questions. What reason demands in this kind of inquiry is that we only accept paradoxical statements when they are forced upon us by our very attempt to be rational – and even then, that we should claim that they are, as it were, 'interim' positions.

Trinity and tritheism

Unfortunately, the doctrine of the Trinity is one of the least understood of Christian doctrines. I recall a discussion with an intelligent Muslim who had attacked the Christian faith because of its belief in the Trinity. I asked him what he meant by the doctrine and he then explained it as if it were a crude tritheism, that is, a belief in three separate Gods who are somehow united. His response indicated that, as so often happens, he was attacking something he had not really understood. This is rather like the situation that arises when people condemn books they have not read, but my Muslim friend had much more excuse because many Christians themselves tend to talk of the Trinity as if it were a kind of tritheism, like the preachers I have already criticized who say simply, without qualification or explanation: "Jesus is God".

Part of the misunderstanding of the Trinity, and a factor that has led to it being confused with tritheism, lies in the use of the word 'person'. Almost every reader will know that in Christian teaching it is said that there is one God in three persons, the person of the Father, the person of the Son and the person of the Holy Ghost (though recently the word 'Spirit' has tended to be used instead of the more archaic 'Ghost'). When the doctrine was first developed this was a reference to the Latin word *persona*, the primary meaning of which is not 'person' in the modern English sense, but 'mask'. In the ancient theatre it was normal for the actors to put on masks which they wore when acting a role. Thus the original language of the Latin and Greek formulations of the doctrine of the Trinity was much less likely to suggest three separate entities, but pointed rather to one actor who, when playing three different roles, wore a different mask for each role. However, this last description must not be taken any more literally than the idea of three separate beings, for when an actor takes off one mask he puts on another, while in the Christian doctrine the three masks or 'personae' of God represent permanent aspects of his nature.

For the present, let us make use of the idea of three *aspects* of God, inadequate as even this approach is, and look at the experiences of God in the Bible that have led to emphasis on these three aspects. Then, as elsewhere in this book, we shall try to relate this Biblical experience to our general experience of life.

Father, Son and Holy Spirit

In the Old Testament, the word 'Father' is not normally used in reference to God until we come to the later books and then only twice, both in the form of a prayer.[1] In Jesus's teaching, however, 'Father' is the usual word for the God of Israel who had spoken to Abraham, Moses and the other prophets and who had led the Jews to the promised land. Mark records Jesus's actual use of the Aramaic word for Father, *Abba*, in Jesus's mother tongue.[2] When we look back from the New Testament to the use of the word 'God' in the Old Testament, there is no doubt that, if we were to use one of the words, 'Father', 'Son', or 'Spirit', it would normally be the word 'Father' that would be most appropriate, as Jesus's custom confirms. The aspect of God that is central in this usage is the idea of God as creator and sustainer of all beings other than himself. One example of a passage that powerfully evokes a sense of this creator-source of the universe is the great nature psalm with its climax in the verse "O Lord, how manifold are thy works: in wisdom hast thou made them all; the earth is full of thy riches."[3] In modern writings, the hymn "This is my father's world" expresses the same theme. Closely associated with this sense of the creator-source is that of the numinous. This, as we have seen, is an intense feeling of an awesome majesty, beyond and within all things. One example that clearly reflects such an experience is the passage which describes Isaiah's vision in the temple and the words "Holy, holy, holy is the Lord of hosts"[4] spoken by the seraphs.

If we are asked to indicate passages in the Bible where the Son aspect of God is revealed, the obvious answer for the Christian is in the life and teaching of Jesus. This answer, of course, is based on the ideas expressed in chapters 4 and 5 and on the general conclusion that Jesus is the Son of God. However, even within the context of the Bible, this reference to the physical life of Jesus does not exhaust the idea of the Son, for the New Testament writers claimed that Jesus did not come into being at his physical birth, nor even at his conception, but that in some sense he had always existed. The incarnation marked a new identification of God with humanity, not the very beginning of his existence. This pre-existence of Jesus is implicit in the very idea of the 'word', or *logos*, that became flesh and it is quite explicit in the Epistle to the Hebrews where the Father is said to have made the world *through* the Son.[5] However, although, from the point of view of theology, the eternal Son is prior to the actual events of Jesus's life, from the point of view of human experience, it is the knowledge of Jesus Christ, as the image of God, that comes first. Hence, while 'Father' refers primarily to the aspect of God as creator-source, 'Son' refers to the image of God as seen in Jesus. Here God, in a sense, is made concrete, so that we can see his character in time and space.

The idea of the 'Spirit' of God pervades both Old and New Testaments and it always refers to a divine energy or power, often manifested in the here and now. Jesus used the analogy of the wind, with its power and unpredictability, to describe Spirit: "The wind blows where it wills ... but you do not know whence it comes or whither it goes."[6] At Pentecost, perhaps the most dramatic of all the experiences of the Spirit, it seemed to be both like wind and like fire.[7] When people feel the power of God actually at work within them, they tend to talk of the Spirit. Thus it is said that the Spirit came upon Samson whenever he was filled with power[8] and in true prayer we sense the Spirit of God somehow actually within us, helping us to pray.[9]

This idea of God within us must be stated carefully. In some religions, notably certain forms of Hinduism, the central core of each person is literally a part of God, part of his Spirit. Some Christians have described their sense of God within them in the same language, but orthodox Christianity has always denied that God's Spirit is identical to ours, rather it can be in a union with ours that assists and encourages our individual spirits. We have the same situation here that I described with respect to mystical experience in the last chapter, where the Christian interpretation of mystical experience is of a union that still respects our individuality. But this universal sense of a God somehow actually at work *within* us is of such immense power that it must be understood as one of the foundations of all religion. Spirit, therefore, refers to that aspect of God that is known as a pervasive power that can invade the innermost recesses of our being.

Here, then, we have the three aspects of God as recorded in the Biblical experience of humanity: three kinds of experience each of which the Christian has wanted to say are experiences of God himself. This is the Biblical foundation for the claim that we know God in three persons.

The Trinity and human experience in general

This section is probably the most difficult part of this book, but I ask the reader to bear with me because there can be no easy treatment of this theme and yet its implications and importance are immense. In particular, I want to dispel some of the simplistic, tritheistic views of God that are held by many Christians and to show that an unblind faith can be moved by serious reflection on the nature of God towards some kind of trinitarian doctrine.

The attempt to relate the Trinity to our general experience is not original; in fact, the claim that the Trinity is actually prefigured in human experience is a fundamental one in St Augustine. Among other analogies, he uses that of human love.[10] When we love another, there is the I that loves, there is the beloved that is loved and there is the love itself that is a kind of bond between the lover and the beloved. But truly there is only one thing here, namely love, although without these three elements there is no manifestation of love. Perhaps an even more helpful analogy is provided by the human mind itself and this is a particularly appropriate analogy if we stress the claim that humanity is made in the image of God. Augustine too suggests an analogy based on the human mind (rooted in the way that memory, understanding and will are jointly constitutive of what it is to be a person),[11] but I am going to develop the analogy in a way that is rather different from his.

When we think of a human being, there is a kind of trinity in the ideas of body, mind and spirit that comprise what we are, but this is not the trinity that I am thinking of because it is possible to conceive of at least two of these elements separately. Whether or not a human mind can exist without a body is a difficult and controversial question, but the fact that many, including Plato, believe that it can, makes these three ideas unsatisfactory as a model for the Trinity. It is essential for true Trinitarianism that the elements be *inseparably* linked. Instead, the model that I want to explore is based on the act of seeing. Here, there is an I, an object perceived, and the actual experience of perception, say the seeing of a tree. No human act of seeing can take place without all three of these elements, yet there is *one* experience; that in which an object is seen. Next, we must note that none of these elements can exist alone. The I only has meaning in the context of the awareness of something. There is a sense in which the mind is aware of itself, but this experience only arises because – most of the time – the mind is also perceiving things outside itself. Meanwhile, the object, conceived simply in itself, dissolves into a cloud of subatomic particles, which in turn dissolve into a cloud of formulae: it is only an *object* in the act of being seen. The redness, hardness, and all the other qualities that we regard as substantial only arise in the context of perception. As for the third element, the perception itself, it is manifest that this demands both an I and an object.

The above is a brief summary of an important and fascinating area of reflection and readers can work through the issues more thoroughly in their own reading and reflection if they so choose. However, it should be clear that the common view in which an I, or real subject, faces a substantial object, which somehow sends out rays to my eye whereby I can see it as it really is, is naive. In every act of seeing, the complex set of data that is coming to me from the object is interpreted and structured so that the act of seeing *any* thing is not the result of just opening my eyes and passively receiving what the object has to show. Rather perception is an active affair, in which one experience is made possible by three elements. There is an I, in the sense of an active mind that structures or processes all information it receives; there is something out there, a reality other than myself; and these two elements come together in the actual seeing, which we can describe as the spiritual *activity* of the person. This is what happens in any act of seeing and it is equally the situation in any other act of perception, such as hearing or feeling with the hands.

It should now be possible to see more clearly what the Trinity really stands for and why even the idea of three *aspects* of God is inadequate. It appears that the mind's knowing is not to be described in terms of a separate self that comes to know an object that is also quite independent of it, but as an *active process*. So it must be, the Christian claims, with God's knowledge or with God's love, if we are to use the words 'knowledge' and 'love' with any meaning. However, there is also an important difference. In this case, it is not that God's awareness must be primarily of an object outside of himself, that is of the created order, for the Christian believes that God has a certain completeness in himself and that creation was a voluntary act. So if God is Mind and Love, which seem the most appropriate of all the descriptions of God, then there must be *activity* within the very nature of God himself.

The analogy of the three elements in the human mind can now be used as follows. The creator-source, that is the Father, eternally loves, not only in some abstract way, but with an actual object of his love called the eternal Son, the image of his nature. Within this image is also the idea of nature, or of anything else that the Father is free to create and which he will then love. But then we can also think of the act of love itself, called the Spirit, which binds together the Father and the Son just as the act of seeing binds together the subject and the object of seeing. It is only in this act of knowing or of loving, parallel to the act of perception in human beings, that anything is made actual or concrete. Thus, while we can properly say that the Father and the Son love, the love itself is most properly applied to the Spirit. Hence St Augustine said: "The Holy Spirit is specially called by the name of love, although in the universal sense both the Father and the Son are love."[12]

The realization that reflection on the Trinity is rooted in our own mental experience should help to carry us a long way from primitive tritheism. The stress is on the unity of the act of seeing and the unity of the divine knowledge and love. At the same time, there cannot be seeing, knowledge, or love, without these inter-related elements. This has been seen by many people in different ways. For example, the novelist Dorothy Sayers has a fascinating way of relating the writer's creative work to a Trinitarian experience[13] and Hegel saw the unfolding of all reality in a Trinitarian way, in which concrete reality must be the realm of Spirit.[14] There is also an interesting similarity with a certain strand of Hindu thought, for example, as expressed in Yan Martel's novel, *Life of Pi*.[15] Here there is a fundamental unity between the creative source of all things, signified by Brahman; the image of this creative source in the representations of Krishna; and the internal energy that flows from this source within each person's spirit. The important difference between this and the Christian version of the Trinity is that instead of a mythical or symbolic image, such as Krishna, there is an actual historical person, namely Jesus of Nazareth. We could go on, but it is clear that once again a fundamental Christian claim is not merely a Biblical or ecclesiastical dogma, it is something rooted in human experience.

The Trinity and the Bible

Strictly speaking, the doctrine of the Trinity is not a Biblical doctrine, for it is nowhere explicitly stated, although there are two occasions when Trinitarian language is used.[16] The Christian claim is rather that the experience of God as found in the Bible, when reflected upon, demands such a doctrine.

Even in the Old Testament, there are suggestive passages where the ideas of the Spirit of God, or the Word of God, or the Wisdom of God, seem to be based on the insight that there are active relationships within God and yet not between *parts* of God. The tendency here, as with the Greek religion of the same period, was to set up notions such as 'Wisdom' or 'Spirit' as semi-independent entities, with an undefined status.[17]

As we saw in the third section of this chapter, the New Testament describes two principal experiences that lead on to Trinitarian thought. First, there is the experience of Jesus of Nazareth and, for the reasons outlined in chapters 4 and 5, Christians came to believe that here was more than a prophet but rather some new initiative of God. This led to the view that Jesus was in some unique sense the image of God and then to the further view that Jesus represented a Word of God that had been there from all eternity. The incarnation was the making concrete, in terms of human nature, of a principle that is eternally true. This is the perfect image that God loves. Second, there is the overwhelming experience of the Spirit, both in its initial outpouring at Pentecost and in the individual experiences of many believers, especially at the moment of baptism.[18] Here was the reality and power of God within our very beings, rising up like an overflowing well of pure water, cleansing and enriching our souls.

I have already suggested that part of the trouble with contemporary Christianity is that many churchgoers do not know the 'in Christ' experience as a living reality. Another way of making the same point is to note how few Christians have undergone the Pentecostal experience. However, we must be very careful here because I do not want to suggest that Christians should all have the same *psychological experience* as the first Christians, for people are very different in this respect. Some contemporary Christians certainly do have the full Pentecostal experience and describe it in the same terms as did the first Christians; such people are sometimes called the 'twice-born'.[19] Others, who may equally know the Holy Spirit within them, do not undergo this kind of experience; these are sometimes called the 'once-born'. The former have to be very careful not to try to force the latter into their own mould, for God may have different roads for different people.

Thus the point of the last paragraph is not that we must all try to make sure that we have the same kind of Pentecostal experience, but that, without a living experience of the power of the Spirit, as known either by the twice-born or the once-born, it is very hard to appreciate the transforming power that underlies Trinitarian thinking. Here, in actual experience, is a kind of present or concrete reality, in which the presence of God is known. The creative source of the universe, made known to us in Jesus, is found as a living power within us. Here God is three and he is one.

The Trinity and the creeds

By now it should be apparent what the creeds are and what they are not. They are attempts to formulate the Christian insight into words, but they are not the directly revealed words of God, nor a simple statement taken out of the Bible. In my view, they can be subject to change and modification, though I would not like to see them altered without the joint approval of the major branches of the church, Orthodox, Roman Catholic, Anglican and so on. The reason for this is that, with one exception, the present formulations of the Apostles' creed and of the Nicene creed were agreed upon by the majority of Christians in the early centuries and, inadequate as they may be, they do tend to bind the churches together. Moreover, the inadequacies of the creeds are basically irremovable because they lie in the inadequacy of human language and human analogy to express the full truth.

For these reasons, provided that the individual Christian can sympathize with the central ideas that underlie the doctrine of the Trinity, I do not believe that he or she should be overly worried about the actual phrases. They are *attempts* to express Christian convictions and they need interpretation. For example, it is not of crucial importance whether or not Mary was a virgin in the strictly physiological sense. Again, we can be free to interpret Jesus's descent into hell either literally, or as a reference to his *spiritual* suffering on the cross. At the same time, on the positive side, we can also exult in the creeds, as patriots can do in a traditional song, and as I do when I hear the liturgy sung with enthusiasm in a church filled with people. Here, however inadequately, fellow Christians unite in expressing fundamental convictions. Most of the language may be obscure for many people, but they can still feel the power of the words as they participate in an ancient act and enter into a tradition that is still alive and that expresses the way Christians see God and his relation to us.

I mentioned 'one exception' to the unity of the churches in the creeds and this ought to be explained. One of the positive aspects of the creeds is the way in which they express the idea of movement or dynamic activity within God. Although Jesus was born as a man at a particular time, the Son, representing the principle of God's word, is not born, but is said to be 'eternally begotten'. This language seeks to express the view that, in terms of the three persons of the Trinity, there is a certain priority in that of the Father, but it is not a temporal priority for both are eternal. The Son, as it were, flows from the Father, as a river continually flows from a lake at its head-waters. Similarly, it is said that the Spirit 'proceeds' from the Father, again giving an idea of movement that has no beginning and no end. The Western church added the claim that the Spirit also 'proceeds' from the Son (in the famous *filioque* clause, which is the Latin for 'and from the Son'), thereby departing from the creed that had been approved by both Eastern and Western churches. The rights and wrongs of this particular issue would take us way beyond the scope of this book, but the controversy helps to explain the most important split within the Christian church. Also, it helps us to see clearly that the creeds are not the unalterable words of God, but human attempts to express the inexpressible. Furthermore, many sections of the Nicene Creed were placed there in order to combat particular false teachings that are no longer commonly found – and this too helps to explain their somewhat remote language.

In concluding this section, I want to make a suggestion with regard to how to teach the Trinity to children, for the approach taken in this chapter is obviously too advanced for them when they are small. I suggest that, in the early stages of Christian teaching, children should be taught that we have known God in three ways and that these correspond to aspects of God that are rather like the three sides of a triangle. The Biblical and general experiences of God as creator, of the man Jesus and of the sense of God's power within, can then be dwelt on. Then the young must be made to learn that their ideas must *grow* along with their growth in body. In the first instance, this can be applied to a richer understanding of prayer, with less emphasis on asking for things and more on our relationship with God. After this, young Christians can come to see that the triangle is a very imperfect model for the nature of God and that if we take seriously the claim that God is 'Love' or that God is 'Mind', then either the Trinitarian formula, or something that is generally equivalent to it, is inevitable. The Muslim, or the Unitarian, who denies the doctrine of the Trinity, has the very laudable intention of stressing the unity of God, but they tend to do this at the expense of ignoring some of the issues that have to be faced in any talk of God as Love or Mind. It is all very well simply to insist that God is Love or that God is Mind, but – I am suggesting – these assertions have more power when they are expressed within a doctrine that sees dynamic principles and activity within God. This is especially evident if we can say "God is Love" or "God is Mind" before, or apart from, the universe which he loves and knows. Christian philosophy has had the courage to see the implications of the claim that God is Love and that God is Mind.

How can we use words to describe God?

I want to end this chapter by returning to a question (raised in Chapter 2) that bothers many people when they start to think about the idea of God. How can we say anything that is true about God when we see something of the awesome majesty of God and the poverty of our language in this context?

Part of the answer has already been given. Christians believe that God has chosen to show himself to humankind, so that it is not simply a case of us striving to reach upwards towards the infinite – it is just as much a case of God reaching down to us. Further, if human beings are made in the image of God, then one of the ways in which God shows himself is through men and women, when they are at their best. Thus there is a kind of 'revelation' whenever we see – reflected in good people – something of the nature of God. As we have stressed, this is supremely true in the case of Jesus, whom the New Testament calls both the *eikon* (that is image) and *karakter* (character) of God, but, to a lesser degree, it is true of all people. In addition to this stress on revelation, we have seen how language can be used *analogically*, that is, how we stretch words so that we can begin to describe things that we only grasp dimly. We need to use language in this way in literature and science as well as in religion.

A further point about religious language can now be made in the light of the last few chapters. Some of the words that we use to describe God have a special relevance and suitability, in particular 'love', 'awareness' (or 'consciousness' or 'mind'), 'creativity' and 'freedom'. In all of these cases, although God has infinitely more of each quality than do human beings, so that we are still using analogies of a kind, in an important sense what God has more of is *the same thing.*[20]

Take the case of the word 'freedom'. I have argued that even though humankind evolved, there is a gap, or difference of level, that emerges with our species. There may be intermediate beings in the sense of semi-humans or animals that have flashes of self-awareness and freedom, but a glimpse of freedom is a glimpse of something *new*, just as the first photon of light to hit a dark screen is the first glimmer of light where before there was *no* light.

The nature of light provides a useful analogy for the phenomenon of consciousness. If one points a telescope at a very distant star, the light that is received comes, as it were, in packages, so that instead of measuring on an infinite scale, one counts photons. Moreover, one cannot measure less than a certain quantity of light; there cannot be half a photon. My suggestion is that, just as there is a radical difference between light and no light (in the extreme case between counting one photon as a kind of blip on a screen and counting nothing), so there is a radical difference between being aware at all and existing on a lower and non-conscious level. However there can still be intermediate positions, perhaps exemplified by several of the higher animals, young babies and near humans (in evolution), who have flashes of consciousness akin to the striking of individual photons on a screen. In contrast, the flashes of consciousness become a *stream* of consciousness in the ordinary human being. An important implication of this language is the confirmation of a point made earlier about Christians *not* being committed to an absolute distinction between human beings and all other animals.[21]

There is a further point to the analogy. The intermittency of light illustrates the difference between non-conscious, semi-conscious and fully-conscious beings. But, in addition to the question of intermittency, there is the question of intensity. God is pure light and, in comparison, the human stream of consciousness is like a feeble lantern. Nevertheless, even a glimpse of light is a glimpse of *light*. Thus any glimmer of awareness is, in some measure, an entrance into the divine light and the beginning of an understanding of Mind.

Along with self-consciousness, and as, I believe, a necessary component of it, comes the phenomenon of freedom, which I shall discuss again in chapter 11. Although one can be more or less free in some senses (for example, in how often one is free and in how strong one is to carry out one's good intentions), in another sense freedom is something you either have or do not have. In this last sense, stones are not free, nor (in my view) are rabbits, but human beings are (except when there is something radically wrong with their brains). As I have said, this does not mean that we are free all the time, but that we have a certain capacity that stones and rabbits do not have. It is rather like the case of prime numbers. Either a number is prime or it is not;[22] in this sense there is an either/or, with no third position. But humankind, I have argued, has the essential capacity for freedom so that we stand, with God, on the side of beings that are free, over against the multitude of things in which this capacity just does not exist because they have not attained this *level* of existence.

As we have seen, the same point can be made with respect to awareness,[23] based on what has been said about God as Mind; about human love[24] as a reflection of God's love; and of our creative capacity as a reflection of God's creativity (though in the last case what should be said would overlap the discussion of freedom). In all of these cases, we find that a word can properly be applied to God, at least within a Christian philosophy, because although God is infinitely greater *in degree* with respect to these capacities, he is not totally different *in kind*.[25]

In contrast, many of the other words that we use to describe God are used much more loosely. For example, when we describe God as 'great', we don't mean to describe his size in comparison with ours, but rather we are using a value term by which we praise God. Again, when God is described as 'jealous' in the Old Testament, this is not an accurate description of God; rather it is a roundabout way of saying that there can be no rivals to God. He alone can satisfy man's deepest longings.

Some readers may find this discussion about religious language very academic, but it has important implications. If it were true that human language could say *nothing* that is true about God, then there would be little point in most Christian teaching. Also, the approach that I have outlined indicates an important contrast with many Eastern accounts of religion (some of which will be referred to in chapter 13). Here there is frequently found the claim that ultimate reality is totally beyond any rational comment or use of human words: we have to rely solely on silence or ecstatic vision. Oddly enough, those who make this claim frequently go on to write long books about God or religious truth! My point here is not to belittle the religions of the East, from which I believe that the Christian can learn much, but to insist that it is not necessary for the person of faith to take such a drastic view of the poverty of human language.

Provided that we are prepared to emphasize the initiative of God in *revealing* himself, then there is no reason why we cannot say *both* that God is transcendent and that he can be described, though very inadequately, by certain words: in particular, "God is Love" and "God is Mind", for the reasons we have already explored. We may also be able to say that God is *Being*,[26] but this raises issues that go beyond what can be explored in this book.

In the light of this reflection on language, a caution should be added about how Christians use the word 'transcendent', meaning 'going beyond' the human dimension. It is misleading to say that God is *totally* transcendent, though this is a phrase one often hears. When this phrase is used as a way of referring to the awesome majesty of God and to our status as creatures, this is perfectly acceptable Christian philosophy. However, when it is taken as an accurate statement about God's nature, it must imply that *nothing* true can be said about God using human words. I have argued that it is *true* to say that God is Love and that God is Mind. Therefore God is transcendent, but not, in the strictest sense, *totally* transcendent. He has chosen to make us 'in his image'.

My final point about language concerns the use of the word 'one'. The claim "God is One" is often treated as a kind of closure statement, asking for an agreement without qualification. However, outside the use of integers (where 'one' is followed by 'two' and 'three' and so on), the word 'one' tends to mean some kind of harmony or unity – as when we say that a family or a country is 'one', or 'at one' on a certain issue. Perhaps, most significantly, the sense in which we, as persons, are 'one' is highly suggestive of a kind of harmony. We see this not only in Augustine's realization that the human psyche is made of different elements (memory, understanding and will) that are not separable 'parts', but also in the way in which our individual souls only find completion within a loving relationship with others, in what John Donne, in powerful and paradoxical metaphor calls 'this dialogue of one'.[27] When monotheists proclaim (correctly) "God is One", this is not the end of the matter, but a *beginning*, in which we are invited to explore the kind of unity that God has. In Islam, for example, God is compassionate *and* God is merciful, and this suggests that compassion and mercy are somehow harmonized within God.[28] In this context the Christian doctrine of the Trinity does not look so strange – it is a variation on the exploration of what kind of oneness or unity is to be found within God.

Notes

1   Isa. 63, 16; pp. 89, 26.
2   Mark 14, 36. On two occasions Paul recalls this word used by Jesus (Rom. 8, 15 and Gal. 4, 6).
3   Ps. 104, 24 – Prayer Book (Coverdale) translation.
4   Isa. 6, 3.
5   Heb. 1, 2–3.
6   John 3, 8.
7   Acts 2, 1–4.
8   E.g. Judg. 14, 19.
9   Rom. 8, 26–7.
10 *De Trinitate*, VIII ch. 10 (VIII, 14).
11 *Ibid.* books IV and X.
12 *Ibid.* XV ch. 17 (XV 31) S. McKenna's translation.
13 D. Sayers, *The Mind of the Maker*, Methuen, 1941.
14 Hegel's Trinity is that of Idea, Nature and Spirit and he saw his elaboration of this Trinity as an expression of Christian doctrine.
15 Yan Martel, *Life of Pi*, Canongate, Edinburgh, 2002, ch. 16.
16 Matt. 28, 19; 2 Cor. 13, 14.
17 E.g., Prov. 8, 22–end, especially v. 30; Gen. 1, 2.
18 Acts 19, 5–6.
19 The terms 'once-born' and 'twice-born' were introduced by William James in his seminal *The Varieties of Religious Experience*, Longman Green and Co., 1902 and later editions, lectures 4 and 5.
20 Technically, this is when theologians use the term 'analogy of attribution'. Here God is (for example) wise in the full or 'pre-eminent' sense, and human wisdom is a pale reflection of this. Nevertheless human wisdom is a true reflection and not just the application of a word with a totally different meaning. Theologians use the term *via negativa* (or 'the *apophatic* way'), meaning 'the negative way', when we say what God is *not*, and the term *via positiva*, meaning 'the positive way', when we say what God is. The use of an analogy of attribution suggests the viability of the positive way because at least some of our language about God is based – I have argued – on the claim that we are made in the image of God. It is not so much a case of building God in our image as of recognizing the stamp of the Creator within us.
21 The absolute distinction is usually based on Aristotle's claim that only humans have 'rational' souls. The truth seems to be that some animals do have significant elements of what can be called 'rationality'. This leads to interesting questions about what future life, if any, such animals may have, if they, too, are made by a loving Creator. I do not explore this question here – and it is a topic where

Christians make different responses. An adequate definition of what it is to be 'human' has to include what is typical of our species, and for this reason it is quite reasonable to include 'rationality' as one of the characteristics of humanity, even if some human individuals, such as anencephalics, lack any rationality.

22   Provided we are thinking of 'natural numbers' or 'prime integers', i.e., 1,2,3, ... ; cf. Descartes' fourth meditation for a similar view of human freedom.

23   Because of its familiarity we tend to take our awareness and self-awareness for granted. However, every now and then we can be struck with sheer amazement at the fact of these gifts. We are not 'things', but centres of feeling and thought. This can give us a glimpse of God's awareness of all that he has made. Our new understanding of how some other animals may participate in this awareness should do nothing to diminish this wonder.

24   Although human love may initially be grounded in a kind of need, it can develop into something infinitely richer. In the true love for a friend, or in the feelings of universal compassion, we have another glimpse into the Mind of God.

25   Here, once again, I am making room for what theologians call the *via positiva*. See note 20, above.

26   Christian philosophy has long insisted that God is 'Being' or 'Existence', partly because of the name of God revealed to Moses (Ex. 3, 14) and partly because God is the source of all that is. However, our being or existence is *dependent* on God's whereas God's Being or Existence must be dependent on nothing outside himself. Many Christians would say that our being is analogous to God's Being in a different sense (of analogy) than our freedom is analogous to God's freedom. The former is a kind of total dependency, the latter a kind of dim reflection.

27   John Donne, from the final verse of *The Extasie*. More material for this theme can be found, among other places, in Plato's *Symposium*, especially in the contribution by Aristophanes which is both comical and deeply serious at the same time.

28   Within orthodox Islam the conventional response to this point is that compassion and mercy are only different from our perspective, while in God they are identical. A similar claim is made by Aquinas. However, this is only one way of seeing the matter, and in the Christian tradition, Duns Scotus takes a different view. There is a case for the claim that just as there are creative tensions within the unity that makes a good person, so, even within God, there are attributes that are in creative and harmonious dialogue – rather than merging into an undifferentiated sameness.

7. Church and Sacrament

Christot and the church

It often happens that one thing can only be understood properly in terms of its relationship with other things. For example, when we learn a word in a foreign language, we need to know how it relates to other words in that language and to its grammar before we can use it correctly. This illustrates why I have followed a certain pattern in this book. We began with faith, then the idea of God and then the idea of a creature made in the image of God. After that, we explored the idea of Christ, who acts as a sort of bridge figure between the ideas of God and of humanity, and then the idea of Trinity. The remaining chapters do not follow such a clear order, but they are interrelated because one part of Christian teaching needs to be understood in the context of the rest.

This interrelationship is especially true in the case of the church, for we need first to look at the idea and the ideal of the church in the light of the earlier chapters before we turn to a reflection on the very human face of the church as we find it in history.

The crucial context for an understanding of the idea of the church is the meaning of the life and work of Christ. Let us therefore summarize Christian teaching about Christ. He is *the* image of God, incarnate as a human person, who opens up to all humanity a new kind of life. 'In Christ' we can be reconciled with God and other persons through a discovery of our true nature. This involves a transformation of the selfish, animal ego, through a death of the selfish individuality that places each person at the centre of their own private stage. Thus the clue to life is a kind of death (to our ego), in which our very being is united with our brothers and sisters in the family of Christ. This is the communion of saints, the body of Christ, and the new creation 'in Christ'.

Thus the idea of the church is that of *community* in which we both lose ourselves and find ourselves, in which love draws us out of our selfishness and in which (as Theresa of Avila put it) we become the hands and feet of Christ in the world. Hence the New Testament can speak of Christians as actually sharing in the work of the cross[1] and as being parts of the body of Christ.[2]

The visible and the invisible church

Unfortunately, Christians come down to reality with a bump when they turn from the lofty idea of the church in the New Testament to its physical manifestation in the world. We must not be one-sided here, for the human face of the church has its glories: its men and women like Francis of Assisi and the lady Julian of Norwich; its magnificent inspiration for art; its role in social movements such as the anti-slavery campaign and so on. Also, at its best, its worship can evoke a powerful sense of the numinous and can help to bind people together in a caring fellowship. But the negative side is also only too apparent: the pettiness of so much church life; the boredom of much of its preaching and worship when the spirit has gone out of them; the corruption of those in high places; the intolerance and pride of many Christians and so on. Behind all of these negative factors, there is the failure of most Christians simply to live up to their high calling in their daily lives. No wonder that we often hear well-meaning people say, "I am a Christian but I don't go to church or hold with most of its doctrines."

The invisible church is the true community of believers in Christ. It contains both departed souls and Christians living in the world. It contains members of every human church and, in my view, many others who are not members of any human institutional church. Thus the division between church members and non-church members in the case of the invisible church is drawn by God and cuts right across the boundaries drawn by us in terms of those who are in this or that – or indeed, any, church. The visible church, on the other hand, consists of the actual churches that can be seen and heard, containing, as in Jesus's parables, both grain and chaff.

The physical institutions of the visible church are both human and divine. They are divine in that they result from the work of Christ and, at their best, they are sincere attempts to represent Christ on earth. At times, undoubtedly, Christ can and does work in and through them. They are human in the obvious sense that the actual day by day life and thought of each church is left to human beings, with all their fallibilities and imperfections.

Can it be said that any one of these human institutions is *the* church, in the sense of having a unique authority to represent Christ, with a direct line of command from the Apostles? Here there is controversy. Some traditional Roman Catholics and, equally, some members of the more radical Protestant churches claim that their church is the only true church, although they rarely insist nowadays that only their members can be saved, which was a common claim in less tolerant days. However, these people tend to say that all other Christian bodies are heretical or schismatic and are therefore separated from the main body of the church. Along with many others (Catholic, Orthodox and Protestant), the mainstream Anglican view, which I represent at this point, is that no one body represents the holy catholic church in a unique way (remembering that the word 'catholic' is the Greek word for 'universal'). Sometimes, *within* a particular nation, one church may properly claim a certain historical priority, as, for example, the Roman Catholic Church in Italy, the Orthodox Church in Greece and the Anglican Church in England. We should note here that the term 'Anglican church', or its Latin equivalent, *ecclesia Anglicana*, is the ancient name for the church in England long before the time of the Reformation. Historically, it is not correct to see Henry VIII as its founder. Moreover, the radical break with Rome dates from the time of Elizabeth I.[3] However, historical claims such as these are only *relative* claims, a way of indicating a particular continuity with the founders of the Christian faith in that country; there need not and should not be an élitist doctrine that places the national church spiritually above the other churches.

The rejection of the claim that there is no *one* church, in the *visible* sense, does not mean that we should not value and treasure the gifts we find within a particular church. Imperfect as a church may be, we may love its special traditions that enrich our lives. At the same time, we may be glad that other churches preserve other traditions that we can learn from and which can also enrich us.

Briefly, there are three rational grounds for the claim that there is no one, true, *visible* church, but rather one, true, *invisible* church.

The first ground is based on an historical argument and is negative in nature, for it indicates that no single church has a substantial historical claim to be *the* church.

The most important part of this argument concerns the claim to primacy by the Roman Catholic Church and this is the only part that I shall try to deal with here. This claim cannot be based on antiquity by itself, for the Greek Orthodox Church is almost certainly older than the Roman Catholic Church by a few years,[4] but this is not the principal issue. The claim is made that Jesus gave authority over the church to Peter in the famous saying "You are Peter, and on this rock I will build my church."[5] However, in addition to the problem of interpreting exactly what kind of authority Jesus gave to Peter in these words, there is a grave historical problem with respect to Peter's succession. There is an ancient tradition that Peter went to Rome and died there, which I think may well represent what actually happened. However, it is quite another thing to claim that he was *bishop* of Rome and that he then handed his unique authority to the following bishops. Of course, the second-century bishops of Rome claimed this, just as bishops and kings down the ages have made dubious historical assertions that suited their claims to authority, but the actual evidence for this claim is thin, especially if it has to bear the whole weight of the case for the primacy of the Roman Catholic church. The first clear evidence of the claim comes in a letter written by Irenaeus in about 200CE. My own view, and that of many others, is that it is most unlikely that any of the apostles took on the role of bishop within a particular city, except perhaps James in Jerusalem.[6] I might easily be wrong about this, but my point is not that Peter was certainly *not* bishop of Rome, but that there is a genuine ground for *doubt* in this case. And if there is real ground for doubt, then this is a poor foundation for the tremendous claims that are made for the unique authority of the Roman see. Let me stress that I do not see this argument as an attack on the Roman Catholic church as such; it is rather an attack on a *particular claim* that is made by it. The historical evidence does not support the view that this, or any other visible institution, is *the* true church. I should add here that many non-Roman Catholics, including myself, would seriously consider the proposal that – for historical reasons – the bishop of Rome should become spiritual head, on earth, of the whole Christian church, provided that among the changes was a shelving of the claim to infallibility.

The second ground for doubting whether there is one true visible church is probably the strongest. Jesus gave us a sort of acid test for deciding whether or not someone was on the side of God: "You will know them by their fruits."[7] In this respect, all the major churches stand in much the same light, for each of them is a crazy mixture of saints and villains. Reflection on this test suggests strongly that the one true church can only be the invisible church.

The third ground is based on the kind of authority that humanity needs. Some Christians argue as follows: "God cannot have left uncertainty in so vital a matter as who is to be his spokesperson on earth, so we must look for that body that now carries his unique authority." Then the argument goes on to show why this or that institution is *the* church. But there are several flaws in this kind of argument. First, it is ridiculous to suppose that God will only save those who happen to belong to a particular human institution, for salvation is a matter of our spiritual and moral state in the eyes of God. Hence the urgency of making sure that one is, as it were, on the right ship, is misplaced. The urgency is there, but it is to be true and faithful to one's vision of the good, the true and the beautiful. If that leads one into a particular church, that is fair enough, but it does not provide grounds for condemning the others. Second, the claim that God must have left a unique spokesperson runs completely counter to our ordinary experience of how God deals with human problems, when, again and again, he chooses to leave human beings to work things out for themselves. Further, the more we reflect on the nature of humanity, the more we can see this is the way it must be, for how else can we learn to be responsible and to care for others and to become rational beings? Thus we can begin to see why God rarely answers prayers for specific guidance in a direct way and, in the light of this insight, it would be odd to expect him to give us direct answers to our fundamental questions through the authority of a particular institution. The point is that fundamental answers cannot simply be *given* (as we saw in the teaching methods of Socrates and Jesus); they have to be *discovered* by each person for himself or herself. True knowledge, like true moral goodness, is an *achievement* and cannot be handed out. Finally, the Christian philosophy that has been outlined so far suggests that there is, and must be, an element of risk in being a Christian. We cannot *know* that our good deeds will be rewarded, we must just do them out of love and, similarly, we cannot *know*, through some specially guaranteed authority, that all our beliefs are true. No doubt there is treasure in the church, but this treasure is in earthen vessels[8] and no single person or institution should be put on a high pedestal.

The role of community

The previous section is unfortunately negative in tone, but I think it is important for Christians to have the balanced view of the church that I have outlined if they are not to become blindly obedient to it on the one hand, or unreasonably critical of it on the other. We can glory in its gifts and triumphs as a divinely ordained community and, at the same time, we can entertain a healthy scepticism about its holiness as a human institution. However, whereas the previous section ended up on a negative note, I want now to stress the positive aspect of the church from the point of view of the individual Christian.

The aspect of church membership that I want to stress here is our identification with, and acceptance of, our fellow human beings, which ought to be analogous to Jesus's identification with and acceptance of us. When non-churchgoers who have a Christian commitment explain why they do not go to community worship, there is often a hint of élitism. "Look at those in the pews; old so-and-so whom I can't stand, Mrs X with her malicious tongue, the Rev. Y with the dreary voice," and so on. Some of these comments may be perfectly apt, but is not the discovery of our humanity an acceptance of such people and a willingness to sit next to them? Further, how realistically have we looked at ourselves if we make such remarks, for is it not odd that the really good do not make this kind of observation? Most of all, Christians should ask themselves where they would be if Jesus had been guided by such sentiments. If he sat down with sinners, is not our élitism put to shame?

There is an interesting difference of emphasis here between the Catholic and Protestant traditions and I am bound to say that I think the Catholic emphasis to be the healthier. In Protestantism, there is a tendency to make the visible church a collection of saved and holy people, marked off from the ordinary person around them. In Catholicism, the stress is on the whole village or town, seen as a worshipping community. The latter stress is likely to touch and influence far more people, but of course it means that within the walls of the church will be a far greater range of commitment and it will be far easier for outsiders to find fault. No doubt there is a middle way here, but I do not want to be in a church community that you can only join when you have proved your spiritual worth. I would rather be in an inclusive church and pay the price of knowing that many of us are poor ambassadors for Christ.

So far I have stressed our duty to identify with a community; equally important is our need of what it can give. Paradoxically, just as it is true in general that in giving we receive, so when we actually participate in a Christian fellowship and give of ourselves to it, we find that we receive far more than we give. As our very nature is social, we need fellowship and that part of the grace of God that can only come in and through fellowship. Who are strong enough on their own, or have the right to believe that they might be strong enough? Someone might reply, "I am not on my own, Christ is with me and in me." Perhaps, but does not Christ come to us not only in our loneliness but also in the fellowship of others, as the Acts of the Apostles makes very clear? Therefore, why should we neglect what he offers us within the community, especially in the Holy Communion (which we shall discuss shortly)? Moreover, if the discovery of our true humanity involves our social nature, in which our selfish ego is transcended, then some aspects of grace *can* only come through a fellowship with which we identify. Once again, they that lose their lives shall find them.

Baptism

The claim that some of God's grace is channelled through the church leads directly to the Christian idea of a sacrament. In its most general sense, a sacrament is 'an outward and visible sign of an inward and spiritual grace',[9] and for this reason the world abounds with sacraments. Nature itself is sacramental, for from its beauty many can sense something of its spiritual source. Human society is also full of small sacramental acts, like hand-shaking and kissing, which when used properly are outward signs with inner, and indeed spiritual, meaning. The Christian idea is built upon this aspect of the physical order and claims that, in addition to this general sacramentalism, there are some specific physical acts that have inner and spiritual meaning and power, given us by Christ himself. Different churches have different lists of how many such acts there are and what exactly they mean, but for almost all of them two such acts are central and a very similar meaning is given to them.

The first is Baptism, in which the outward act is either being immersed in water or sprinkled with it. The rite was not invented by the Christians, but they took it over from other religions, together with its universal symbolism of washing and rebirth, and gave it a specifically Christian meaning. Passing through the waters of Baptism signified a sort of dying to the old self-centred life and a passing into the new life 'in Christ'. For Christians there was the added symbolism of passing over the waters of the Red Sea and the river Jordan. For adults, this act symbolized forgiveness of sins as well as rebirth and when children came to be baptized, which probably happened quite early because of the tendency to treat whole families as units, this symbolized the child's reception into the Christian family as well as the forgiveness of 'original sin'.

It follows from what has been said about original sin that this last aspect of baptism must be reinterpreted in our time. As a result, some contemporary Christians want to confine baptism to believing adults (as the Baptists have always done), or at least to those young people who can make a realistic choice and profession of faith. Others maintain that infant baptism still makes sense, even though the baby cannot literally be said to need forgiveness, because incorporation into the Christian family marks such an important step. My own view is that the early church almost certainly practised infant baptism, in part because of the references to converts being baptised with their whole household,[10] and in part because of the greater sense of community solidarity that characterized the times.

It is clear that the subject of infant baptism is one concerning which there is understandable disagreement between Christians, with some approving it, some claiming that it is always a mistake and others saying that it is alright in principle, but inappropriate in our contemporary world where the peer pressure is often stronger than the family pressure. However, there is no need for this disagreement to prevent Christians from working and worshipping together in the same church. Perhaps those churches are richer which tolerate different views and practices on matters that are not essential. Moreover, the basic meaning of Baptism is the same for all groups. Outwardly we are washed with water, and this symbolizes the gift and power of the Spirit that the Christian receives and the grace that flows within the Christian family.

The Holy Communion

The second great sacrament that comes directly from Jesus's teaching is the Holy Communion, often called the Mass or the Eucharist or the Lord's Supper. Here, again, Christians did not invent the basic idea of a sacramental meal, but Jesus gave it a new meaning.

Behind all uses of a sacramental meal lies the fact that meals taken together are focal points in family or group life, moments that help to bind people together. A fellowship is both expressed in and strengthened by this corporate act. Many of the Old Testament sacrifices were essentially communal meals in which it was believed that God somehow took part in the fellowship and there are parallels in many other religions.

Finding parallels between Christian rites and those of other religions is sometimes thought to be an embarrassment for the Christian faith, but it should be seen as a strength. Christian philosophy should not be a negative one, but a positive one in which all that is good in ordinary human life is taken up and used with new purpose and meaning. Accordingly, Aquinas used to reiterate that God's grace does not destroy natural goods, but completes them. So Jesus took a friendly social meal, that may also have been a passover supper with special significance for the Jews,[11] and gave it added meaning. The occasion when he did this is described in three of the gospels and in St Paul's letters[12] and it is evident that the remembrance of this last supper soon became the central act of Christian worship, as it is for most churches today.

The bread and wine are said to become the body and blood of Christ during the celebration of this sacrament. How is this to be understood? To begin with, we must heed Jesus's warning: "It is the spirit that gives life, the flesh is of no avail; the words that I have spoken to you are spirit and life."[13] These words were said, we must note, immediately after some of the disciples were shocked at Jesus's statement that they would have to eat his flesh. Clearly, therefore, we have to look at the symbolic interpretation of flesh and blood and not at their literal meaning. One way of putting this is to speak of the 'real presence' of Christ as symbolized in the body or flesh and the 'life' of Christ as symbolized in the blood. We may remember that Jews to this day have to drain any animal of blood before it is eaten, because the blood is the sacred symbol of life. Thus, in the context of this meal that recalls the last supper, God uses the outward eating and drinking of the elements of food and drink to draw us together and to share in the life of Christ. He is there, in and through the sacramental act.

It is worth suggesting at this point that there is no need for Roman Catholics and other Christians to be divided on this matter, despite the controversy that has raged over 'transubstantiation' (the Roman Catholic doctrine that the bread and wine become 'in substance' the body and blood of Christ). Recent studies have shown how much this old controversy is based on misunderstanding. The definition of the doctrine is in Latin and there has been a tendency to use inappropriate English words in the translation. Thus, while the doctrine asserts that there is a change *in substance*, it also asserts that the 'accidents' of sight, taste, touch, etc., are unchanged. In modern English, it is precisely these things that signify the *physical* nature of something, so that it would be more accurate to say that the bread and wine are *physically* unchanged than to say that they are changed. In any case, recent theological debate between Roman Catholic and Anglican theologians has tended to find that in essence their views are similar and that for both of them the heart of the Holy Communion is the meaning of the action, in which we receive God's grace and experience communion with Christ and each other.

One other aspect of the Holy Communion should be touched on here, and again the point is to stress Christian unity where there has sometimes been conflict. Christians have frequently argued as to whether or not this sacrament is itself some kind of sacrifice, with many Catholics (Roman and Anglican) claiming that it is a renewal of Christ's sacrifice and Protestants tending to claim that it is only a memorial of a sacrifice made once and for all at Calvary. I suggest that Christians should not accept either of these accounts in their simple form, but should say something like what follows, whether they are Catholic or Protestant in emphasis. "The work of Christ has a timeless quality. Although Jesus lived an historical life, its meaning is eternal and it has to be taken up and made our own in whatever time and place we are living. Thus, when we recall the life and death of Christ, in particular at the powerful sacrament of Holy Communion, we are neither re-enacting, not simply remembering what was done, but rather we are *re-entering* a reality that transcends our ordinary level of living. Certainly we remember, but in doing so we become caught up in an event that stands for an eternal truth. The sacrifice of Christ is then *present*, in that we can receive grace from it and share in it, but strictly speaking it is not *re*-enacted. Drawn by God's love we offer our gifts (the bread representing our life and work and the wine representing our leisure and our joys) and God accepts them and transforms them, as he does all things that are offered to him. So they become unto us the very presence and life of Christ within us." This is not the whole story of the Holy Communion, but it is a kernel that can unite all Christians around one table.

Notes

1 E.g. 2 Cor. 1, 7; Phil. 3, 10; 1 Peter 4, 13.

2 1 Cor. 12, 12–14.

3 At the time of the Reformation in England there was an essential continuity of (i) most worshippers and clergy, (ii) the essential core of beliefs (other than the role of the Pope), (iii) the same church buildings, (iv) the same basic liturgical practices of Baptism and Holy Communion, and (v) the same basic ethic. A similar misunderstanding concerns the notion of the 'head' of the church. In so far as the Anglican Church as a whole has a head 'on earth', this should probably be thought of as either the Lambeth conference or the Archbishop of Canterbury. In the case of the Church of England, since the time of Elizabeth I, the sovereign is 'head *on earth*', or more accurately 'supreme governor' (under God). The 'head' of the Church of England, in the full sense of the term, has always been seen as Jesus Christ. (On this matter see John Overall's *Convocation Book*, 1606, II Canon V, and John Hales, *Works*, Glasgow, 1765, I, p. 106.)

4 *cf.* Acts, 11, 26, "the disciples were first called Christians in Antioch".

5 Matt. 16, 18.

6 This is the position defended by the scholar and bishop, Joseph Lightfoot.

7 Matt. 7, 16. In the case of the Roman Catholic Church, perhaps the greatest single charge concerns the official support for the torture of heretics from 1252 (in the papal bull *Ad extirpanda*) until the beginning of the nineteenth century (when the Spanish Inquisition and its practices were wound up). In the 1700s Voltaire was one of those who condemned the contemporary torture of Protestants.

8 II Cor. 4, 7.

9 Prayer Book catechism.

10 E.g. Acts 16, 15.

11 I Cor. 11, 23–6. According to John, the last supper was the night before the Passover (so that Jesus's death corresponded with the death of the sacrificial animals); according to the other three gospels, it was held on the Passover night. It is possible that both are right, because it has been suggested by some scholars that on account of the large number of visitors to Jerusalem there may have been one official Passover for the more orthodox and another one for some of the 'outsiders' or visitors.

12 I Cor. 11, 23–6.

13 John 6, 63.

8. Eternal Life

Is immortality important?

The prospect of the afterlife loomed large during many periods of the church's history. For example, fear of hell and the promise of heaven were large factors in medieval sermons, and Locke, writing about Christianity at the end of the seventeenth century, described virtue as 'the best bargain' because of the promise of heaven.[1] More recently, there has been a reaction and many Christians, sensing that this concern with the afterlife was a long-term version of pure selfishness, have gone to the other extreme. Surveys of church opinion have shown the surprising fact that many practising Christians do not believe in personal survival at all except through our family and friends and the influence that we leave behind us. This is a very similar view to the Old Testament tradition and to that of the Sadducees in the New Testament. Although I shall be arguing against the view of the Sadducees, the fact that they did not believe in any personal afterlife, despite their belief in God, can help to dispel the claim that people have only believed in God because of the hope of immortality.

I have sympathy with the negative reaction to heavenly rewards, but I shall argue that it has gone too far. The sympathy is based on a real disquiet at the low idea of God that is implied by hell-fire sermons and the egoism of much of humanity's concern for heaven. Genuine love, as I have stressed, is motive-free so far as oneself is concerned. It is only this kind of love that can begin to explain the point of Christ's life and the kind of response that we can give. As a famous hymn puts the matter, "My God, I love thee; not because I hope for heaven thereby".[2] The hymn ends with the explanation that we love "solely because thou art my God, and my most loving king."

However, a Christian belief in personal immortality need not be based on a selfish desire for oneself, but on three quite proper grounds. The first is the implication of the Christian faith for our personal future. If individual persons are precious in the scheme of things, there is something odd in the suggestion that they are simply discarded at death, like worn-out cars. I shall pursue this point later. The second quite proper ground for belief in personal immortality is the Christian doctrine of hope. There is always the danger of this hope sliding off into either selfish desire or wishful thinking, but in itself it is neither of these. We are meant to love and care for our own souls so long as this love does not displace the love of God and fellow humans. Moreover, we can perfectly well separate the belief that personal immortality is the *result* of our love, from the belief that it is the *motive* for our love. When the former is the case, then there is a quite proper and joyful expectation of a loving union with God and our friends that death itself cannot destroy. Such a hope is not properly described as a *selfish* hope because the self is not placed above the other and, indeed, the true self is seen to be discovered only in losing our selfishness. The third ground is the implication of the resurrection of Jesus, which will be discussed later. Overall, there are grounds for a Christian hope, both for ourselves and for those we love, that is part of an unblind faith.

Resurrection versus immortal soul

I am sometimes asked whether I believe in the Christian doctrine of the afterlife, to which I usually reply: "Which Christian doctrine of the afterlife?" Christians have believed many different doctrines, all – allegedly – supported by the New Testament. The most important divergence is between the resurrection view, which is strong in Protestant circles, and the immortal soul view, which is often found in popular presentations of Christianity, but that does not truly represent official doctrine in either Protestant or Roman Catholic theology.

Briefly, the resurrection view argues that there is nothing in our nature that survives of its own right and, therefore, no *separable* soul that can exist without a body. The word 'soul' refers to an aspect of a living and animated body.[3] Hence the future life does not depend on something that belongs to our nature purely as thinking animals, but on the grace of God who can recreate us, body and soul, by resurrection. (This was the belief of the Pharisees over against the older Jewish belief that immortality was only found within the family and the tribe.) This view is significantly different from the immortal-soul doctrine because it places the emphasis on the merciful act of God. In contrast, the immortal-soul view, in its typical form, holds that the essential self is a pure spirit or soul that can exist without a body. According to some, a soul of this kind is 'infused' into the embryo at the moment of conception; it survives the destruction of the body and then goes on to whatever state it is worthy of. In itself it is eternal, although it can be destroyed by God.

It must be admitted that both views run into difficulties when subjected to careful analysis. Consider first the resurrection of the body view. What is it that makes the new, resurrected John the *same person* as the John who had lived before? If we say that it is the same matter that is miraculously brought together again, we face awkward questions. All the time the matter in our bodies is changing and, more importantly, when it comes to the resurrection, it is very unlikely that the matter that now comprises us is *identifiable*. The particles that make up our bodies are not like eternal billiard balls with numbers on them; they are more like wave motions or equations, so that it is not clear what it means to say that this is the *same* particle as moved in my body a hundred years ago. Perhaps, then, it is the pattern or structure that makes me the person that I am. But if this is the whole story, then the person that was John could, in principle, be recreated a thousand times at once with identical bodies (except for their spatial and temporal coordinates) and which one would be John? This question does not arise within this life because we have a continuity of body, but once this body is destroyed, there seems to be nothing to indicate that this new body really is John, even if the structure of the old John is remade. Science-fiction accounts of people being 'transported' or 'teleported' raise similar issues.

Such reflection may lead to the suggestion that, if there is to be a meaningful personal afterlife, there is a problem with identifying the person that is John with *this* physical body, even in terms of its structure. What might be called the 'essence' of John needs to have some continuity and some kind of 'reality' that can survive the destruction of this body. However, in my view, this should not lead us to return to the immortal-soul doctrine, at least in its popular form, for this too runs into severe problems. For example, how can such an immortal soul have a beginning or be created? How can such a soul move a body, including its own? (This was a major problem for Descartes.) Is such a soul independent of God for its existence? How can such a soul manifest itself or be identified when it is not in a body? And so on ...

I do not have satisfactory answers to any of these questions except in so far as I believe that whatever my ultimate nature is, it is somehow known to God, and preserved in his Mind. I may not have or be 'an eternal soul', but I may be 'an eternal idea' in the Mind of God. This leads me to the conviction that the Christian doctrine of the future life should be one in which it is held that God has some future for us based on a loving relationship with him, but that what form it takes is something we cannot know. In sum, I am supporting a version of the 'resurrection of the body' approach because of the emphasis on God's action. However, the exact manner of our future should be an area for Christian agnosticism of the kind already defended. Nevertheless, I shall go on to indicate what I believe is a *possible* doctrine in the light of the difficulties that have been brought forward and which I offer in the form of a tentative proposal for those who feel the need for something more to be said.

I argued in chapter 3 that, as the human level emerges and with it the appearance of self-consciousness, freedom, creativity and love, so a new kind of being comes into existence that has what can be called a spiritual dimension (since it is a reflection of God's Spirit). I also argued that this view is quite compatible with a 'materialistic' view of the human person, in which thought essentially *is* a neurological activity within the brain, provided that such 'physicalism' is interpreted in a non-reductive way (so that, for example, we need something like intentional language adequately to describe the mental level).

Although my own preference is for a 'materialistic' position, I do not mean to say, however, that more 'dualistic' accounts of human nature must be wrong, or (still less) unChristian. There are intelligent people who take a 'dualistic' view, in which the human soul or spirit is not only believed to be essentially non-material, but also capable of existence without a body. Some of these people are Christian, some Hindu, and – among others, perhaps rather surprisingly – some atheistic. As elsewhere in this book, I am supporting an inclusive view of Christianity.

Because the human level is new in respect to the rest of creation, there is no adequate analogy for it in terms of *things*. We may call the human spirit a spiritual substance if we like (although I prefer not to). It cannot be described purely in terms of matter or 'reduced' to it. However – according to mainstream Christianity – it needs a body of some kind in order to express itself or to be recognized. With the destruction of the body, it is still in existence as a unique spiritual reality *in the Mind of God*, but, without a body, it has no place and can neither act nor express itself, nor be said to live (except in God). To live fully, it has to be given a physical or quasi-physical body (like the resurrected body of Christ). God gives it this body and, therefore, in a sense, the doctrine of the resurrection of the body is true. However, a purely physical description of my body does not capture the whole of what I am. Therefore when some people say that the body is the clothing that I must have in order to live, although this is misleading, such language (along with references to our immortal souls) points towards a truth.

Whatever the reader may think of this speculation, it has the following logic. God alone is pure spirit, while matter and the created order as such stand in contrast as the realm of nature. Humanity, in a way that is unique in our experience stands somewhere between the principles of spirit and of nature. I leave open the possibility of other forms of intelligent and responsible life that we have not met, whether physical in form or angelic. I also leave open an adequate account of the way in which non-human animals also, in their own way, are made in the image of God. We are creatures, but we are also spirit, or rather we can become spirit as we emerge into personhood and find union with God. Hence we must be wary of simplistic accounts of humanity that deny this ambivalence, like modern behaviourism. If we think of a thin sheet of solid ice with liquid water below it and air above, then this may represent our status as we live in a hinterland between the realms of nature and spirit. We are both flesh and spirit.

The New Testament ground for hope

The New Testament can be used as a quarry for all sorts of doctrines of the afterlife, such as resurrection at the last day, immediate transference to heaven or hell, or a journey to a place of purgation. I propose to argue that there is only one unambiguous claim in the New Testament concerning the afterlife and that is that God's nature and power are such that the faithful shall continue to live in Christ, but how or when or where we cannot know. The grounds for this unambiguous hope can be found in three contexts.

First, there is Jesus's direct teaching on the subject, brief as it is. He clearly sided with the Pharisees on the subject of some kind of resurrection when, to the Sadducees, he said: "You know neither the scriptures nor the power of God ... He is not God of the dead, but of the living."[4] Thus it is our experience of the nature of God and of our relationship to him that is the principal ground for the Christian hope. We shall live because we are loved by God, and in so far as there is a key to understanding the nature of the universe, this key is to grasp the full significance of love. To put this in another way: in a Christian philosophy we not only discover that love helps to make life better (a discovery with, as it were, a small 'd', that is shared with secular humanism), we also Discover that love is the clue to how the universe is meant to be ruled, and why it is there at all (reflecting a belief that there is here a Discovery with, as it were, a capital 'D').

Second, there is the resurrection of Jesus. No New Testament passage puts this ground more strongly than St Paul in the fifteenth chapter of 1 Corinthians, which was probably written some twenty years after the crucifixion. He begins by listing the apostles and other disciples who, he knew, had claimed to have witnessed the risen Lord, ending with himself, for he evidently regarded his own experience on the road to Damascus as of a piece with the other resurrection experiences. Then he discusses the Christian hope that he bases firmly on the resurrection of Christ: "If Christ has not been raised, then our preaching is in vain ..."[5] In Chapter 12 I shall discuss how Christians describe the nature of the resurrection of Jesus.

I am not one of those who believe that here there is a *proof* of the truth of Christianity, because it is *possible* to give psychological accounts of the primitive Christian experiences that do not depend on a real resurrection and, indeed, this must be so if we are to walk by faith and not by sight. I have also claimed that there has to be an element of risk in Christian commitment and faith. However, there is certainly a solid ground here for the Christian hope that puts it miles apart from blind faith. In the first century, we have evidence of a dedicated group of men and women who claimed to have known the risen Christ and who were willing to die for their faith. It is not unreasonable to say that some astonishing event triggered this faith.

The third context for the ground of the Christian hope is the experience described as life 'in Christ' which has already been discussed. The point here is that, if the accounts of this life are taken seriously, then there is already a foretaste of a kind of life that transcends the dimension of time as we know it. This is why

Christians tend to talk of *eternal* life, rather than *endless* life (which suggests a going on and on of the same kind of life that we find in nature). The nearest analogy in ordinary living for this new life occurs when we are caught up in a moment of love or beauty and do not notice the passage of time. Similarly, as people approach God, they come to share in his timelessness.

In this section I have not referred to what some people call 'proofs positive' for a future life, based on claims of contact with the departed. I have spent some time examining these claims (as a former member of The Society for Psychical Research). My own conclusion is that some of the evidence is both puzzling and suggestive, but that it is always possible for an intelligent sceptic to come up with alternative explanations, so that – as in the case of alleged miracles – it is a mistake to think that there is primary evidence here that ought to convince all people. I prefer, therefore, to ground my belief in an afterlife in my belief in the nature of God. At the same time, for some people – especially those who have what seem to them to be personal encounters – there are certainly 'straws in the wind'.

Reincarnation

In the contemporary scene of a growing dialogue between the great religions of the world, it may be helpful to add a note here on a Christian approach to reincarnation, given the importance of this idea in many religions. Another reason is the recent appearance in scientific work of evidence, or at least apparent evidence, for reincarnation, through hypnosis[6] or the testing of children who claim to remember past lives.[7] I am not suggesting that reincarnation has been proved to be true, but that the evidence is interesting and shows that if it is not true we have to admit extraordinary powers of constructive fantasy in the unconscious mind, or the existence of some 'paranormal' ways of knowing about the past.[8]

It may come as a surprise to some readers to learn that many Christians have believed in reincarnation, including Origen and his followers in Alexandria in the third century. So did many of the Cambridge Platonists in seventeenth-century England, although they insisted that once one knew Christ there was no need for further earthly lives. The evidence also suggests that many ordinary Christians have believed in the doctrine, despite its rejection by the established churches.[9]

Given the variety of Christian views on the afterlife, I cannot see any absolute incompatibility between reincarnation and the Christian hope, provided that one says, with the Cambridge Platonists, that when one fully knows Christ, the circle of rebirths will end. However, I am not personally persuaded by the arguments for reincarnation, and even if I were, I certainly would not want to see it made into official teaching. It seems to me that this is another area for reverent agnosticism, wherein some Christians may see reincarnation as a likely possibility and others not, while all hold the same basic Christian hope of a fuller life in Christ.

The last things

We have already come across the Greek word *eschatos*[10] meaning 'last' in the order of time and this is the source of the Christian word 'eschatology' which means the last things, that is, heaven, hell, judgement and the second coming. As with the Christian doctrine of the afterlife, once we leave some basic statement, there is considerable divergence among Christians on these issues. This book is not meant to resolve these, but it ought to give some understanding of what they are about and some suggestions as to how they fit into an unblind faith.

Heaven is the *state* of being with God in joy and thereby united with our friends. It follows that it is perfectly reasonable to speak of some people having a foretaste of heaven in this life. There is a suggestion in Jesus's teaching that there may be many levels of heaven[11] and some Christians have taken this to imply that there can be an eternal progress towards God or into God, which can begin here. The poetry of T. S. Eliot suggests this kind of eternal journey. Perhaps, at the lower stages, there is the experience of a further physical or quasi-physical period and then, as one moves to new levels, anything comparable with the physical dimension becomes more and more remote. Perhaps some people stay on the lower levels. These possibilities, like all other matters of detail, including the possibility of intermediate stages like purgatory, should be left to our reverent agnosticism.

Hell is the opposite of heaven, the state of separation from God, which must involve alienation from our fellow human beings and from one's true self. We shall see in chapter 13 that Karl Marx has a lot to teach us here. Some Christians believe that, as part of his identification with humanity, Jesus experienced at least the *feeling* of separation from God when he cried, "My God, my God, why hast thou forsaken me?"[12] Thus it is clear that the central idea of hell is a spiritual one and not a physical one. In fact, the preaching of a physical place of everlasting torment has done great damage to the Christian faith, for it turns God into a moral monster and distorts the grounds for the Christian response to God. But this does not mean that the idea of hell should be treated lightly. The references to hell in the New Testament are perfectly appropriate provided we remember that suggestions of a physical hell are symbolic. Some of them are references to the rubbish pit outside Jerusalem and indicate the uselessness of the soul without God, not its eternal punishment. Whether those in hell will all be reached by the love of God in due time, as the 'universalists' believe, we cannot know also. Those who are attracted to this idea may take comfort in Francis Thomson's poem *The Hound of Heaven*, which suggests that God's love will forever seek those who are lost.

The idea of judgement is closely related to the ideas of heaven and hell. In former times, most Christians thought in terms of a literal day of judgement in which there were two somewhat contradictory themes. One was an account, as kept by a recording angel, with the good and bad deeds added up to see where we stood. The other, based on the insight that no one is worthy of God's love and that we all depend on his grace and mercy, saw the judgement in terms of whether or not we were 'justified' before God by our acceptance of what Christ had done for us. Many Christians still think in terms of one or both of these ideas when they talk of judgement, but I suggest that there is a third approach to judgement which is more likely to be on the right lines and which borrows something from both of these themes. Our good and bad deeds, and our response to or our rejection of grace in whatever form it is offered, do not lead to an adding up of scores, but to an immediate and, in a way, natural result, in terms of what happens to our spirit. There is some similarity here to the Hindu idea of karma, a spiritual law of cause and effect, but it is extended to take far more seriously the Christian insight into the reality of grace. Thus there is no need for a recording angel, because when we respond to the good our spirit grows and we become capable of more joy and more growth. There may not be an immediate reward, but in its own way and time the reward is natural and inevitable, not because we acted *for the sake of* the reward (which would frustrate its attainment), but because we have moved to a higher level of being. Similarly, every refusal of grace and every mean act drag us down. Again there may be no immediate and obvious punishment, but inevitably we have hurt ourselves at the deepest level. We may be able to retrace our steps, but only at the price of the pain of dying to 'the old man'. Thus there is judgement, but not the keeping of accounts.

Finally, what should we make of the second coming, that doctrine which is at the centre of the preaching of many radical Protestant churches and which is relegated to a distant and hazy future by the more traditional churches? The principal reason for the uncertainty and disagreement here is that the crucial New Testament passages that refer to the second coming are open to several possible interpretations. For example, in the thirteenth chapter of Mark, was Jesus referring to an historical event after the spread of the gospel, or was he referring to the dramatic meaning of the cross and resurrection that were about to occur, or was he using picture language to describe inner and spiritual events; or were these words never spoken by him but put into his mouth by some in the early church who expected an imminent return of the Messiah? It is most unfortunate that many preachers bang the pulpit and declare what the Bible teaches about the second coming, when what they actually give us is *their interpretation* along one of these lines.

I do not want to claim that the doctrine is unimportant, but, as the reader will by now have been led to expect, I think that we should be agnostic about exactly how and when it will be fulfilled. What I believe to be of permanent importance in the doctrine is the note of *urgency* in the Christian gospel that the more traditional churches tend to neglect. It is not that there cannot be another opportunity for us to respond to God for we cannot know whether or not this will be the case; it is that each presentation to us of the good, the true, or the beautiful, in its own way may be a unique opportunity. The chance to do service for God of a particular kind, or for a particular person, may be gone forever. Also, there is much to be said for living each day with a sense that it may be our last on earth.

Two of Jesus's parables express this note of urgency with special power. One is the parable of the wedding feast, where some of the bridesmaids are not ready with their lamps when the bridegroom comes: "Watch therefore, for you know neither the day nor the hour."[13] The other, which I would closely associate with this in its meaning and which comes later in the same chapter, is the parable of the great assize. At the last day the unrighteous say, "Lord, when did we see thee hungry or thirsty ... ?" and the Lord replies, "As you did it not to one of the least of these, you did it not to me."[14]

Perhaps, one day, the heavens will open and we will literally see the return of Jesus in power, but what is certain is that every day and almost every hour Jesus comes to us and challenges us in the way we treat our fellow men and women. If we are faithful in this latter challenge, there is no need to worry about what will happen to our souls if the world ends unexpectedly.

Notes

1   J. Locke, *The Reasonableness of Christianity* (1695), *Works* VII, pp. 150–1 in the 1823 ed.

2   No 80 in the English Hymnal. The original is attributed to Francis Xavier, c. 1552.

3   *cf.* Gen. 2, 7. The Old Testament word *nephesh*, which is usually translated as 'soul', is used in this way and not for an entity that could exist separately.

4   Mark 12, 24–7.

5   1 Cor. 15, 14.

6   H. Wambach, *Reliving Past Lives: The Evidence under Hypnosis*. Harper and Row, 1978 and Hutchinson, 1979. The interesting part of this book is not the fact that so many people, under hypnosis, appear to recall a former life (which could be a construct of the mind) but the statistical analysis of the alleged former lives, in terms of gender, social class, race, etc.

7   I. Stevenson, *Cases of the Reincarnation Type*, University Press of Virginia 1975. Professor Bruce Greyson, of the University Virginia, is presently (2010) continuing the experiential work of Stevenson.

8   The word 'paranormal' refers to faculties, or alleged faculties, such as telepathy and clairvoyance. A paranormal explanation would often be contrasted with a scientific or 'naturalistic' explanation. However, a paranormal explanation does not require the concept of 'miracle', and indeed, it is one for which a 'scientific' explanation might become available in the future.

9   See, for example, E. L. Ladurie, *Montaillou*, Penguin, 1980, pp. 163, 194, 206, etc.

10   See the last section of chapter 3.

11   John 14, 2.

12   Mark 15, 34.

13   Matt. 25, 13.

14   Matt. 25, 44–5.

9. The Essentials and the Non-essentials

Is belief important?

Many Christians have all sorts of particular beliefs that other Christians regard as untrue, or as unimportant even if they are true. Thus, if Christians of many kinds are to share a basic unity, we need to be able to distinguish the essentials of the Christian faith from the non-essentials. The latter can then be an option for those who happen to believe them, or for those churches that want to stress them, but they need not be sources of division.

When we ask what are the essentials of the Christian faith, the first question that arises is whether *any* belief is essential for our salvation. It seems odd that anyone should be saved or doomed just for believing or not believing that something is the case – that is for belief in the sense of 'belief that'.[1] What people have believed, in this sense, is enormously influenced by their culture, upbringing and temperament, and to suggest that God would regard such beliefs as essential for a person's permanent salvation seems to make God capricious (rather like the God whom some Calvinists believed in who predestined many souls to hell before he had ever made them). This view has only seemed plausible because preachers have tended to slide over from talking about belief in the sense of 'believing that', to belief in the sense of 'believing in', wherein some kind of commitment and way of life is involved, and then it is quite reasonable to say that a belief might affect our salvation.

I do not want to say that belief, in the sense of 'belief that', is unimportant, in part because we need to have a general respect for truth, and in part because some of these beliefs may have long-running effects on what kind of people we are. But this kind of belief cannot be *essential* for salvation as belief in the sense of 'belief in' might be.

Next, we must note another ambiguity in the question "What is essential?" This might mean what is essential for one's life and growth as a person, or it might mean essential if a person is to be a Christian, which is not necessarily quite the same thing, as I shall explain. Further, it might mean what is essential for the church if it is to represent Christ's teaching. Again, this is not necessarily the same as what is essential for the individual Christian. For example, it might be essential for the church to have a statement of faith like the Apostles' creed if it is adequately to carry out its teaching function, but it may not be necessary for someone to be in a church with such a creed in order for them to be a Christian.

A three-tier system

The distinctions I have just made between the different senses in which we can talk of something being *essential* lead me to a suggestion that I believe could go a long way in forwarding Christian unity. It would enable people to see where agreement really matters, where it matters less and where it is unimportant. The heart of this suggestion is that we should adopt a three-tiered system of belief. Level A is the fundamental one and refers to the belief that is essential for identifying a Christian. It is basically summed up in the first creed: "Jesus is Lord" or "Christ is Lord". Level B is what is essential for the church as a whole in order to maintain its nature and to fulfil its charge to spread the good news revealed in Christ. According to my suggestion, this comprises the basic content of the Apostles' and Nicene creeds. Level C refers to the mass of particular beliefs of individual churches, for example, the belief in the physical assumption of Mary within the Roman Catholic Church. Within a particular church, beliefs in level C may be thought important for the full growth and richness of the church, but there is no need for anyone to argue with other Christians about them as if they were matters of vital importance. I also doubt whether any church is wise to insist that all its members must hold to its beliefs at level C, for a Christian might love and respect a particular church, but be driven out of it if they are compelled to swallow their doubts about all of its beliefs.

We shall now look at each of these levels more carefully.

Level A. Christ is Lord

Nowadays, few Christians believe that they alone can be saved, although this was the official teaching of some of the major churches in former times. From what we have said of the nature of God and of humankind in earlier chapters, it follows that the one *essential* condition for being a person, and therefore in a fundamental sense for being 'saved', is to respond to the good in whatever form it comes, but especially as it confronts us as the morally good, or the true, or the beautiful. The liberal Christian believes that whenever we are confronted in any of these ways, we are in fact being confronted with God. But a genuine response to the good or the true or the beautiful does not necessitate that one *knows* that these are reflections of God. Thus the good person of any religion, or of none, can still respond to God. Moreover, when we see that Christ is the incarnation of the *logos*, or word of God, as it comes to all people, we must also see that in a sense such response is response to Christ. So whoever respects the good, the true and the beautiful has begun to treat Christ as Lord.

Congruently, it makes sense to say that whenever an atheist thinks lovingly of another person, they may discover that – unknowingly – they have in fact been praying for them, so far as God is concerned.

However, it does not follow that all good people are *really* Christians, for to say this tends to make for woolly thinking and confusion. It is one thing to say that a person is responding to the *logos* and is, therefore, being saved in a fundamental sense and that as a result will more easily come to recognize him whom they have unknowingly served; it is another thing to say that all good people are Christians. In order to avoid confusion, it is better to use the word 'Christian' not simply as another term for 'a good person', but for one who believes *that* Jesus is the Christ *and* who believes *in* him. There is the additional problem that, unfortunately, Christians are not always 'good persons', as that term would normally be understood! So Christians have the joy of stating what they believe to be the truth about God and humanity and have the responsibility of living out this conviction and sharing it. In other words, what is literally essential for all people is *articulated* by Christians when they say "Christ is Lord".

Here, I suggest, is the solution to the basic confusion over the notion of what is essential. When we ask what is essential for salvation in the strictest sense, the answer is a response to the good, which is, however unknowingly, a response to God. When we ask what is essential for being a Christian, the answer is to believe and to articulate that "Christ is Lord" (or the variants, "Jesus is Lord" or "Jesus is the Christ", which are essentially the same). We can see this both from the logic of the situation, that is from what follows from the nature of God and of humanity, and from the history of the church, where we find "Christ is Lord" to be the first creed. The first Christians were asked to renounce their sins and to assent to this one simple statement of faith.[2]

It should be noted that the adoption of this creed as the first tier or level of Christian belief places people with all sorts of doubts within the Christian fold. To say and mean "Christ is Lord" is to commit oneself to the way of Jesus in life and prayer,[3] to make him Lord of one's life, and most of all, to adopt his example of love. All sorts of people with all sorts of doubts are attracted to Jesus because he is seen to represent what is good or true or beautiful. All these people can make Jesus their Lord and, in doing so, find that they are not alone, but are within a great company that draws its strength from this commitment.

This emphasis on the possibility of combining doubt with a Christian commitment can be illustrated by the remark of a thoughtful friend who said to me, "At the end of the day, if ever we are in a position to know the whole truth, I would rather find that I had been wrong – in the company of the likes of Francis of Assisi – than right – in the company of the typical cynic."[4]

A powerful example of the impact of the person and character of Jesus is provided by Terry Eagleton's recent book *Reason, Faith, and Revolution*.[5] Here both 'actually existing religion' (49) and the 'straw-targeting of Christianity' by doctrinaire atheists such as Richard Dawkins and Christopher Hitchens (52) are subjected to ruthless attack, while Jesus himself is sympathetically presented as a figure of challenging importance. I am not suggesting that Eagleton would endorse most of my theology, but there is much common ground at this level.[6]

Level B. The church and the creeds

In some ways, it would be nice if this first creed were all the theology that we needed, but although it is all that is essential in the strict sense that I have described, it is not enough for the health of the church nor for many of its members as individuals. The reason for this is that we are, potentially at least, rational animals with minds as well as hearts and it is the whole person that God seeks to draw to himself. Thus intelligent people must seek a *philosophy* of life in which they try to understand and interpret God, humanity and the world, as far as they are able. I do not mean that all who can ought to take philosophy courses at a university, for this may or may not help in the quest, but that in their own reflection and reading each person should try to develop this understanding. This search soon leads to a realization of the limits of our ability to answer many of our fundamental questions, but there is still the demand to stretch our mind up to these limits. The alternative is the folly of blind faith or of the equally blind unbelief that is so much in evidence. Blind faith can lead to the horrors mentioned in chapter 1.

The church too, as an historical institution, needs a basic Christian philosophy that it can teach its members, otherwise it will not be able to pass on the insights that it has gained into the relationships between God and humanity and the world. I am not saying that this is the only, or even the primary, task of the church, for that is to introduce people to a way of life – through prayer and liturgy and communal life – and this way of life is not primarily a matter of what we believe. Not every member of the church should be expected to accept every part of this philosophy, because we have seen that the one essential criterion for church membership should be the creed "Christ is Lord". However, it may be perfectly reasonable for the church not only to teach more than this as its official teaching, but also only to appoint to teaching positions within it those members who subscribe to its basic philosophy. Hence the distinction between levels A and B. Level B can be taught as official church teaching, but only level A is demanded as a test of church membership.

What should be included in level B? It is partly in reply to this very question that I have written this book, for what is presented here is precisely the sort of teaching that I would advocate as the basic Christian philosophy that is appropriate for level B. Where do the two basic Christian creeds (the Apostles' and the Nicene) fit into level B? In my view, they are both acceptable summaries of this basic Christian philosophy, *provided* that one allows for a certain latitude in their interpretation. For example, out of respect for the Orthodox churches, when Western Christians say that the Holy Spirit proceeds "from the Father *and the Son*", they should be allowed to interpret this as meaning "from the Father *through* the Son", which is a compromise formula that has been suggested by many. Also, when the creed says "born of the virgin Mary", some Christians may see this as a reference to a literal and technical virginity, others as an ancient title that is a way of expressing, in mythical form, the spiritual significance of Jesus's birth. Also, the 'descent into hell' has several possible interpretations, such as a reference to Jesus's spiritual agony instead of an actual journey, and the 'resurrection of the body' can also mean different things to different Christians, depending on whether the 'body' is taken is taken in a physical or a spiritual sense. In all these matters, we must be wary of making our interpretation an orthodoxy that is imposed on others. If people can say the creeds with sincerity, using this latitude in interpretation, then let them be counted within the number of those who accept level B.

Inevitably there will always be borderline cases. For example, should John Smith be ordained when his view of the incarnation seems about half-way between the official view and that of the Unitarian church (where it is generally held that Jesus was not essentially different from any other great prophet)? There can be no formula for sorting out such questions beforehand for they are typical examples of questions that demand judgement, or discrimination. The need for such judgement arises not only with religious questions but with many of the ordinary issues that people face in their daily lives, for example, "Am I be being dishonest in leaving something unsaid in this letter to a friend?" However, when there is doubt, I suggest that the spirit of charity should lead us to err on the side of comprehensiveness rather than that of exclusiveness. Furthermore, honest disagreements can play a positive role, for as J. S. Mill said (in the context of political and social disagreement) we can all learn and benefit from opinions that are different from our own, and hence we should tend to value them rather than shun them.[7]

Level C. Traditions and superstitions

When we approach the more particular beliefs of different churches, there is both a positive and a negative aspect to note. The positive aspect is the colour that a particular tradition can give to a church, without which the world culture would be much poorer. Some of this colour may have little or nothing to do with belief, for example, a particular tradition in cathedral music, but in other cases it may be closely connected with beliefs, for example, in processions and pilgrimages connected with certain saints. An important example of level C is a belief in the value of a church order that includes bishops, priests and deacons. Personally, I think that there are good grounds for this belief,[8] but I do not want to put it on the same level with the issues that I have been discussing and that is why it would be out of place to defend this kind of church order here. I am concerned in this book with the exposition of level B. Another positive aspect of some beliefs at level C is the way in which they can foster particular forms of liturgical practice or private prayer, and therefore help to build up corporate or individual spiritual life.

The negative aspect of these particular beliefs is the extent to which they lapse into superstition, or make important what is true but unimportant. In the worst instances, Christians are expected to accept, on sheer authority, beliefs that are downright absurd.

Notes

1   See chapter 1, *Unblind Faith*.

2   Acts 2, 38.

3   It must be stressed that the basic Christian commitment included *both* the attempt to follow the moral teachings of Jesus and his way of prayer. From chapter 1 it should be clear that prayer of a kind is possible even during periods of doubt, and even if honesty makes us begin each prayer with something like, "O God, if you are there." As stressed before, it is certainly possible to be both a Christian and an 'agnostic', in the strict sense of the term. Could one be both an atheist and a Christian (who sought to make Jesus the model of how to live, and who therefore proclaimed "Jesus is Lord")? This would be an odd position to take, just because following Jesus would normally imply following his way of prayer as well as his way of life – but I am reluctant to be too certain of the answer, especially in the light of the huge variety of disciples.

4   I am not suggesting that these are the only options, but the remark succeeds in indicating that (as with William James) faith can contain an element of choice.

5   Terry Eagleton, *Reason, Faith, and Revolution*, Yale University Press, 2009, pp. 19–21, 26, 28–9.

6   Eagleton holds that Jesus's "sense of history seems to have been a little awry" (15). I would argue (probably in disagreement with Eagleton) that if we accept the need for an historical church, much of what I call level B becomes necessary in order for the message of Jesus to

be effective. Elsewhere, Eagleton has an interesting take on the term 'Son of God' (which, he points out, is not the term Jesus himself used most of the time in reference to his nature, preferring the term 'Son of Man'). In his introduction to *The Gospels*, annotated Giles Fraser, London, Verso, 2007, xxv, he writes "To call him the Son of God is to claim that the solidarity he shows others, not least his profound acceptance of their moral frailty, is an authentic image of the Father." While in no way suggesting that Eagleton would accept much of my theology, there is common ground here. See also his description of Jesus as a 'stumbling block' to orthodox belief (*ibid*, xx).

7   J. S. Mill, *On Liberty*, especially ch. 2.

8   The grounds include respect for an ancient tradition and the practical benefits of having a 'pastor of the pastors'. In some Protestant denominations moderators or superintendents effectively fulfil this role, whether or not they have the title of bishop. If it could be established that Christ himself established the three-fold order this would, of course, virtually settle the matter for Christians, but the evidence suggests that the three-fold ministry developed gradually in the first and second centuries, with a lot of local variation. In the New Testament the word *diaconoi* is naturally translated 'deacons', but the term for what are later called 'priests' is *presbuteroi*, which, strictly speaking, should be translated as 'elders'. For the Jewish priesthood, the word *hieroi* is used, which – according to the New Testament – is abolished, except for the work of Christ, and for the way in which the whole church, collectively, fulfils the intentions of the Old Testament rituals at the temple in Jerusalem. The basic meaning of the term for 'bishops' (*episcopoi*), is 'overseers'. Many scholars believe that *episcopoi* were not, originally, a higher *order* than *presbuteroi*, but were simply elders with a particular administrative function. Gradually, in the second century, they became a third and higher order of ministry. Many modern scholars take the view that 'deaconesses' in the early church were women deacons, and not – as many traditionalists still claim – a different and lower order of ministry than that of deacons. In Rom. 1, 16, Phoebe is called a 'deaconess', but this term can be either a general term for 'servant', or a term for a member of the *order* of deacons. From the foregoing it can be seen that my approval of the three-fold ministry is not dependent on it being established either by Christ or by the apostles, but on respect for an ancient tradition that has practical benefits – provided that it does not become 'authoritarian' in a way that diminishes the voice of the laity.

Part Two: Problems for the Christian Faith

10. Evil and Suffering

Why is there a problem?

It is not difficult to see why the existence of evil and suffering presents a problem for many believers, not only in Christianity, but in any religion where God is said to be good and all-powerful. "Why is there evil in the first place?", it may be asked, meaning by 'evil' the intention to reject the good or to cause harm; and, "Why does God permit the main result of evil, namely suffering?" If God is good, he cannot desire evil or suffering and, if he is all-powerful, why does he not prevent them?

The problem was acutely felt in the Old Testament just because the writers were coming to believe in a loving God. This was particularly evident in the authors of Job and of many of the psalms. They asked, why do the righteous so often suffer and the wicked prosper?[1] Several answers were suggested, the most common of which went something like this: "I myself have seen the ungodly in great power: and flourishing like a green bay tree. I went by, and lo, he was gone."[2] Unfortunately this pious answer just will not do, at least not by itself. The wicked are not always brought down and they often die in their beds of old age, full of riches and honour, while others, including innocent children, die in concentration camps. Where is God's justice in this?

Some religious people think that the problem can be answered by bringing in the next life. The writer of the psalm just quoted is unlikely to have been thinking of this since, as we have seen, the idea of personal immortality only came into Judaism after the return from exile and was not universally accepted doctrine even in the time of Jesus. Nevertheless, many Christians have suggested that the justice of God will be worked out because both the wicked and the righteous will be suitably rewarded in the next life.

However, in conversation with an intelligent agnostic or secular humanist, I have always felt that this answer to the problem of evil and suffering, at least by itself, was too easy a way out. In the first place, it does not begin to tackle the problem of the existence of evil. Next, it asks the critic to take on trust the existence of the next life. Moreover, the more we stress the role of the next life, the more the critic is likely to say something like this: "This is a very convenient answer, for it avoids having to see any effects of your loving God in this life. If all justice is to be found in the hereafter, then *whatever* happens here is compatible with God's love. Does not this mean that there is no divine influence or providence in this world?"

In the light of this kind of reaction, Christians need to say much more if they are to have an unblind faith.

How far is freedom the answer?

At this point, many Christians will say more by adopting the following argument. God has chosen to make a universe in which there are many kinds of creature, including, as part of its fullness and richness, self-conscious beings who have freedom as an essential part of their nature. Such are human beings and possibly other kinds of intelligent beings that we have not met. Since it is part of their nature to be free, it must be possible for these creatures to choose something other than the good, for the whole point of their life is that the love whereby they can choose the good has to be freely given, and therefore has a value of a kind not found elsewhere in the created order. Because of the unique value of this love, a universe in which there are human beings, with both love and evil, is better than a universe with no human beings and neither human love nor human evil.

This emphasis on human freedom entails that we must be very careful in the way that we talk of the omnipotence of God. For the man of blind faith, omnipotence often refers to the belief that God can do literally anything, but Christian philosophers have rarely believed in this kind of absolute omnipotence. For most of them, God cannot will a contradiction, nor can he will evil, as this would be contrary to his nature. Being sensitive to how we should use language, Aquinas insists that it is better to say that it makes no sense to speak of God doing contradictory things, or doing evil, than to say that God is 'limited'.[3] God's omnipotence refers to the belief that God can do whatever it is *logically possible* for him to do. Thus he can make people who are free, but he cannot *make* these people good; he can only encourage and assist them to be good, otherwise it would not be *their* goodness, but a necessity of temperament imposed upon them by God. We would have nicely behaved robots, but not loving persons. Human goodness, by its very nature, has to be *achieved* not given.

Here, the position I am defending is in sharp contrast with the teaching of John Calvin. He argued that God knows all future events not because he has foreknowledge of them, but because he has absolutely decreed them – including the "plans and intentions" of all human beings. Hence, it is purely God's grace that *makes* people good. Although Calvin sometimes refers to 'free will' this can have no significant place within such a bleak philosophy – in which, from all eternity, some people are foreordained to eternal hell by the absolute decree of God.[4]

The proper understanding of omnipotence is so important for an unblind faith and is the source of so much misunderstanding that we must go into it more deeply, even if the language may seem somewhat technical for some readers.

Let us note that the idea of absolute omnipotence, meaning an infinite capacity to do anything, is not essentially tied to the idea of God, even when it has developed into the one creator-God of the great monotheistic religions. In ancient Israel, for example, God was the one supreme creative power, but the word 'infinite', in the modern sense, cannot properly be applied for they simply did not have the concept that the word 'infinite' now suggests.[5] In the Bible, there is sometimes the suggestion that God can do anything,[6] but this must be understood in the context of a culture that did not distinguish between logical and practical impossibility.

What precisely is this distinction? Something is *logically* impossible when it implies a complete contradiction. Thus a square circle is logically impossible, provided that we use the words 'square' and 'circle' in their ordinary senses. Mathematics gives us many other instances. For example, it is a contradiction to say that the angles of a triangle do not add up to 180 degrees (assuming that we are talking of triangles on a plane surface, for other geometries are possible). In contrast, what is *practically* impossible does not in itself involve a contradiction, but it is beyond our powers. For example, it is practically impossible for a human being to run a mile in 10 seconds. Here, 'practical' does not mean 'almost', as in the popular use of the term 'practically impossible', but 'completely impossible given our powers'.

The important point can now be made more clearly. Most Christian philosophers have claimed that just as it makes no sense to think of God making square circles, so it makes no sense to think of him *making* people morally good, because this too would involve a logical contradiction. To expand on a point already made: if God made people good, they would no longer be 'persons' in the full sense of the term, because, for human beings, moral goodness has to be a kind of *achievement* – even though, Christians would add, one that needs the help of divine grace. However – as we have seen – it is misleading to describe this as a 'limitation' on God's power, for when the Bible speaks of God's power this is a reference to the fact that he has the power to do all things that for us are *practically* impossible.

The conclusion we reach here is of a piece with many other emphases in this book. While a blind faith frequently makes careless and sweeping claims on behalf of God and of Christianity, an unblind faith often finds that the ancient doctrines contain basic truth, but that they have been misunderstood and expressed in inappropriate ways. We have found this to be so in the case of original sin and it applies equally to an understanding of omnipotence.[7] Once the true nature of God's power is seen, it follows that, in making free beings such as us, God chose, by that very act, to accept that there are some things that cannot be done. So long as human life involves freedom, then evil and suffering are the price that must be paid for human love and joy.

Natural evil

Although the approach suggested above brings the discussion of evil and suffering to a higher level, it is still insufficient for an unblind faith. An intelligent and friendly critic of the Christian faith might well take up the argument as follows: "Fair enough, you have shown how evil must be a possibility once human beings are created and you have shown how this evil must be able to lead to suffering, but what about all the suffering that is not caused by human evil, namely the suffering that is sometimes called 'natural evil'? Examples are the consequences of earthquakes, cosmic disasters, animal suffering within the ordinary course of nature and so on? *Some* of this is caused or encouraged by human choice (such as the result of choosing to stay in an earthquake zone after repeated warnings of an imminent disaster, or the failure to spend enough money on cancer research), but much of it is completely independent of any human choice. How can such things be allowed by a loving God?"

This question demands a further reply and Christian philosophers have usually responded along these lines. Any created universe must manifest an *order* if it is not to be chaos and if it is to be a possible context for human life. Events have to fall into a pattern and to be generally predictable, otherwise, although we might be able to *will* good or evil for another person, we could not produce actions that were likely to bring about this good or evil and eventually it is doubtful whether it would even make sense to will anything at all.

One way in which this necessary order could be produced so that we could predict the outcome of our actions, with some probability, would be for God to direct every event, by his sheer will, in such a way that events appeared to fall into regular patterns. However, Aquinas, and most Christian thinkers who have followed him, argue that this is not how God has chosen to make things happen. Instead, he has created something that should be seen as still more marvellous, namely a universe that is *made to make itself.* The created order is then given its own laws, its own causality and its own relative independence or autonomy. Aquinas called this the domain of 'secondary causality'. Thus nature is not to be seen as a sort of marionette theatre in which the finger of God directly controls every movement, but as an *order*, with a genuine, though not absolute, independence. This enables us to engage in science as we seek to understand the working of this order and generally to live a human life in which events are predictable.

But if this is the way that God has set up his creation, then God *must* generally respect these laws of the universe and allow physical nature to take its course; otherwise he simply destroys the environment that is necessary for growth. On rare occasions, he might suspend these laws, or operate in terms of higher laws that appear to suspend them, and then the Christian may talk of 'miracles'. However, we have no right to demand that God act in this kind of way whenever it suits us. Suppose, for example, that a thunderstorm threatens the life of someone whom we love. God *could* intervene, for it is not logically impossible for him to do so (as it is impossible for him to make our friend good), but if we expect him to intervene on this occasion, then we must equally be prepared to ask him to intervene whenever someone is threatened by a storm, or by anything else in the course of nature. But as soon as we see the results of a consistent use of God's saving power, we find that the necessary context for human growth, in which nature can be relied upon and in which we have to learn responsibility, has been set aside.

The foregoing argument has led some liberal Christians to deny that miracles, in the strict sense of the term – which implies that a purely natural explanation could not be given – ever happen. As we shall see in chapter 12, some would even apply this conclusion to the way in which they interpret the resurrection appearances. My own view is that although this is one possible reaction, it does not necessarily follow from the need for nature to have its own autonomy. However, this is one of many areas where this book – it is hoped – may provoke further thought.

Belief in the autonomy of the natural order means that we should be extremely careful when we say, "It is God's will", after some misfortune. There is a sense in which all that happens is *permitted* by God, and some writers have paid lip service to God's omnipotence by saying that, for this reason, his 'will' is always accomplished. However, this misleads the ordinary person. When a child is killed in an accident, it is *not* God's 'will' in any ordinary sense of the word and great misunderstanding has arisen because so many religious people have talked as if it must be God's will whenever tragedy occurs. The child's death is probably due to human evil, negligence, or carelessness, in which case it comes under the inevitable consequences of freedom. Sometimes it may come purely from physical and unpreventable causes, in which case it is still not God's will, but the effects of the *order* which the world must have if we are to learn to be responsible and to love.

This, at least, forms the beginning of a Christian response to the problem of suffering and more will be added in the next section. However, it is understandable that many thoughtful people are still not satisfied, and this is why those who have an unblind faith are sympathetic to those who find the problem of suffering so great that they cannot feel able to commit themselves to Christan belief. Whereas many atheists and agnostics are irrational, because they have rejected a caricature of Christianity (or of other forms of religion), those who base their lack of faith on serious reflection on the problem of suffering have a legitimate position. This is particularly evident in the case of those people who have suffered personal tragedies, and ask, quite reasonably, "Where was God when this happened?" In such cases it is both unhelpful and superficial to say something like "It was all part of God's plan".

There are two things I want to say to thoughtful people who take an atheist or agnostic position of this kind. First, it is one thing to reject belief in the kind of Providence that many religious people have, in which it is believed that God is directly controlling every event; it is another thing to reject the kind of Providence defended in this book – in which God is *with us* in all our sufferings, but does not manipulate the world in the way that we think he should.

One example of how God can be felt to be *with* us in our sufferings is provided by those people who are imprisoned, especially if imprisoned unjustly, who sense a kind of solidarity not only with others in prison, but with Jesus, following his betrayal, when he awaited his execution the next morning. Obviously, this does not amount to an escape from prison – the world is not manipulated for our benefit – but it can amount to a profound change in attitude that, in turn, may have powerful consequences.

Here it is worth reminding readers that Charles Darwin did not lose his faith and become an agnostic on account of his theory of evolution. He gradually lost his faith for several reasons, one of which was the morality of much of the Old Testament. Another, according to several commentators (but not proved), was because of the premature death of some of his children, especially Annie. At the end of his *On the Origin of Species* (1859) he writes of the grandeur and beauty of the world, and in later editions he added a reference to the 'Creator', who had 'breathed' power into forms of life. Like the more liberal theologians of his time (such as Frederick Temple and Charles Kingsley) and many fellow scientists (including his friend, Asa Gray, who was the leading botanist of his day and a devout Christian), Darwin saw no necessary conflict between his theory and belief in the Christian God, and a letter of 1879 (12041) explicitly claims that one can be a 'theist and an evolutionist'. I suspect that the chief reason for his growing agnosticism was the traditional belief in a Providence that ordered the cruelties of the Old Testament and determined the tragic death of children. Had he been confronted with the view of Providence suggested here (and more generally, in the liberal tradition), and with a different view of Biblical inspiration, it is possible that his response might have been different.

Second, some people who reject the idea of Providence, even

in the more liberal (non-interventionist) version, may still wish to affirm 'Christ is Lord', and to associate themselves with the lifestyle that Jesus proposed.

The role of Providence

If we accept the argument of the last two sections, it follows that there is no absolute inconsistency in believing in a God who is good and powerful and in the existence of both moral and natural evil. One is the result of freedom, the other of the autonomous order that God has to make as an environment for us to live in. However, an unblind faith can take a further step in its understanding of evil and suffering, even though we cannot hope to see the whole picture nor to satisfy every sceptical enquirer.

Let us suppose that a friendly agnostic returns to us with the following comment: "I can see from what you have said that there might be a loving God in spite of the human and natural evil that we find, but what difference does this God make to our world? If God cannot interfere with human freedom, nor interrupt the autonomy of his order, does this leave any significance to the idea of God? What difference does it make whether there is such a God or not, except perhaps in the next life, and surely you don't want to say that God is only relevant in the hereafter?"

This is an important comment because it reflects the thinking of many intelligent people once they have moved away from the naive idea of a God who alters the world or our fellow men and women in accordance with our requests. In my view, the Christian reply to this comment should be along these lines.

Much of the discussion of evil and suffering has taken place in the context of the assumption that the *end* of life is human happiness. But perhaps a better perspective is this: *the* end or final purpose of human life is both a joy that can only come from union with God and our fellow human beings, and a nobility of character that has an intrinsic value (and moreover, a nobility of character that is itself important for our relationship with God). But both of these depend on our growth as persons to the point where our selfish egoism is replaced by a genuine love of God and of humanity. Therefore, the primary purpose of this life must be seen in terms of this growth rather than in terms of happiness. This does not mean that happiness is unimportant here and now, let alone that we should neglect the

NE PAS AFFRANCHIR

NO STAMP REQUIRED

By air mail
Par avion

IBRS/CCRI NUMBER:
PHQ/D/1154/OX

REPONSE PAYEE
GRANDE-BRETAGNE

Oneworld Publications
185 Banbury Road
OXFORD
GREAT BRITAIN
OX2 7BR

IF YOU WISH TO BE PLACED ON OUR MAILING LIST, PLEASE RETURN THIS CARD

NAME: _____

ADDRESS: _____

ZIP/POSTAL CODE: _____ COUNTRY (IF OUTSIDE UK): _____

EMAIL: _____

O N E W O R L D

O X F O R D

To ensure we send you the correct information, please could you answer the following questions:

In which book/catalogue did you find this card? _____

If in a book, where did you purchase it? _____

Which of these best describes your interest in our books? Please tick as appropriate:

☐ You use them for personal use or as gifts

☐ You work in book retail   ☐ You are an academic

☐ You are a student and our book(s) are recommended   ☐ If so, do you have responsibility for selecting books for course adoption?   Yes/No

☐ Other reason? _____   If yes, for what course? _____

PLEASE INDICATE ANY AREAS OF PARTICULAR INTEREST

☐ Comparative Religion   ☐ Inspirational

World Religions: ☐ Mysticism

☐ Hinduism   ☐ Buddhism   ☐ Bahá'í Faith   ☐ Science and Religion

☐ Judaism   ☐ Christianity   ☐ Other (specify)   ☐ Philosophy

☐ Islam   ☐ Sufism   _____   ☐ History

☐ Modern Spirituality   ☐ Psychology and Self-help

    ☐ Other (please specify) _____

For further information, please e-mail us at info@oneworld-publications.com or visit our website at
http://www.oneworld-publications.com

happiness of others, but that is not *the* end.

If we accept this perspective, then we shall have very different expectations about what we think the world ought to be like and, in particular, about how we expect God to answer our prayers. We shall expect God to make a difference and this must be stressed in reply to the comment of the friendly agnostic, otherwise we do indeed make God irrelevant to this life, but the chief expectation is not that God will mould the world as we would have it, but that he will help us to live in the world as it is. He will not so much change the world as change us, and then the world through us. The world will be the kind of place where noble character both can and does develop.

'Providence' is the word usually used for God's government of the world and his active involvement in it and I have written more extensively of its meaning elsewhere.[8] What I have suggested – as already intimated – is that it is God's providence deliberately to make a world that makes itself. Thereafter, God may steer it in certain directions, but – at least typically – by use of a kind of persuasion rather than through an overwhelming force. Perhaps on certain occasions he brings about an event by some direct use of his power and then some Christians would talk of a 'miracle', but this cannot be the general means of his government if we are to have human character and a context for human growth. God's daily providence, therefore, is active principally through the influence he has on us, a power that is analogous to the way in which we influence our friends for good, without manipulating them or forcing their response. Through the good and the true and the beautiful, he draws us every day towards himself and towards our own growth and fulfilment, whether or not we recognize that God is the source of the good and the true and the beautiful. So he is active, but in the only way that is possible given his decision to make creatures who can freely respond to him in a world that has its own order. The earlier passages dealing with the atonement are consistent with this emphasis on God working through the persuasive power of love rather than through force.

An important illustration of this perspective on the purpose of human life and of the working of providence is the Christian attitude to sickness, old age and death. Within the context of seeing happiness as *the* end of this life, all of these seem pointless, except perhaps for a speedy death in order to make room for other people. Within the context of the view of providence that I have suggested, they can all have a positive significance. It is not that God wills *this* sickness or *this* infirmity or *this* manner of death. The point is rather that God has made a world in which all of these things must occur and when they occur they can be used creatively. Further, given his decision to make human persons, God *had* to make a world in which these things would occur. A particular occurrence may be evil, often because it is the result of some human neglect or hatred, but the permanent risk of such happenings is a necessary part of the human situation. At the same time, each occurrence opens up new possibilities as we respond to God. For one, sickness, old age or approaching death is the signal for a tragic personal decline, for another, any of these can be the signal for a heroic response in which a person comes to terms with the world as it is, accepting what cannot be changed and seeking to change what can be changed (which is often something within us). If we look around us, we can find many examples of this positive approach to sickness, old age and death, especially in certain old people who have developed a serenity which shows not only that they have learned to accept what cannot be changed, but that paradoxically they have achieved a level of happiness that they did not know in their youth.

In all the reflections made in this chapter I am not suggesting that there are neat answers to every problem raised by the presence of evil and suffering, but that thoughtful Christians are not simply faced with a blank wall so that they must either give up or blindly accept contradictory statements about God. The more we reflect on the issues, the more we are led to think more deeply about the meaning and purpose of life and as we do this we find that the Christian philosophy of life makes at least as much sense as any other philosophy. Once again, we can be Christians with an unblind faith, especially if we feel that living the life of faith 'makes a difference' to how we are able to experience life, here and now, with a real measure of fulfilment and inner happiness.

Notes

1   E.g. pp. 73, 3–5.

2   Ps. 37, 36–7 Prayer Book (Coverdale) translation.

3   See Thomas Aquinas, *Summa Theologiae*, 1a, Question 25, A. 3, *cf.* A. 4 and 1a 2ae, Question 93, A. 4.

4   Calvin, *Institutes*, 3, 22, 8; *cf.* 1, 16, 8-9; 2, 3, 13; 3, 21, 5 and 22, 1–6.

5   In translations of the Old Testament we often find the word 'almighty' for the Hebrew *shaddai*.

6 E.g. Matt. 19, 26.

7 Some Christians would make a similar point about how to interpret the doctrine of omniscience, saying that God can only know – at least in detail – what it is logically possible to know, given the free will of persons and the indeterminacy of sub-atomic particles. This issue is much complicated by the Neo-Platonic argument that God knows the future because he sees all things from an eternal standpoint. (This argument is essentially different from and more subtle than the Calvinist argument that God knows all things because all events, including the thoughts and intentions of every person, are determined by his absolute decree.) In response, a number of Christians, following the lead of A. N. Whitehead, argue that although God is, in a sense, eternal, in his relationship to us he has accepted certain time restraints, including some that relate to 'future contingents'. This is one of many issues where this book does not seek to give a definitive answer, but to raise awareness.

8 Michael J. Langford, *Providence*, SCM Press, 1981.

11. The Problem of Freedom

The old and new versions of the problem of freedom

We have seen that the Christian response to the problem of evil and suffering depends in part on the conviction that human beings are free. But are we free? And what does it mean to claim that we are free? The thoughtful Christian who mixes with scientific materialists and Marxists is bound to find another set of questions here for an unblind faith.

It is important to see that the issue of freedom, although an ancient one, has taken on a new form with the rise of modern science. In the ancient world, freedom was frequently challenged on a number of grounds. One was a fatalism that saw a blind fate ruling over every event and this often lay behind the attempt to prophesy in the crystal ball sense. Another view was that the gods played a kind of chess game with mortals; another that astrological powers determined our lives. This last form of determinism is specifically attacked in the New Testament.[1] Yet another view saw one omnipotent God as the controller of every event, human and natural. The basis for this was a concern to guard God's omnipotence, but I have argued that this is a mistaken approach since the view that God has chosen to create a world that has a kind of internal freedom is, in fact, the result of a still loftier idea of God.

The contemporary scene is different. Astrology is still a force in some quarters, but its followers usually think in terms of the influence of astrological forces on our characters rather than in terms of detailed predictions about the future, so that whatever we may think of astrology, for most people it is not a radical threat to freedom. However, a certain contemporary approach that is held to be scientific does pose a threat. This is the view that just as we have come more and more to know the causes of natural events, like rain, so in principle we can come to know the causes of human thought and action. In principle, so it is often argued, all events are totally determined and predictable; the only difference between human thought and action on the one hand and the falling of rain on the other is that the former is so complex that detailed prediction is impossible. But even if detailed prediction is never possible in practice, the very claim that it is possible *in principle*, say to an enormous computer, is a threat to freedom. The underlying suggestion is that we are totally conditioned by our genetic structure plus the stimulations we receive from within our bodies and from the outside environment. Many hold that this view is inevitable once we accept the scientific spirit of our age and reject the superstitions that we allow whenever our private wishes are involved.

The essence of freedom

If we reject the deterministic position and hold to a belief in freedom, as I believe that an unblind faith must,[2] can we say what we mean by freedom?

Negatively, it is quite easy to say what freedom means: it is the claim that, although we are *influenced* by the factors of which the determinist speaks, we are not *totally conditioned* by them. There is still an area in which what we call free choice can operate. But we don't have to maintain that we are free all the time, for example, under the pressure of certain drugs, or in intense pain, or during a breakdown in brain chemistry. All that is necessary is that the ordinary human person can make a number of significant choices to select A rather than B. When we do so, we are pressured, but not determined; influenced, but not totally conditioned.

However, this is only a negative claim, a way of saying that free action is *not* random action, *nor* like the movement of a weighing machine in which the pressure on one side of the scale will inevitably bring it down. But can we also say *positively* what freedom *is*?

The difficulty here is that, outside our experience of human action, we have no experiences of freedom from which we can frame an analogy. In other words, we cannot describe human action in terms of natural or artificial models, like the balance scale, without effectively denying freedom. We are back with the claim made in chapter 3, namely that with the arrival of the human level, freedom emerges along with self-consciousness, creativity and love, as a new aspect of our being, or as some would say, as a new 'category'. Human beings are not complex machines, nor even complex animals (who may also have a measure of freedom), but a new creation.

It is just here that many determinists miss the point and continue to ask for some model to describe freedom that, if offered, would beg the very question at issue. But there is no conflict with the scientific spirit here. The claim is that with human consciousness there is a new level of reality which sciences like physics and chemistry and even biology are not set up to deal with. Of course our bodies have a physics and a chemistry and a biology, but to insist that this is the whole story of humanity amounts to a dogmatic assumption of the determinist position.

Three arguments for freedom

It follows from the preceding account of the nature of freedom that no strictly scientific argument can be put forward either to prove or to disprove the reality of freedom.[3] However, it does not follow that there can be no rational defence of freedom, but that (as with arguments about the reality of God) the arguments cannot have compelling force. Rather, they are designed to suggest that the idea of freedom helps to make sense of our overall experience and that the denial of freedom leads to at least equal difficulties in our account of human experience. Here are three of the arguments for freedom.

First, a belief in freedom of the will seems to be demanded if we are to be able to make sense of our moral life. We commonly distinguish between actions for which we can blame people and which we call 'voluntary', such as striking someone with intent to injure, and actions for which we do not blame people and which we call 'involuntary', such as falling through a floor and injuring someone below. Without this crucial distinction, it is hard to see how we could use words such as 'ought' and 'should'. The fact that our moral language has developed on the basis of this distinction does not prove absolutely that the distinction is there in reality, but it does permit us to make the plausible claim that human language reflects an insight that is based on a real distinction.

Further, we should note that it is not enough to say that voluntary action has causes that lie within us, while involuntary action has causes outside us (a distinction which – as Aristotle showed – is useful for many purposes). When we cannot act freely because of a severe mental breakdown or an inherited brain defect, the cause is essentially within us, but we are still not free. The point is rather that free action is not caused at all in the way that purely natural events are caused. Free actions are influenced by many factors, but the crucial 'cause' is our will. Nor are free actions characterized by a kind of randomness or 'wild leap' – as Jean-Paul Sartre seems to have believed. They are causally related to our thinking processes, but not in the same way as other events in nature are causally related to physical processes.

The second argument concerns the paradoxical position of determinists. If they are consistent, they have to apply determinism to themselves, including their own thought processes. It follows that all the determinists' conclusions, including the one that says that determinism is true, are totally conditioned by the influences that bear upon their thinking. But if they realize that the belief in determinism is itself determined, then there is something odd about the conviction that it is *true*.

As with the first argument, this is not a strict proof of freedom, or rather, in this case, a strict disproof of determinism, for the discovery that determinists have dubious grounds for their beliefs does not prove that the beliefs are false. However, the belief in freedom emerges as something more coherent and plausible than the determinist position, because if I believe in freedom of the will I also believe that I have freely chosen this belief in the light of the evidence. In fact, any claim that a certain position is actually true seems to be predicated on the assumption that we can make a decision about the merits of a truth claim that is not totally predictable and conditioned. As a result, this is one of the places where most scientists and theologians sing, as it were, from the same hymn-book. Both believe that they are – in their different ways – searching for some kind of objective truth, and for both, equally, this means that the mental processes by which we seek truth cannot be thought of as totally deterministic.[4]

The third argument goes like this. The more we come to understand the causes that go to make us what we are and to influence how we think, the more this very knowledge allows us to transcend conditioned ways of thinking in which our thoughts tend to reflect different pressures that bear upon us. For example, consider the Darwinian theory of evolution. Assuming that it is true – as I believe it to be – that human beings have evolved more or less along the lines suggested by this theory, then this very knowledge *itself* produces a new situation. Instead of being controlled by the process, we can now control the process ourselves and, within certain natural limits, we can decide how the human species will evolve from now on. This involves a new freedom for the human species as a whole and I am suggesting that there is also an equivalent freedom for the individual when we know the physical, psychological, or social pressures that have helped to make us what we are. This is the reason why psychological analysis is sometimes a *liberating* experience.

A similar line of argument applies to the neuroscientist who is working on the actual processes that are taking place in the brain when we think. The neuroscientist is in the strange (some would say paradoxical) position of examining these processes by thinking about them, when this very thinking is also seen as a neurological process. It seems to me, that in order to argue convincingly for their conclusions, neuroscientists need to say either that their thinking in some way 'transcends' the purely biological processes they are examining, or that it is better to say that all thinking *involves* neurological processes rather than to say that all thinking *is* such a process.

Personally, I prefer the former of these two options. As we saw in chapter 3, the 'physicalist' claim that thought essentially *is* a kind of neurological event is not necessarily inconsistent with a Christian philosophy, provided it does not include a 'reductionism' that denies any kind of transcendence to the human mind.

The point here is very like that of the second argument. It is that *human* knowing and understanding cannot be made sense of without the category of freedom. Far from our thinking being caused in the way that the rain is caused, we think *about* causes and we think *about* the pressures that bear upon us and such reflection is an aspect of that higher level of life which human existence is all about.

The spiritual meaning of freedom

When we begin to explore the problems connected with the Christian faith, it often happens that, after an initial process of weighing the pros and cons of a position, we are driven to look more deeply into the meaning of the faith. This turned out to be true in the case of evil and suffering and it is equally true of freedom. Following a discussion of the dispute between freedom and determinism, we are finding that we need to look at the spiritual meaning of freedom in order to understand more fully what it is.

Part of the fascination of freedom as it is explored, for example, in great literature, is that whenever it seems almost in our grasp we shrink from it, as if at the last moment we lack the courage to seize what we most prize. Some people have called this phenomenon 'the fear of freedom'.[5] This fear seems to me to be an indication of the spiritual struggle that is the experience of every person as we emerge from the animal to the personal level. This fear can also help us to see why the ancient human virtues are interconnected. Courage is needed to accept the frightening responsibility that freedom brings; at the same time, freedom cannot be enjoyed without temperance, or we become slaves to our animal passions; when we have courage and temperance, wisdom becomes possible as we can make our own judgements; when we judge wisely we become just.

Thus freedom can be seen more clearly to be an integral part of the nature of the mature person, along with self-consciousness, creativity and love. It cannot be described in terms of lower levels of being, but it is one of the preconditions of the truly human level and it is, at the same time, a manifestation of that level.

If freedom is an aspect of the spiritual nature of the person, it would seem to follow that God himself is supremely free, and this is puzzling to many people for, surely, it might be said, God *cannot* do evil, he must do what is best, and so what 'choice' can he have? However, this remark overlooks the significance of creativity. It is no doubt true that God and, perhaps, also the perfectly good person, cannot do evil. They are 'able' to do it in one sense, but 'could not' in another. In the *Analects* of Confucius, when the ages of life are reviewed, the sage can say: "At seventy, I could follow the dictates of my heart; for what I desired no longer overstepped the boundaries of right."[6] But there is still choice, for there can be many good things to choose between and it is not always the case that one of them must be the best when we are thinking of creative action or creative thought. Consider a great painter in front of a fresh canvas. We can predict that they will produce a great work of art, but not what the work will be. By analogy, if God is to create a universe it is inevitable that it will be good and beautiful, but nevertheless, it could be very different from the one in which we live. Some theologians believe that God has, in fact, created other universes – all of them good and beautiful, but different.

It follows that it is only in a very restrictive sense that the good person loses the freedom to do evil, because for every evil door that closes, two or more good doors open in response to creative genius. This is what should make the idea of heaven dynamic and exciting, in contrast with the boring portrayals of heaven with which we are often presented. Heaven may include an eternal exploration of the beauties of God's universe and an eternal series of challenges to our creative capacities.

Freedom and grace

As we are led to think more deeply about the meaning of freedom, we must come in time to face the ancient problem of the relationship of freedom to grace, perhaps the most fundamental of all the spiritual questions that concern freedom. The Christian faith appears to claim two contradictory things at the same time: first, that human beings are free and responsible for their own acts; second, that we depend utterly on the grace of God – that free gift whereby we are first created and then redeemed or recreated in Christ. Thus St Paul frequently asserts that he would be nothing without Christ, for "by the grace of God I am what I am";[7] and Christian preachers continually contrast the impossible way sought by the person who tries to reach goodness by their own efforts (like those who try to lift themselves up by their own bootlaces) and the transforming way of those who find that they are loved and accepted as they are, and that "while we were yet sinners Christ died for us".[8]

This seems to be a typical case of where we are asked to hold two truths together in a kind of tension, for both the experience of human freedom and of the unmerited gift of grace seem to reflect profound aspects of the Christian life. But how can we maintain both aspects without adopting a blind faith that accepts stark contradiction?

Here are two suggestions that may help us to see that freedom and grace only appear fundamentally opposed from the narrow perspective that most people have, while from a more adequate perspective they support each other.

First, freedom to choose the good as we see it does not have to involve the even greater freedom to reach our full potential in the life of the spirit. Christian teaching has traditionally distinguished between the natural end of humanity (a full and happy life by earthly standards) and the supernatural end (a transformation of the person through union with God and fellow human beings that brings eternal life). It has gone on to say that fallen persons can achieve neither without grace. But perhaps the natural end is theoretically possible without grace, at least in the sense of the means of grace that are available to us through the work of Christ. I have argued that *it is possible* for people to live without actual sin, even though the odds of any individual doing so may be very small, for otherwise it is hard to make sense of human guilt as a consequence of sin. John Wesley was among those who argued, similarly, that if we make use of the grace that is available, it is possible for all human beings to live without sin, even though exceedingly few actually succeed in doing so. However, the naturally good person would probably be the first to see the potential for a further end, for which he or she needed a relationship with God that demanded more than ordinary moral goodness. Thus the grace that comes from communion with God would be seen as absolutely necessary for our spiritual end, but not, in the strictest sense, absolutely necessary for our natural end. There is a more general sense of grace that refers to the gifts of God that we need continually, even to exist. In this sense, of course, no achievement is possible without grace.

Second, there is something artificial in looking at the problem as if freedom gets us so far and then grace, as it were, lifts us over the next hurdle. It is like the artificiality of seeing perception as simply a subject looking at an object, when, as we have seen, there is rather a subject-object relationship and neither the subject nor the object can exist in isolation. Subject and object in themselves are mere abstractions. Similarly, freedom and grace are not things that can exist outside the context of relationships, but are aspects of an encounter between ourselves and God. As we reflect on this encounter, we can emphasize either one side or the other of the relationship. We can look at the subjective side and stress the importance of our response and our capacity to be drawn by love. Alternatively, we can stress the 'givenness' of God's grace, equivalent to the 'object' in the act of perception. Strictly speaking, however, there is only one experience, just as there is only one act of perception. Thus, just as an adequate account of God's knowledge or God's love meant that we had to speak of Father, Son and Holy Spirit and not confuse them even though God is one, so in our encounter with God we need to speak of freedom and of grace, without confusing them, even though there is a unity in our experience of God.

It begins to look, therefore, as if the apparent contradiction between freedom and grace results from the human tendency to look at ourselves as pure subjects, set over against the world of things and of other persons, and from the failure to see that truly human living only arises in relationships with others. We can, of course, choose to become something approaching a pure subject, but in the end this is to choose death. Only when we give up the ego that we try to cling to can we find real life. Once again we have to learn that it is only through a kind of dying that we can live!

An additional note on 'Pelagianism'

The relationship of freedom and grace has often been discussed under the topic of 'Pelagianism', based on the views, or alleged views of a British monk who lived from about 360 to 420CE. Unfortunately his writings are only known from extracts found within theologians, such as Augustine, who were attacking his views, so that a balanced view of what he actually said is hard to achieve. Some theologians define 'Pelagianism' as the view that we can achieve salvation solely by our own efforts, and do not have to depend on the grace of God – except (as indicated earlier in the chapter) – for the grace that creates and sustains us all in being. It should be clear from this chapter that, like almost all Christians, I reject this view. However, there is also a position that is often called 'semi-Pelagianism' (which *might* have been the actual position of Pelagius himself). This is described in different ways, but a plausible formulation would contain the following theses – all of which I would support:

(1) Although it is proper to describe the state of human beings as 'fallen' (which, for more recent Christians, does not need to refer to an historical event) – our nature is not *totally* depraved, as claimed in the writings of some Protestant Reformers. On this matter the Catholic and Greek Orthodox accounts of human beings being weak, but retaining some genuine capacity to reason and to choose the good, is sounder.

(2) Non-Christians comprise both evil and 'naturally' good people, some of whom achieve a significant level of both moral goodness and genuine happiness. Whether or not this goodness is the result of an unacknowledged work of grace within them, this means that Christians should take a positive view of many non-Christian achievements – as did Matteo Ricci. Nevertheless, 'natural' goodness could not merit the kind of eternal life that is offered to people 'in Christ'. Moreover, many people find that without special grace, even a modicum of natural goodness is beyond their reach.

(3) When Christians respond to the special grace of God which is offered to us in Christ, this response should not be regarded as

itself *purely* the work of grace within us – which effectively removes all genuine freedom from human choice, especially in respect to the *acceptance* of the grace that is offered. Certainly we may find God's grace working within us (as in Rom. 8, 26) but this is an encouraging, not a compulsive force. It will not do, for example, to claim that some angels did not fall only because they were given more grace than those who did fall (as in Augustine's *City of God*, XII, ch. 9).

Such is the degree of misunderstanding and confusion surrounding the terms 'Pelagian' and 'semi-Pelagian', that I personally refrain from giving an opinion on these positions until they are defined with some measure of clarity. When this is done, it often turns out that disagreements are not as sharp as was supposed.

Notes

1   Gal. 4, 8–11.

2   There are some philosophers who think that we can be both scientifically determined and, in a significant sense, 'free' – a view sometimes called 'compatibilism'. I believe that this view is mistaken, but I do not have the space to pursue the argument here. Those who continue to be worried by an apparent conflict between free-will and respect for science should bear the following point in mind. Increasingly, scientific method does not depend on absolute and mechanical laws, but on regularities of a general or statistical nature. This is especially true in the human sciences, so that a scientific approach to humanity does not need to assume that every individual is totally predictable, even in principle. There is a useful discussion of this matter in D. D. Raphael, *Moral Philosophy*, Oxford University Press 1981, pp. 91–104.

3   However, strictly scientific arguments or discoveries can have some relevance to the issues. For example, further discoveries about the nature of the brain might make the deterministic position more or less tenable.

4   One of the counter-arguments to my position is based on the claim that all traditional truth claims, even in science, are based on an unsupportable belief about there being an 'objective' truth, as it were 'out there'. Those who adopt this point of view often call their own (apparent) references to truth claims (for example, about there being no truth claims) as 'ironic'. Clearly, this position warrants a much more extended treatment than I can give it here, but I would insist, at the least, that this disbelief in an objective truth is part of

a philosophical position that can be rationally challenged, so that
commitment to it is likely to involve an element of faith!

5   See E. R. Dodds, *The Greeks and the Irrational*, University of California
     Press, 1951, ch. 8. Also, Jean-Paul Sartre's play, *Huis Clos*.

6   Book 2, 4. Arthur Waley's translation.

7   I Cor. 15, 10.

8   Rom. 5, 8.

12. The Bible: History, Myth, or Legend?

Historical religions

Christianity is one of the historical religions. This means that certain events that are claimed to have actually occurred in a definite time and place are important or, in some cases, crucial. Judaism and Islam are also historical religions while Buddhism is not. This is not to downgrade Buddhism, but is simply to highlight a difference in character. In Buddhism, no historical event is crucial, only the teaching. For example, if it could be proved that Guatama, the original Buddha or 'enlightened one', never existed, this would not unduly worry an educated Buddhist, whereas if it could be proved that Jesus had not died on the cross, then Christianity as we know it could not be sustained.[1] There is a good case for the actual existence of an historical figure behind the stories of Guatama, but this does not have the central importance that the Jesus of history has for Christianity.

It follows that an unblind Christian faith must have grounds for believing in certain key events in history. Not all Christians agree about exactly what these events are, but almost all would include the life, death and resurrection of Jesus, though the last of these is interpreted in different ways. Thus, the question "How reliable is the New Testament?" is a vital one for the Christian, for, outside the existence of the church and a number of apocryphal gospels of uncertain date, the New Testament is almost the only evidence for the events in question.

In this chapter, I shall argue that there are reasonable grounds for holding that the New Testament and the most important parts of the Old Testament do have historical value and can support the basic historical claims that the Christian must make. However, it is worth noting that there are some other sources of evidence, few though they may be, and that is why I referred to the New Testament as 'almost the only evidence'. One of these sources is Pliny the Younger, whose letter to the emperor Trajan, written in or about 112CE, discusses the Christians in his province, who sing hymns to a certain Christ, as to a god. He also appears to refer to the Holy Communion at which the Christians assembled. At almost the same time the historian Tacitus wrote in his *Annals* about the persecution of the Christians under Nero in 64CE and he describes how the sect sprang from a 'Christ' who had been put to death under Pontius Pilate. A few years later, another Roman historian, called Suetonius, has two references to the Christians, one of which confirms Tacitus' account of the persecution. However, more telling than any of these non-Christian sources, though somewhat later, is the evidence provided by a letter that has survived from shortly before 200CE, written by Irenaeus. In this letter, Irenaeus reminisces about his early student days and his personal memory of Polycarp who had died as a martyr in about 155CE at a great age. Polycarp, he remembers, used to tell stories about 'John, the disciple of the Lord' whom he had known when he was young. We cannot be sure exactly which John is referred to here, but this letter does constitute personal testimony of a most valuable sort: "Irenaeus, then, in France shortly before 200CE, was able to recall at only one remove a man who had known Jesus intimately."[2] To some readers this may seem a pretty remote kind of evidence, but when we consider the smallness and apparent unimportance of Christianity in its first few years, it may seem surprising that any evidence was preserved outside the sacred writings that the church treasured. However, I stress that these extra-biblical sources are not being held up as proofs for the vital historical events; they are rather 'straws in the wind', that is to say, suggestive and intriguing items of evidence that help to support our picture of the early church and thence of the man who founded it.

The fundamentalist debate

I shall argue that Christians do have reasonable grounds for the central historical claims that they must make, but before outlining this argument there are some important matters of clarification to deal with. The first concerns the term 'fundamentalism'. Unfortunately, this word has been used in several ways, but I shall use it to refer to the belief that (*a*) every word of the Bible is *verbally* inspired by God, so that there can be no possibility of error save through faulty transmission of the original text, or through poor translation; and (*b*) that all the Old Testament stories, including those concerning Adam and Eve and the patriarchs are essentially historical and not mythical accounts. We must note that there is no logical necessity to combine beliefs (*a*) and (*b*), for God might have verbally inspired a series of holy myths, but in practice these two beliefs tend to go together.

The most obvious objection to fundamentalism, which is actually of much less importance than two others that I shall refer to shortly, is that the Bible abounds in apparent contradictions. For example, it is suggested that Jerusalem fell to the Jewish assault on Canaan,[3] but this is then denied in another passage.[4] Again, John appears to make the last supper take place the night before the passover, while the other gospels make it a passover meal. However, for someone who is convinced of the total and infallible accuracy of the Bible, it is not difficult to get round such contradictions; all that is needed is to make one's explanation more complicated, just as some scientists do when they try to accommodate awkward evidence with their theories. Thus one might say that Jerusalem was taken, but then lost again almost immediately, or that two different cities of the same name are referred to, and so on. Personally, I am not impressed by such suggestions and see no need to attempt such a defence of the verbal inspiration of the Bible, but this is principally on account of the two major objections to fundamentalism that follow.

The first of these is the moral objection. If fundamentalism is accepted, then it would appear that God commanded the slaughter of thousands of innocent women and children, for example at Jericho and Ai. He would also appear to have struck down Uzzah, most unreasonably, for trying to stop the ark from falling. For the ordinary Christian, these and a host of similar examples do not provide significant objections to the Christian faith, because, as I suggested in chapter 2, what we read is not what God said, but what the Hebrews of the day *believed* that God said. This, for example, was the teaching of the Quaker preacher, Hannah Barnard.[5]

Further, what we find in the Bible, especially in the Old Testament, is a growing *development* in the human understanding of God. However, this is an attitude that we can only take if we reject fundamentalism.[6] We do not have to reject *inspiration*, for there can be many kinds of inspiration, as when someone sees a vision and then tries to express this vision in their own words. What we have to reject is *verbal* inspiration. The words of the Bible – or at least the vast majority of them – even those of the most original text, are human and open to the errors and limitations of vision that human beings are subject to.

The second major objection arises from a reflection on contemporary experience. It is logically possible that God dealt with the people of Biblical times quite differently from the way in which he deals with them now, but there is something very unsatisfactory in such a suggestion for it makes the Bible far less relevant to us. But if the experience of God in our time is any clue to the experience of God in the past, then we must accept the fact that when God works through men and women he does not literally take them over and use them like puppets. Instead of this, we find that God inspires some people with a vision of the good or the true or the beautiful, and then leaves it for them to work out what this means and to express the insights in their own words or science or art or music. Moreover, this approach to inspiration is the only one that makes sense in terms of the understanding of humanity's relationship to God that I have described, for God seeks to *draw* us by the example and power of his love, and Jesus suffered just because God so respects our freedom that he will not, and in a sense cannot, *force* us into his mould. So it is that, in the last two hundred years, more and more Christians have reinterpreted their understanding of the inspiration of the scriptures in order to fit in with this understanding of God and humanity.

There is another major objection to fundamentalism, or at least to that aspect of it which stresses the historical nature of Genesis, which has already been mentioned in the third section of chapter 3. This is the necessity of an historical dimension to human character, which makes it contradictory to speak of the instant creation of an adult man or woman. This makes a literal interpretation of Genesis not only improbable, but rationally impossible. There *could* not be an 'instant Adam', with anything recognizable as character and virtue.

One of the important consequences of the rejection of fundamentalism is that Christians are not obliged to regard all the books of the Bible as being of equal value. Consider, for example, the book of Revelation. This is very likely a second-century document produced during a time of persecution by a Christian who really believed that this world would soon end. The churches argued for years as to whether to include this book within the Bible and eventually most accepted it, although two important branches of the church (the Copts and the indigenous church in India) still reject it. My suggestion is not that Revelation is valueless – on the contrary it contains some magnificent examples of Christian poetry and insight – but I doubt whether it should be treated with the same authority as those that come from the first generation of Christians, that is from those who were eye-witnesses of the central events, or who knew such eye-witnesses, which is the case with most, perhaps all, of the other books in the New Testament. Yet it is on an irrational reliance on the verbal inspiration of Revelation that Jehovah's Witnesses and many other fringe sects depend. In arguing with such (usually well-meaning and kindly) people, I question whether the book of Revelation has full Biblical authority, hoping thereby to enter into a creative discussion concerning why this, or any other book, should have authority, and of what kind. In particular I ask Jehovah's Witnesses how they would respond to a well-informed Coptic Christian who argued that the only reason for including Revelation in the Bible (given the evidence of its late date) is because of the authority of the church – which is an authority they totally reject.

Myth, legend, parable and allegory

The rejection of verbal inspiration and of the literal historicity of some parts of the Old Testament suggest that much of the Bible is myth or legend. However, we must be careful how we use such words.

In popular usage, the word 'myth' tends to mean 'untrue', but this is not the strict meaning of the term. A myth is a traditional story in which, very often, divine or semi-divine beings take part. Moreover, because it is a traditional story, not – at least typically – one made up for entertainment, a myth nearly always has great psychological significance. For example, the ancient myth in which Zeus, the chief of the Greek gods, murdered his father, Chronos, is of great importance for our understanding of the importance of the psychology of the time (and according to Freud, of all times). In terms of factual accuracy it is best to say that myths are neither true nor false, for they are not meant to be taken as literal fact. However, in a secondary sense they can be true, in that they can reveal how people have felt or thought. Many cultures still have their myths, for example, 'the American dream' or 'the belief that computers save paper', but nowadays the stories or ideas that are used to express a nation's sense of its role in history rarely involve divine beings.

It follows that to describe the Adam story as a myth should not be seen as downgrading it, but rather as pointing to its symbolic and psychological significance. It might even be called a 'true' myth, in that it presents human beings as creatures of God whose moral and spiritual problems centre on their desire to make themselves the centre of the world.

In contrast to myth, a legend is a traditional story that claims to be about historical people and which is either totally untrue or much exaggerated. Sometimes there are grains of historical truth behind a legend. For the most part, they are not of great psychological significance, but some are important, for example, as expressions of the heroic pride of a people. In the Old Testament the book of Judges clearly contains much material of this kind, but it is more common to find in the Bible a mixture of myth and legend, as in the story of Noah. Here, some great flood (but not one that covered the whole earth) probably does lie behind the story, but it is ingeniously worked into a mythical account of God's dealings with humanity. As such, the story can be of great power, but there is absolutely no need to insist on the historical accuracy of the whole tale, and indeed doing so raises major ethical issues about a God who chooses to drown so many people, including children.

Next, we must distinguish both myth and legend from parable. A parable is a story that is deliberately made up in order to illustrate a moral or spiritual lesson, whereas myths and legends tend to grow or evolve without the same element of deliberate invention. Examples in the Bible are the stories told by Jesus and the story of Job in the Old Testament. There can be an overlap with myth or legend when one of these is worked over and turned into a parable, as, in all probability, in the case of Jonah.

Finally, we should clarify the word 'allegory'. This is a myth or a legend or a parable that is used in a particular way, so that the separate parts of the story can be given meaning. For example, Jesus himself allegorized his parable of the sower when he compared the seed that fell among thorns with those for whom the word is choked by the cares of the world and delight in riches,[7] and Paul allegorizes the wanderings of Israel in order to explain the experience of the Christian church.[8] It is important, however, to note that some parables cannot be turned into allegories without absurdity. For example, the parable of the unjust steward (Luke 16, 1–9) indicates how odd it is that we tend to be careful about worldly matters, while neglecting much more important spiritual matters. If we allegorize the story, for example, by likening the unjust steward to God, we destroy the point of the parable.

The historical core

A rational evaluation of the Bible brings out the fact that it is a rich mixture of history, myth, legend, parable, allegory and poetry – in addition to other kinds of writing, for example, law and proverb. It cannot be stressed too strongly that many thoughtful Christians find this realization a help and not a hindrance to faith. Although the modern study of the Bible, which treats it from some points of view as it would any other ancient document, sometimes raises awkward and challenging questions, it also brings out the great richness and quality of the Bible and the strength of the basic historical claim that Christians must make. Moreover, the alternative is a blind faith in the authority of the Bible that is ultimately fragile, for as soon as real doubts or legitimate questions are allowed to creep in, one's whole faith is liable to be shattered. This is why some fundamentalists have an 'all or nothing' approach to the Bible (either it *is* the word of God, or it is just an ordinary book), which is the opposite of the *discrimination* we are expected to show in most departments of life.

Let us now turn to the historical core, meaning by this the history that is essential for a traditional Christian faith. In the New Testament, this consists of the existence of Jesus as an historical figure, the principal characteristics of his ministry and teaching as recounted in the gospels, his crucifixion and resurrection, and the emergence and spread of the early church. Exactly what is essential in the Old Testament is more arguable, but, tentatively, we might say the flight from Egypt, the forming of a covenant at Sinai, the settlement of the Jews in the promised land and the development of the prophetic tradition with its hope for a Messiah. In the case of the flight from Egypt, I do not mean the detailed account as given in the book of Exodus, but the claim that a group of former slaves – perhaps much smaller in number than is claimed – escaped from Egypt and settled in what is now Palestine.

Whatever may be our doubts as to the details involved in all these events, there is a strong case for the truth of this historical core, except perhaps in the case of the resurrection, with which I shall deal separately. If we take the historical evidence for other ancient events, such as the battle of Marathon, there is usually no more, and in many cases much less evidence than there is for the historical core to which I refer. In general, with regards to the past, when controversy is not raised and no one is thought to have an axe to grind, then the smallness of the hard evidence tends to be forgotten.

In the case of the historical core of the Bible, there are five strands of evidence that I want to mention, though this does not exhaust what could be put forward.

First, there is the need to explain the very existence of Israel and of the church. When we look at the extraordinary history of the Jews, with its incredible continuity despite thousands of years of wanderings and persecutions, there is a very strong case for saying that some dramatic set of group experiences forged this people. Freud was one of those who argued powerfully for this claim. The events that surround Sinai, even if mixed with myth and legend, are utterly congruous with such a forging. Similarly, the very existence of the early church demands some dramatic set of experiences that could forge the followers of a dead leader into the dynamic body that we find in history. Again, the core of the gospel story is utterly congruous with this.

Second, there is the evidence of the actual documents. It is probable that the vast majority of the New Testament was written between around 48CE (the earliest of St Paul's letters that have survived) and 90CE. A large number of ancient manuscripts have been found, the most famous collections being known as the Chester Beattie and Martin Bodmer papyri, both of which contain fragments, and in some cases whole New Testament books, from around 200CE or even earlier. One papyrus fragment, containing part of St John's gospel, found in Egypt in 1920 and know as P52, is possibly the oldest surviving manuscript of the New Testament, and – astonishingly – is dated by most scholars at around 125–150CE.[9] In terms of ancient documents, this is an amazingly short time between holograph (the original manuscript) and the copies that have been found, for manuscripts were continually being copied and recopied and there is often a gap of hundreds of years between the holograph and the earliest copies that scholars can actually handle. In particular, it is extraordinary to think of St John's gospel (probably written in Ephesus) being read by a community on the banks of the Nile, before 150CE. Of course, this is not proof of the accuracy of the New Testament, but it is an important strand in the argument that much of the New Testament goes back to the time of eyewitnesses.

Third, there is the growing awareness of the role of oral tradition in primitive cultures, together with the realization that this tradition could faithfully record the exact or almost exact words of a poem or story over many generations. Modern people, with their reliance on books and machines, tend to forget the role of both ordinary memory and of professional 'rememberers' of tradition in the ancient world. In this context, the gap between the witnessing of events in the New Testament and the writing down of these events in the gospels and the Acts of the Apostles is a very short time indeed, probably between thirty and fifty years. The value of oral tradition is even more important when we try to assess the possible accuracy of the Old Testament where some of the stories may have been passed down orally for hundreds of years until they were written in their present form.[10]

The fourth strand of evidence, similar to the third, is the extent to which many passages are in the form of stories, as in the parables, or poetry, such as the psalms and the beatitudes.[11] These are the forms of speech that it is easiest for people to remember with accuracy. Indeed, story and poetry were often used deliberately with this in mind. Moreover, in chapter 4 I tried to show that the parables contain the core of Jesus's teaching.

Finally, I would stress the many indications of eyewitness reporting that occur in the gospels. Most interesting of all, perhaps, are those passages in St Mark's gospel (probably from around 65CE) that appear to be critical of the disciples, passages that have been toned down in Matthew and Luke, because by the time those gospels came to be written (probably around 80CE), the disciples had become heroes.[12] This is exactly the kind of internal evidence that scholars use in order to evaluate the links between different texts. It should also be born in mind that the early church rejected many alternative gospels, some of which can be found in the New Testament apocrypha, largely because they were not thought to date from apostolic times. Many of them contain stories of miracles performed by the infant Jesus that were very attractive to the pious. However, from early times there was a realization of the difference between what was edifying and what was an authentic and primitive record.

The claim that eyewitnesses lie behind the New Testament has been given added support by Richard Bauckham's recent and scholarly book, *Jesus and the Eyewitnesses*.[13] This should be essential reading for those wishing to pursue this strand of the argument of this chapter.

I would strongly urge that those who believe that the church suppressed the alternative gospels simply because some of them were heretical, should actually read the many that have survived. The books, generally known as New Testament Apocrypha or Pseudepigrapha are readily available in larger libraries. For the most part, not only are these gospels of much later date, even the most interesting of them, and probably the earliest, *The Gospel of Thomas*, contains questionable material, such as stories of the young Jesus cursing a boy who teases him, and thus causing his death.[14]

As is often the case, the force of the argument for the genuineness of the historical core is a cumulative one, and depends on putting together many things, including these five strands. One of the things is the question of whether the picture that emerges 'makes sense' in terms of contemporary experience, for all historians use this criterion, however solid the documentary evidence seems to be. An absurd story tends to be disbelieved – and rightly so – however many documents and witnesses are produced. It is at this point that objective and scientific factors in the evaluation, including the five strands just discussed, tend to get mixed up with personal feelings and prejudices. It is not surprising, therefore, that we find disagreement about a subject that raises such emotion as the historical basis for the Christian faith. However, my claim in this chapter is that, when all the evidence is put together, there is a stronger case for the historical core with which I am concerned than with many other historical events that are generally accepted without question.

One further point needs to be made. Rational people recognize that in order for a scientific breakthrough to occur, there often has to be a radical thinker who is prepared to entertain what most think of as 'heresy'. This is particularly evident when some apparently strange or unusual event is said to happen. For example, most scientists rejected the phenomenon of ball lightning until some 'qualified researchers' actually witnessed it – and then began a search for an explanation of something that undoubtedly does occur. There was, in other words, an understandable reluctance to accept as real something that was outside normal experience. Let us now suppose that the core of the Christian story is true, and, in particular, that in the life of Jesus, the creative source of the universe was, in some unique way, at work. In this context it would not be irrational to think that accompanying this unique event were some signs, and therefore, that the 'extraordinary' could not be ruled out, as it might be by most of us when hearing a traveller's tale. In his *Jesus and the Eyewitnesses*, Richard Bauckham makes a similar point with respect to the 'unique uniqueness' of the holocaust testimonies. Without the testimonies that have survived, no ordinary person would be likely to believe the story of Auschwitz – the testimonies are in a significant sense unbelievable, "since they are *prima facie* scarcely credible and since they defy the usual categories of historical explanation."[15] Although the testimony of eyewitnesses in the New Testament is different in many ways from that of the holocaust survivors (as Bauckham explains), there is a significant analogue here. The generally important criterion of "what makes sense" in terms of contemporary experience, is not an adequate test for evaluating either the actualities of the holocaust (which we know to be only too real), or events surrounding an actual incarnation of the spiritual source of the universe.

The resurrection and ascension

The last paragraph provides a good starting point for considering the resurrection, and in particular the questions "Is the resurrection part of the historical core?" and "Is belief in the resurrection essential for the Christian faith?" The initial problem here is that Christians adopt at least three different kinds of position with respect to the resurrection. For some it signifies a literal, physical event, in which there was both an empty tomb and the flesh and blood body of Jesus brought back to life. For a second group, there is an empty tomb and the appearance of the risen Christ, but what was seen was not the former body, but a new or spiritual body of which we can know little. For this group the phrase 'physical resurrection' is not really appropriate because it suggests that it was the physical body that was seen, whereas they wish to stress the transformation of the physical body. Further, it is not necessarily the case, according to those who adopt this second position, that a camera would have recorded anything on film. A third group go further, and think that the resurrection, while still in a sense 'true', consisted of a series of dramatic encounters in which the disciples were aware of the presence of Christ. For them, even if Jesus seemed to have a body in some of these encounters, this is unimportant, as is the empty tomb. If the bones of Jesus were found hidden somewhere, many of these Christians (unlike the others) would not be greatly disturbed because this would not contradict the genuineness of the experiences of Christ, for example, at Emmaus. In many cases, those Christians who take this third position also stress the continuity between the New Testament experiences of being in the presence of the resurrected Christ, and later experiences, throughout history, of Christians who sense the presence of Christ. Those who take the first and second positions do not deny such post New Testament experiences, but tend to put them in a different category from those that occurred between Easter Sunday and the ascension.

My own preference is for position two, but at the same time I hold that it is important to adopt an inclusive faith in which – as argued earlier – the only absolute demand for being a Christian is the creed "Jesus is Lord".

In the light of these different positions, how should we say that the resurrection is related to what I have called the 'historical core'? I suggest the following summary: when the resurrection refers to the claim that Jesus is alive and that Christians can know him either directly or through others, then this is so central for the traditional faith that it should be included in what is counted as central to church teaching (that is at level two of the three levels described in chapter 11). Also, it is almost certainly part of what individual Christians mean whey they say "Jesus is Lord" (that is at level one).[16] In other words, it would be very unusual to find a Christian who did not affirm the resurrection in terms of one of the three positions just outlined. However, for those who take the third position, it would be misleading to say that – for them – a strictly historical claim is involved, because personal encounters with the presence of Jesus would normally be considered as 'private',[17] rather than as either public or 'historical' events. Nevertheless, when it comes to official teaching (at what I refer to as level two) my own view is that the church should go further than the third position, and suggest that there was indeed an empty tomb, which is a strictly *historical* claim (leaving open whether this accords with position one or two). This historical claim cannot have the full evidential support of events like the crucifixion, but there is still evidence of a kind.

Part of this evidence, as I have already intimated, lies in the very existence of the church, along with the claims made by those first disciples who went around proclaiming that they had seen the risen Lord and who were prepared to die for their faith. Apart from the gospels, the strongest reference to these early Christians occurs in the fifteenth chapter of I Corinthians where St Paul, writing in the early 50s CE, lists those who claimed to have seen the Lord, ending with an appearance to some 500 disciples. If these witnesses were all mistaken, then we need to posit some kind of mass hallucination that, it might be claimed, is almost as problematic as belief in the resurrection. Another part of the evidence is drawn from the experience of those Christians in every age who have claimed in some way to know a living Christ.

I am not suggesting that non-Christian interpretations of these experiences *cannot* be provided, for this would be to overstate the case and to play down the element of faith. For example, one can entertain the possibility that there was some kind of group hypnosis, or a complex plot to which many people were party. These would both be examples of non-Christian views of the resurrection. There could also be radical but Christian views that did not see the resurrection as an historical event, such as the third position mentioned at the beginning of this section. Thus I think that Christians are mistaken if they claim that the resurrection can be *proved* to have taken place as an historical event, as some books have attempted to show. My point is rather that non-Christian explanations of the events surrounding the foundation of the church are, in their own way, as perplexing and troublesome as the Christian claim.[18] Also, I suggest that there are grounds for the Christian claim both in the experience of the first Christians and in the experience of the Christian life as it is lived through in every age. This last point is of great importance, for, as I argued in the case of the five strands of evidence with respect to the whole historical core, the argument must include what 'makes sense' in terms of one's own experience.

Once again, we find that we are dealing with the possibility of an unblind faith. From a strictly historical point of view, the resurrection cannot have as solid a foundation as the crucifixion, but there are grounds for it within history and, for the person of faith, these grounds can take on something approaching certainty if they are matched by a personal experience of the power of the living Christ.

My conclusion can be put in another way. In the past, many Christians have tried to argue from the alleged occurrence of miracles, including that of the resurrection, to the truth of Christianity. I prefer to argue the other way round. Because (quite apart from the question of miracles) I believe in a personal God, and because I also believe that this God reveals himself to us in a very special way in the life of Jesus, I think that miracles could happen within the events that surround this unique encounter between God and humanity. In other words, my beliefs change my rational evaluation of what 'makes sense' and of what might be possible. Similarly, my belief that "Jesus is Lord" changes the way in which I read the resurrection stories.

The 'ascension' marks the event – traditionally forty days after the resurrection – when the resurrected Jesus ceased to be present with the disciples (except in the sense that they believed him to be with them, spiritually, at all times, and especially at the breaking of bread). Clearly, the pictorial representations of this event are metaphorical (including the somewhat amusing examples of some stained-glass windows in which the disciples are looking up at the soles of Jesus's feet as he disappears into the heavens). This is no more a picture of the actual reality than that of Jesus sitting 'at the right hand of the Father' – which again can be presented in paintings as a kind of metaphor. Theologically the ascension is important because Christ is not now specially located in one place, as Jesus was during his earthly ministry, and – although in a different way – during the resurrection appearances.

Is the Bible the word of God?

Some Christians will be uneasy about this chapter because I have rejected the doctrine of verbal inspiration and the literal historicity of certain parts of the Bible. However, I have tried to present an overall view of the Bible that sees it both as an historical book that can be studied with an open mind and as a book of unique richness and importance for the Christian. In other words, the Bible *can stand up to* the examination demanded by any critical and educated intelligence and emerge as a challenging and impressive testament to a living faith. Of course, not every reader will arrive at the same conclusions, but Christians can ask non-Christians to read the Bible, applying their own standards of critical judgment, and then to ask themselves the question that Jesus asked: "But who do you say that I am?"[19]

Does this or does this not mean that the Bible is the word of God? The answer must depend on exactly what we mean by the 'word'. In the strictest sense, every Christian must say "No", for Jesus himself alone is *the* word. If we mean that the actual words of the original text were dictated by God, then some Christians would say "Yes", but I have again argued that we should say "No". However, if we use the idea of 'word' in the broader sense of the means by which God speaks to people, then not only is the Bible *a* word of God, in an important sense it is *the* word of God, for, so far as the *written* evidence goes, it is *the* Christian source for our knowledge of Jesus, for the events that led up to his life and for the events that immediately followed it. Also, it has an extraordinary power to evoke a sense of the wonder of God's creation, of his dealings with humanity and of the character and challenge of Jesus. For these reasons, I have no doubt that the writers were 'inspired'. So what I have presented is not a negative view of the Bible, but a positive one that at the same time allows for an unblind faith and not the blind acceptance of authority.

Finally, let us note what the Bible, taken as a whole, succeeds in achieving. It presents the reader with the person of Christ. It does this not by simply giving us the story of Jesus, but by putting this story into the context in which the meaning of his life can be seen. This is why we need history, myth, legend, parable, poetry, prophecy and so on. All of these are part of the tradition in which Jesus spoke and which, together, explain the meaning of his life. Luther put the point perfectly when he said: "The Bible is the cradle in which Christ is laid."

An additional note on the resurrection

An 'experiential' account of the resurrection is often associated – though misleadingly – with a famous statement by David Jenkins, when Bishop of Durham, in a BBC interview in October, 1984. Many newspapers reported him as saying that the resurrection was 'a conjuring trick with bones', when in fact what he said was almost the opposite, because he prefaced that phrase with 'much more than'. Ever since, there has been a totally unfair representation of the Bishop as a Christian who denied the reality of the resurrection. However, it is true that in his writings the importance of the resurrection is seen as lying, primarily, in the *experience* of the living Jesus with his disciples, rather than in any kind of special event.[20] As we have seen, it is also true that some Christians think the whole issue of a literally empty tomb is unimportant. For example, this is the position of many of those in a movement associated with the 'Sea of Faith', the title of an influential book by Don Cupitt.[21]

The issue here is explored in a published set of exchanges that took place between Don Cupitt and Charles F. D. Moule (at the time, Lady Margaret Professor of Divinity in Cambridge, and a representative of an intelligent version of a more conservative position).[22] Cupitt does not actually deny claims concerning special events, but responds to suggestions about them with "I do not know" (p. 30). However – apart from the experiences of the disciples (which were 'events' of a kind) – the occurrence of 'events' is not essential to the theory he supports. Moule accepts the importance of the theological meaning of the resurrection, but *also* supports a version of the 'event' theory, and central to his argument is his claim that the Easter experiences were prior to the Easter interpretation (p. 37) so that the situation was much more complicated than a certain theological theory giving rise, by itself, to a way of seeing the life of Jesus. The stories are far more than 'picturesque expressions' of the Easter faith (one of Cupitt's terms, p. 30). In particular, there was an element of surprise and astonishment that helped to shape the theology, rather than the other way round.

A more recent variation on the 'experiential' position can be found in Geza Vermes' *The Resurrection*.[23] Vermes is dismissive of the evidence for any kind of physical event, but is sympathetic to claims about a series of personal experiences, which he classes with the 'mystical' (p. 149), as a result of which the disciples were re-empowered, so that there was a kind of "resurrection in the hearts of men".

I suggest that there is a stronger case for some kind of event theory than Vermes admits, partly because of Moule's argument concerning the evident surprise caused by the resurrection experiences, and in part from the following consideration. I have argued that the reflective Christian comes to the New Testament stories in several stages; first, an awareness of the extraordinary nature of Jesus of Nazareth – relying only on perfectly plausible accounts of his life and character and teaching; second, a reasonably grounded belief in a personal God who genuinely conveyed a message through the prophets; third, a decision that this Jesus is the Messiah to whom the prophetic tradition looked forward; and then, fourth, a re-reading of the gospel stories in the light of these steps that have been taken. In this context, without any gullibility, a reflective person may be unwilling to dismiss outright the historical reality of some actual events of an extraordinary and, perhaps, unique nature, even though they remain extremely puzzled about exactly what happened. Certainly there are contradictions and inconsistencies in the accounts – but given the fact that the records come from different sources, and that they are from twenty[24] to fifty years after the event, this is not sufficient for a rational denial that some astonishing 'event' – in addition to a series of personal experiences – lay behind them. After all, if Jesus does represent a unique encounter between God and humankind, then unique events are not so incongruous.

There are other ways in which Vermes' position can be criticized. For example, he insists that the shock experienced by the disciples over the events surrounding the cross and its aftermath indicates that Jesus did not, at least in any clear manner, predict that something like this would happen. However, this insistence involves a rejection of a whole series of Jesus's sayings (e.g. Matthew 16, 21), basically, only because they do not fit his theory. Moreover, the shock experienced by the disciples (concerning the reality of which I agree with both Moule and Vermes), can equally well be accounted for by the commonly observed fact that people often only half listen to what they are told, and tend to select for special attention those parts that they really want to hear.

I want to end this section with another of my suggestions that some readers may find helpful in the formation of an unblind faith. When Aquinas discusses miracles (*Summa Theologiae* 1a 105, 7; 114, 4), he makes a most interesting distinction between what he calls miracles, in the strict sense (which are events *within* nature, that cannot be explained in terms of natural, 'secondary' causality), and still more marvellous happenings that are not *within* nature, such as creation and redemption.

I wonder if, just possibly, this could apply to the resurrection as well; although what I am about to suggest is speculative. My reasoning goes as follows. In the case of all the other alleged miracles, in the strict sense of the term, it is quite possible for liberal Christians to say that they do not think they are necessary for an understanding of Jesus's message, and therefore that they are not essential for Christian belief. One can still believe that extraordinary things tend to happen in the context of walking 'in tune' with God and nature and other people, so that the Acts of the Apostles can still read like a 'saga of the Holy Spirit', but such a reading of the New Testament does not require miracles, in the strict sense. However, in the case of mainstream Christianity, even in the liberal tradition, it is difficult to apply this agnosticism to the case of the resurrection, which has been, for good reasons, so central to Christian teaching. It is possible to get round the problem by arguing (as I have indicated) that the true meaning of the resurrection is only to be found in the experienced presence of Jesus with his disciples, but to some people this looks like a fudge – and moreover, a more significant fudge than a claim about the metaphorical virginity of Mary.

Let us return to Aquinas's teaching about creation. This, he argues, cannot be a 'miracle', in the strict sense, because it is not an event within the natural order, but the setting up of this order itself. He also argues, for similar reasons that 'redemption', although a profound truth, is similarly not such an 'event', and if I am right about the essential non-importance of the virgin birth, then one can argue that the same is true for the incarnation (because no single event in the natural or historical order is crucial for its truth).

In the light of this, could we say – and this is a suggestion that is not central to the argument of this book – that the resurrection, too, is an extraordinary theological truth that cannot be encapsulated in any single event? Is it a truth about how the perfect image of God must for ever be 'alive' in God,[25] and how those who are united with Christ, are similarly eternally united with God (so that we are, even now, risen 'in Christ', Col. 2, 12)? In a similar vein, Rowan Williams has written: "The untidy character of the stories leaves the reader or listener with work to do. Whatever else this is, it isn't the account of an event happening just to someone in the past ... if you do meet him, there is an influx of some vision and energy that takes you beyond your normal frame of reference."[26]

If this view is emphasized, then although a particular historical event may have a special *association* with the resurrection, the truth 'transcends' any single event (just as the truth of redemption is associated with an historical event – the cross – but is not, strictly speaking, definable in terms of it). The resurrection is a truth about the nature of life in God, and no single historical event can be said to be exactly equivalent to it. However, at the same time, there have been some 'events' (including experiences of the disciples) that have been necessary for the theological understanding to develop.

Notes

1   I do not think that Christianity would disappear completely if all the historical claims were shown to be false, but it would lose many followers and those who remained would have to reinterpret many of the basic doctrines. It would probably become very similar to Mahayana Buddhism with Christ being seen as a kind of Bodhisattva.

2   C. H. Dodd, *The Founder of Christianity*, Fontana, 1973, p. 27.

3   Judg. 1, 8.

4   Josh. 15, 63; Judg. 1, 21.

5   Hannah Barnard, a preacher from Hudson, New York, scandalized some London Quakers during her preaching tour of Britain (1799–1802), when she taught how the Old Testament often represented what people of the time *believed* that God commanded.

6   Some fundamentalists try to avoid the moral objection by claiming that if God commands the slaughter of women and children, or anything else, this makes it right. However, this is a desperate line of defence, for it renders the statement "God is good" effectively meaningless, for 'good' is defined purely in terms of God's will. Traditional Christianity has always rejected this view of morality, claiming that goodness is rooted in God's whole nature, not just his will. In the third century, Origen (in his *Homilies on Joshua*) argued that the passages were to be read as allegories, and referred to the spiritual battle with evil in our hearts.

7   Matt. 13, 22.

8   I Cor. 10, 1–11; *cf.* Gal. 4, 24.

9   See B. M. Metzger, *The Text of the New Testament*, Oxford University Press (3rd ed.), 1992.

10   One commonly held view among scholars is that most of the Old Testament books were edited and put into their present form after the exile, around 400BCE, although some favour an earlier date. The earliest extant manuscripts are found in the Dead Sea scrolls, some 200 years later. Some of the written sources used may have been much older, because Jeremiah, for example, mentions the use of scrolls.

11   Matt. 5, 3–12; Luke 6, 20–6.

12   E.g. Mark 10, 35–41; *cf.* Matt. 20, 20 and Mark 9, 18; *cf.* Matt. 10, 1 and Luke 10, 17.

13   Richard Bauckham, *Jesus and the Eyewitnesses*, Grand Rapids, Eerdmans, 2006.

14   This gospel, according to many scholars, could date from the early second century, or just possibly earlier, and might contain some genuine historical material.

15   Richard Bauckham, *Ibid*, p. 493.

16   It is unlikely that anyone who proclaimed "Jesus is Lord" would be unable to accept *any* of the three views of the resurrection I have described. However, it is possible, hence the word 'almost' at this point.

17   By 'private' encounters I don't necessarily mean 'individual' encounters, but those, whether to an individual or a group, which could not be tested by scientific procedures open to all. Jesus's resurrection

appearances in the New Testament were always to the faithful, with the possible exception of Paul (who was a fervent believer in God).

18   The atheist or agnostic will almost certainly reply that mainstream Christian explanations of the resurrection depend on the acceptance of the 'supernatural', while explanations, say, in terms of mass hallucination, do not. There is a legitimate point here, but the complete rejection of the *possibility* of divine action can be just as dogmatic as that of a blind faith that automatically assumes the presence of the supernatural.

19   Matt. 16, 15.

20   *Cf.* David and Rebecca Jenkins, *Free to Believe*, London, BBC Books, 1991. After writing of how Jesus was with the disciples after the crucifixion, the authors write "This is what the Resurrection meant" (45, *cf.* 149).

21   Don Cupitt, *Sea of Faith*, London, BBC, 1984.

22   Published in Don Cupitt, *Explorations in Theology 6*, London, SCM Press, 1979, pp. 27–41.

23   G. Vermes, *The Resurrection*, London, Penguin, 2008.

24   Twenty years is about the right time for St Paul's claims in *First Corinthians*.

25   Some Muslim scholars see this as the real meaning of Qur'anic references to the death of Jesus. This enables them to admit that Jesus did 'die' on the cross, in a purely physical sense, and lessens any apparent contradiction with Christianity.

26   Rowan Williams, 'Easter – the awkward time of year', *The Daily Telegraph*, News Review on Saturday, 26 March, 2005, p. 21.

13. Christianity and Other Religions

An approach to the great non-Christian religions

At the beginning of this book I suggested that sooner or later an intelligent person who has been brought up as a Christian is bound to ask questions such as: "Am I a Christian just because of my upbringing?" or "If I had been brought up as a Buddhist would I now be a Buddhist?" Such questions must lead the thoughtful person to wonder whether Christianity really is different from the other great religions of the world and, if it is different, then why one religion should be accepted rather than another.

In this chapter, although it is quite impossible to do justice to the issues involved, I want to suggest an approach to the subject of world religions which is consistent with an unblind faith and that can also be the basis for each reader's further exploration.

From the start, we have to steer a middle course, as in so many other things. On the one hand, we must be suspicious of a superficial rejection of other faiths that is not based on a genuine knowledge of them. For example, I once saw a booklet available at the back of a church which gave a one page description of each of the great non-Christian religions followed by a one page refutation of their central views. Finally, it was concluded that Christianity is the only true religion. Such an approach is basically dishonest, and is also insulting to the intelligent Christian as well as non-Christian, for how can one know to be wrong what one has not properly understood?

On the other hand, we have to be equally suspicious of the assumption that all religions are really the same, an assumption that is a very natural reaction to the superficial attempts to prove that one religion is better than another. It *may* be true at a deep level that all the great religions are the same, but we have no right to assume this without a careful study. It could be a legitimate *conclusion* of such a study, but not a premise adopted before we start.

Unfortunately, we know that a careful study of every great religion is impossible, except perhaps for a few specialists who make this their profession, so what is the ordinary Christian to do? If we are at present Christians, or are attracted to Christianity, I suggest that we adopt the following four-pronged approach.

(1) We describe ourselves as Christians, but avoid saying of any other great religion[1] that it is false, *unless* we are honestly persuaded of this after careful study. Moreover, even if we conclude, after careful study, that a particular doctrine is false, it would not normally follow that a particular religion, taken as a whole, is 'false'. In fact, although I consider myself to be a Christian, I have personally concluded that some doctrines that have often been held to be part of Christian teaching – such as the doctrine of original guilt – are false. In other words, we should keep open the possibility that if Christianity is *true*, it does not necessarily mean that another great religion is *false*. Unless we adopt this approach we cannot be justified in adopting a Christian philosophy until we have actually carried out our study of all the other faiths, and for many people this is virtually impossible.

(2) So far as time allows, we should feel obliged to study both our own faith and that of others, so that we can come to understand more fully what many people regard as the most crucial questions about life.

(3) We recognize the important distinction between the fundamentals of a faith and the incidental trappings that surround it. Further, we must also try to evaluate good examples of what each religion stands for, not the caricatures that are so easily found. For example, if we are examining the essential teachings of Hinduism, then although we may quite properly reject the caste system in India, this would not, by itself, be an adequate ground for dismissing the religion at its best, because many devout Hindus also reject the caste system.

(4) When we start to explore a central teaching in any faith one of the questions to ask is "What is the *emphasis* that is being brought out?" It is possible that all the great religions are saying the same thing at a very deep level and that they are all responses to the same spiritual reality, but at the same time that they are significantly different in what they emphasize. I shall pursue this point in the next section.

Differences of emphasis

In the following sections, I am going to make brief comments on four of the major alternatives to Christianity: Buddhism, Hinduism, Islam and the Bahai faith, and follow this with some comments on Marxism and on traditional Chinese religions. Several other religious traditions deserve inclusion, including Judaism, Sikhism, Jainism and Zoroastrianism, but the examples I give indicate a kind of approach that could be extended. It is important that the purpose of each of these sections be understood, for they are not meant to be attempts to prove that these religions are false. In the case of Marxism, it is perhaps better to say 'system of thought' rather than 'religion' – but we shall note how Marxism displays many of the characteristics that typify a religion. However, there is no doubt that these religions do have different emphases, not just at the superficial level that I have described as the 'trappings', but at a more significant level. Nevertheless, I am still leaving open the possibility that at the deepest level these differences of emphasis may be relatively unimportant, so what I am referring to in this discussion of the 'emphasis' of a faith is a sort of intermediate level – somewhere between the trappings and the ultimate core – if that can be found. Thus, in the following sections, where I explore some of the potential tensions between Christianity and other faiths, I shall frequently examine an emphasis that is found in one religion rather than another. This should help the reader to see where, at this level, there are real differences between the world religions. Then, in those cases where I think it possible to see where a creative dialogue might begin, I shall suggest how the differences might disappear, or become relatively unimportant, at a deeper level of discussion.

Before describing some of the emphases one finds in the great non-Christian religions, the chief emphasis of the Christian faith should be underlined. One is tempted to say that this is love, and in a fundamental way this is true, but because so many of the other great religions also stress the importance of love, or of the similar notion of compassion, it is misleading to put this down as the chief *distinctive* emphasis, even if one believes, as I do, that the Christian faith has something to say about love that is not easily found in other faiths. Therefore, in the case of Christianity, the emphasis I would stress is the idea of the incarnation, whereby it is held that God has *identified* himself with humanity, in the manner explored in chapters 4 to 6. Many other religions speak of the 'incarnations' of God, but they tend to mean that God can be seen in the inner core of every good person (or perhaps, of every person) because of people's potential. This inner core is both a human spirit and part of the divine Spirit.

This is one of the cases where we have to be very careful about our use of words, for here we can easily be led into thinking that there is no significant difference because the same word – in this case the word 'spirit' – is used for different ideas. While Christians do not deny that we can see something of God in the spirit, or soul, of every person, when we speak of the 'incarnation' of God in Jesus, we mean to assert something more than the claim that the inner being of a person has something of the creative stamp of the creative Spirit within it. We mean that the creative source of the universe, who is ultimately *other* than his creatures, although he can be united with them, chose to identify himself with humankind in an act that, so far as we know, is unique.[2] Jesus not only reveals God because of his goodness, he reveals the *initiative* of God because he is the express image of God, united with humanity so far as it is possible for the eternal to be so united.

As a result of this emphasis, many Christians say that although other great religions are not false, and indeed may be true in what they teach as fundamental, they are nevertheless *incomplete* in comparison with Christianity. Because I believe in the reality of the incarnation, I have some sympathy with this view, but would immediately add that in a way Christianity may also be incomplete, in that it too can learn things from other traditions.

Buddhism

The aspect of Buddhism that I want to single out is the response of the individual to suffering. Central to Buddhist thought is the claim that suffering is caused by attachment, or desire, and therefore that the way to remove suffering is to remove desire. From this comes the familiar picture of the Buddhist saint who acquires complete tranquillity by finding *detachment*. The goal here is very similar to that of the great Stoics, who held that while in one's actions one must do everything in one's power to alleviate suffering, in one's inner heart and mind one must be unmoved and detached both from the sufferings of others and of oneself. For example, the great Stoic Epictetus said that when you see others suffer you must be prepared to groan with them, in order to help them, but one must not groan in one's inner being, only outwardly: "Sigh, but do not sigh with the heart."[3]

Here there is a startling contrast between the tranquil and detached Buddhist or Stoic and Jesus on the cross, where the demand to love involves *both* outward action and inner suffering or empathy, powerfully expressed when Jesus wept over Jerusalem.[4] This suffering is not morbid and useless, first, because in many instances only this kind of identification seems really to help, and second, because not only are endless vistas of suffering opened up (so long as there is animal or human suffering), but there are also endless vistas of joy opened up, which can only come with fellow-*feeling*. Thus the Christian is told: "Rejoice with those who rejoice, weep with those who weep."[5]

So it appears that the Christian ideal of love involves a demand to be *attached* in a way that both exposes us to suffering and opens up a new joy in the communion of saints. Also, we are called to have an identification with all humankind that can mirror in its own small way Christ's identification with us at Bethlehem.

This can be put in another way. We are sometimes told that the command to love our neighbours is not a command to *like* them, because this may be impossible, but a command to the will to act for their best interests. I think this is misleading and indicates an easy way out of the hard challenge made to us by Christ's command; it also helps to explain much of the callousness of some periods of Christian history. The New Testament picture of love is one of both doing *and* of caring in one's heart. Of course we cannot, by a mere act of will, immediately *feel* for our neighbour, and this is what gives plausibility to the cold doctrine just expressed. But we can begin to love in the full sense by taking the steps that we pray will lead to a complete love through the work of the Holy Spirit. For example, we are told not only to *act* with charity, but to pray for others in a way that will open up our hearts to feeling. Jesus not only *acted* with kindness towards sinners, he had *compassion* for them and he commanded us to love with heart and soul and mind and strength.[6]

It follows that at this intermediate level there is an important contrast between the Christian ideal of love, symbolized and climaxed in the cross, and the Buddhist ideal of detachment. How then can I suggest that at a deeper level this distinction may be superficial? The answer goes like this. We have assumed too easily that we know what the Buddhist means by 'desire'. The Buddhist also speaks of compassion and of a search for blessedness, so that perhaps we tend to misunderstand each other through the words we use to translate subtle ideas. For the Christian, there is a right desire and a wrong desire, the latter connected with the fulfilment of the selfish ego. However, the famous 'eightfold path' of Buddhism[7] includes the notions of 'right thought' and 'right effort', which suggest that for them too there may be a right and a wrong way to have what we normally call a 'desire'. If Christians and Buddhists could sit down and explore together the kind of desires that we ought to have and those that we ought not to have, then perhaps it might turn out that many or all of the differences vanish. Meanwhile, I suggest that the presence of Buddhism should challenge Christians to think more deeply about the kind of love and compassion that we should have for our fellow human beings, for ourselves and for animals.

Finally, the great variety of beliefs found within the Buddhist tradition must be appreciated. The earliest stream (*Theravada*, or 'the tradition of the elders') has no interest in the concept of a personal God, but some of the other streams do.

Hinduism

The aspect of Hinduism that I want to single out has already been referred to in chapter 6. It is the claim that when our souls have finished their journeys and have become perfect, they are joined with the great soul, or that ultimate reality, *Brahman*, on the analogy of a drop of water being reabsorbed into the ocean from which it came. For Hindus who belong to the *Advaita Vedanta* school of Hinduism,[8] this means that our present individuality is a sort of transient illusion and that when we truly find ourselves, there is a losing of ourselves into the great 'One'. Some other schools of Hinduism, for example, the one that follows the teaching of Madhva, have a very different perspective, and do make room for the value of individuality.

On the surface, *Advaita* teaching has some similarity to many things in Christianity, for Jesus taught that we must lose our life in order to find it, that he and the Father are one, and that the kingdom of God is within. However, most Christians have interpreted these sayings in a way that is different from *Advaita* doctrine, as we have seen during our brief discussion of Christian mysticism.[9] The Christian would tend to say something like this: As we die to the old self, a new kind of unity with others and with God becomes possible; but this unity is not an *identity*, it is rather something symbolized in the union of two lovers in which there is still an I and a Thou. Thus, in the incredible richness of God's creation, there is believed to be a continuing place for the person that is you and the person that is me, though both must be transformed.

However, even in the case of *Advaita* Hinduism, once again we can begin to see the lines along which a deeper study might find common ground. We keep using words like 'self' and 'unity' with only a dim understanding of their full meaning, and with inadequate analogies. Furthermore, we need to be careful how literally we take metaphors, like that of a drop of water being absorbed into an ocean. For example, Theresa of Avila wrote: "Spiritual marriage is like rain falling from Heaven into a river or stream, becoming one and the same liquid, so that the river and the rain water cannot be divided; or it resembles a stream flowing into the ocean, which cannot afterwards be disunited from it."[10] However, as a Catholic Christian, Theresa certainly did not mean to imply that the individual human soul ceased to exist, rather that the experience of unity is so great that this metaphor is a way of pointing to the experience. In consequence, in the presence of *Advaita* Hinduism, the Christian is challenged to think more deeply about the nature of humanity and of that unity which we should all seek.

Islam

Islam, like Christianity, suffers from the problem that its alleged representatives often present a total caricature of the religion at its best. Suicide bombers who kill innocent civilians are an obvious example, for they are as far removed from the real spirit of Islam as were the crusaders from the true spirit of Christianity. However, there are three particular doctrines in commonly-found versions of Islam that are very widely held, and that, in my view, raise real difficulties. Nevertheless, I take the view that none of these doctrines is actually essential to Islam, and that a liberal version of Islam is already emerging in which the difficulties I am about to describe might disappear.

The first is the belief that the Qur'an (as delivered to the prophet Muhammad through the medium of the angel Gabriel) is *verbally* inspired – a claim that raises similar issues to those that arise from a fundamentalist Christian view of the Bible. The problems in this case centre on (i) some of the punishments that are commanded in the text, such as the severing of the hands of thieves (5, 28), (ii) the different rules that apply to women and men in areas such as divorce and giving witness (2, 229f.; 2, 282; 4, 15), and (iii) the claim that Jesus did not really die on the cross, but only seemed to die (4, 156–7). To put the matter frankly, many people have difficulty in believing that these sayings, particularly the one referring to the cutting off of hands, are the actual words of God himself. However, we can observe the gradual emergence of what might be called a 'liberal' version of Islam, in which the same kind of change is beginning to happen in the way that divine inspiration is believed to work as has happened in Christianity. At present, for all kinds of political reasons, it is simply unsafe to proclaim this more liberal version of Islam in many Islamic countries, but it is growing and, as it grows, it will become easier to appreciate the positive aspects of the faith, and a number of the more obvious objections will simply fade. Thus, according to one liberal version of Islam, some parts of the Qu'ran, including all or most of the passages I refer to, are not from 'the eternal message of Islam', but from the social and practical parts that do not have to be seen as verbally inspired.[11]

The second doctrine concerns the way in which the sovereignty of God is given a kind of absolutism in which neither logical necessity nor the moral necessity of working within the realm of the good, is appreciated. As we have seen, from the time of Aquinas at least, mainstream Christianity, has stressed the need to see how God's will necessarily operates in the context of his loving nature. Calvin was a dissenter from this more rational approach, and his view of God's absolute sovereignty has much in common with that of popular Islam. Fortunately, in this case, Islam itself can give us an example of how the faith can begin to come to terms with the requirements of reason and of goodness – notably in the Mu'tazilite tradition, within Islam, of the eight and ninth centuries. In other words, once again the kinds of objection that are likely to be made can be seen as objections to 'popular' Islam, and not to Islam at its best.

The third doctrine concerns the way in which, in traditional Islam, civil or state law is integrated with religious law (*shariah*). This reflects the different histories of Christianity and Islam. In the case of Christianity, the church was a persecuted minority for most of its first three hundred years. After that there was a period in which (in 'Christendom') state law and religious law were often intertwined – but the more recent tendency to separate the two realms of law (civil and religious) has been made much easier because most Christians see this separation as a return to an earlier system, and many regret the integration of civil and religious law after Constantine. Hence many Christians favour a kind of 'secularism' in which the church is not directly involved in government or law, provided that the voice of both individual Christians and of churches can have an appropriate influence. However, in Islam, the political as well as religious success of the first generations of Islam meant that the systems of law were entwined from the beginning, and their separation is therefore more difficult. However, it can be achieved, as evidenced in modern Turkey, where the population is predominantly Muslim, but the civil law is basically secular.

Other difficulties remain, such as the fatalism of 'popular' Islam (whatever happens, "It is God's will" – a sentiment also found in some conservative versions of Christianity), but again this refers to 'popular' Islam, and does not necessarily represent the faith at it best. Also, the claim that Muhammad is the *last* of the prophets raises difficulties, particularly for Bahais, who herald a nineteenth century prophet. Nevertheless, dialogue is possible, in this last case by concentrating on exactly what one means by a 'prophet'.

The Bahai faith

I shall indicate here three aspects of the Bahai faith that invite comment. The first is the emphasis on *continuing revelation*, which is a central theme in the religion founded by Baha'u'llah (1817–1892). This is almost an opposite emphasis to that of a *last* prophet. On this theme, Christians would tend to describe the continuity of revelation rather differently than Bahais. The Christian would speak of continually uncovering what is implicit in the work and words of Christ, whereas the Bahai tends to speak of the disclosure of new truth. Personally, I do not see a need for fundamental disagreement here.

More difficult and controversial is the claim that Baha'u'llah is *the* prophet of his time (apart from his forerunner known as the *Bab*), whose message demands a new religion and who will not be succeeded by another great prophet for one thousand years. This claim, which helps to account for the present persecution of Bahais in some Muslim countries (because of the denial that Muhammad was the last prophet), raises, once again, interesting questions about what we mean by a 'prophet'. For example, how should we describe

Baha'u'llah's older contemporary, the Japanese woman teacher Nakayama Miki, founder of the religion known as Tenrikyo. This was at first a religion confined to Japan, but is becoming a world religion with a special emphasis on healing. This religion is also remarkable in emphasizing the complete equality of women, even before the similar emphasis in the Bahai faith. (The first religious movement I am aware of adequately to expound this equality is that of the Quakers, around 1650.)

A third aspect of the Bahai faith is the stress on the need for a world community. Here there should be – in my view – universal agreement among the great religions of the world that Bahais have blazed a trail that others should follow. This does not mean that there should be no place for individual states, with their own customs and laws, but that – rather as in a federal system – these states should acknowledge a more general and universal human society of which they are part, and to which all people owe a moral allegiance. Only then is it likely that there will be universal peace.

Marxism

Some readers may be surprised to find a section on Marxism within a chapter on the great religions of the world, but even if we are not happy about referring to Marxism as a religion, we can see that it shares many of the same characteristics. In particular, we can see how it demands and receives a loyalty from many of its followers that is extremely like religious faith. Also, there is a doctrine, often taught with all the enthusiasm and dogmatism with which Christianity used to be taught to whole nations in the Middle Ages. There are 'holy' books such as the Communist Manifesto and Chairman Mao's red book, which are given a special status and authority.[12] There are 'holy' places, like – under Stalin – Lenin's tomb, and many other parallels to religion as it is commonly found. Most important of all, in some parts of the world it has been a rival to Christianity, or to the other great spiritual religions, for the hearts and minds of people. It is appropriate, therefore, that it should be considered here.

I propose to mention two of the basic problems with Marxism, both of which have led many Christians to the view that Christianity offers a more coherent philosophy of life than does Marxism. Then I shall indicate how, despite these problems, Marxism has something positive to say to Christians. However, I must make clear that in this section I am going to discuss Marxism rather than the views of Marx himself, which sometimes differed considerably from the later interpretations of his thought. For example, it was Lenin, not Marx, who propounded the view that a small party, who thought that they *knew* what was truly good for humanity, had the right and duty to take power by force, whatever the wishes of the majority. Again it was Lenin who stressed that all aspects of traditional morality were secondary to the over-riding moral command to hasten the revolution of the proletariat. Further, the following criticisms are of what might be called 'classical Marxism', because there are many people who call themselves Marxists because of an understandable sympathy with many of Marx's ideas, but who would not uphold the doctrines I am about to criticize. In a similar way, many intelligent people call themselves Catholics even though they do not uphold all the official teachings of the Vatican.

In a fuller discussion of Marxism, I would concentrate on the Marxist theories of materialism and of economic determinism, and the way in which these neglect the spiritual side of human beings. Here, however, I am concentrating on two specific problems. The first is the claim that Marx and Engels discovered *the* science of history and economics, their work being equivalent to the discoveries of Darwin in biology.[13] The hallmark of scientific knowledge is that the truth of a claim is virtually forced on all rational minds who study the evidence and the argument. However, large numbers of brilliant historians and economists are not convinced by Marx's writings, and it is absurd to suggest that they are all simply stupid. In other words, the claim to have discovered *the true science* in these fields is thoroughly dogmatic and 'unscientific'. Christians, as we have seen, do not normally claim to *know*, but rather to believe, although they claim some rational grounds for their faith. The result is that, somewhat paradoxically in view of what is often said, Christianity is much less dogmatic than Marxism.

The second major problem is the claim that human materialism, meaning our selfish and unsocial drives, is essentially environmental. This is necessary for the Marxist belief in the eventual possibility of a classless society in which there will be no state and no coercive law, but in which all will work willingly for the common good. The Christian view is that, although much of our selfishness may be environmental, much of it also flows from our nature, as we saw when discussing the notion of original sin, a doctrine that, although it needs restating, seems to contain a profound truth. It may be possible for a particular individual to grow up without any selfishness, but for a whole society to grow up in this way seems to most Christians to be based on a naive view of human nature. In the light of the historical and anthropological evidence, the picture I have drawn of humanity needing to struggle with an animal nature in order to emerge into the spiritual or personal realm is far more realistic than the Marxist view. Similarly, Aquinas argued that we would have needed some kind of political order, even if there had been no fall. To put this another way: Christians are not committed to belief in an *historical* fall, but they are committed to a doctrine of the fall – to the belief that we have individually and collectively fallen below our calling.

On the other side of the story, there are three positive aspects of Marxism that have led some Christians to see Marx as a sort of misguided Christian prophet. First, there is his stress on the economic aspects of human life, especially those relating to our work. Even though – at least potentially – we are spiritual beings, we have to manifest our spiritual nature in our everyday life, and this includes the economic and social system of which we are part. Christians, and others, have paid too little attention to the implications of this, and in particular to the need for social *structures* that help the poorest. Second, and closely related to the first point, is Marx's teaching on alienation. It is an 'alienation' from the work of our hands, forced upon many people because of the context in which they work, which tends to alienate us from our neighbours, from nature and even from ourselves. As Marx put it: "A direct consequence of the alienation of man from the product of his labor, from his life activity and from his species life is that *man* is *alienated* from other *men*."[14] What Marx has to say here is of profound importance, for what 'alienation' means to him has many similarities to what 'sin' means to the Christian. In other words, much of what Marx has to say of human alienation can enrich the Christian understanding of sin and of the sources of sin. Third, and related to both of the above points, is the need for a critical appraisal of our social and political system. It is not that the Christian message can be translated into a purely social gospel, for this is to be blind to other vital aspects of the gospel as they relate to our understanding of God and of humanity. However, our social and political systems have such enormous effects on the lives of ordinary people and influence their freedom and opportunities for development so intimately that they cannot be ignored. In my own view the required critical approach does not entail anything like the introduction of classical communism (partly because of the deplorable results in terms of human freedom of all such sweeping changes that we can observe), but it does suggest the desirability of some radical changes to the kind of capitalism that is current in the West.

I want to put the last point in another way. A concern with the welfare of the poorest and most marginalized people is one of the chief priorities of the prophetic tradition in the Old Testament and of Jesus's teaching in the New. One of the implications of this is that in order to improve the lot of the poor and to promote social justice we ought to be concerned with the social and political order in which we live. However, no *one* system is demanded by Christianity, and there can be legitimate differences of opinion about exactly how a particular society should be governed.

Traditional Chinese religions

Until recent times the majority of Chinese were either Confucian or Daoist, or Buddhist – and sometimes an individual might have an allegiance to more than one of these traditions, because they were not necessarily seen as exclusive. Each of these traditions deserves both respect and a thoughtful study which would go beyond the confines of this book. In the first chapter we took note of an interesting example of a missionary who found insights in the great Chinese classics and who actively studied the traditions, Matteo Ricci.

In China it is much harder to draw a sharp line between philosophy and religion than in the West, and the scene is complicated by claims that there were at one time at least one hundred 'schools of thought' within the country. I propose to introduce just five of the 'sages', in order merely to indicate a huge area that merits attention.

A sage (*shengren*) is a wise person, whose sayings or writings take on a special kind of authority, and are subject to numerous interpretations. They are not necessarily 'saints' in the Western sense, although some of them are certainly believed to be people of heroic virtue. Nor are they prophets, in the Western tradition, but something akin to revered teachers who are heads of schools. The extent to which the traditional writings actually come from a particular sage is a matter of much scholarly dispute, but – as with other 'Scriptures' – this does not necessarily matter. The key point is that a particular tradition, encapsulated in a body of ancient writings, is given special respect.

Confucius (the Latinized form of Kongzi, *c.* 551–479 BCE) is the most famous sage. In his teachings there is no reference to a personal God, but there is a strong emphasis on loyalty and reciprocity, explored in a series of moral duties, with important differences according to where people are placed in the social hierarchy. There is a particular stress on filial piety. The Golden Rule, in its negative form, is also present ("Do not do to others what you would not have them do to you"). Despite what might be called the 'secular' tone of much of the teaching, morality has a kind of metaphysical or religious grounding in the need to seek a way of life that is in harmony with the ways of heaven (*tian*).

Mencius (the Latinized form of Mengzi, *c.* 372–289 BCE) is a later follower of Confucius. Like his master, he emphasizes our different obligations to different sets of people (unlike Mozi, below), but placed even more emphasis than did Confucius on the moral qualities desired of a ruler, including his need for compassion. His recommendations for how this should lead to change in terms of social welfare and land reform read like something from a much later source.

Laozi (historically an even shadowy figure than the first two sages, who – if an historical person – may have been a contemporary of Confucius) is the leading sage within the Daoist tradition. Here we find something much closer to a religion in the Western sense, with a strong emphasis on meditation and the search for harmony with the whole of nature and thereby with an 'ultimate principle' (the *Dao*). Nature, properly understood, is a kind of ultimate reality, but although within Daoist philosophy one might be tempted to use the word 'god' for this ultimate reality, there is nothing that corresponds to the personal God of the Abrahamic traditions.

Mozi (sometimes referred to as Mocius), who flourished around 400 BCE, is in some ways the most interesting of all the sages, although his influence declined after strong opposition from the Confucians. Three things are especially remarkable about this sage. The first is his teaching about the importance of *jian'ai*, meaning 'impartial care' or 'concern for everyone', but more often, somewhat misleadingly rendered as 'universal love'.[15] This hugely interesting theme is in contrast with that of most Chinese sages, especially in the Confucian tradition, with its emphasis on the difference between duties owed to different classes of people; indeed this was the main reason for the attacks on Mohism from the Confucians. The second was his valiant and often dangerous attempt to persuade local war-lords that they should not embark on aggressive wars. Here he anticipates one kind of Western just-war theory, exemplified by the seventeenth-century Quaker, Isaac Penington, who (unlike his friend George Fox, who taught that all war was wrong), believed that war was justified when your homeland was invaded – but not otherwise. Third, was the manner in which he interpreted the demands of 'impartial care' in an extremely practical way that parallels, to a surprising degree, the philosophy of Western utilitarianism.

Mozi is often criticized for his dour outlook on life, especially in relation to his attack on music. However, it should be remembered that he affirmed the capacity of music to cause delight; his strictures were on the ruler spending money on music, and on other art forms, when the common people went hungry.[16] In my view, the role of the arts is, nevertheless, seriously undervalued by Mozi, but his views must be seen in context.

One of several ways in which Xunzi, c. 298–238 BCE, anticipates some aspects of the rationalist Enlightenment of eighteenth-century Europe is his attack on superstition. The ancient funeral rites and sacrifices (which – unlike Enlightenment thinkers – he wanted continued, although for purely social reasons) are merely ways of expressing the grief of the living. Moreover, in his view, long-term rewards and punishments for our actions do not depend on heaven, but occur naturally, in a kind of mechanical way. Further, as part of his rationalistic and naturalistic approach, he rejected Mencius's belief in the golden age, claiming that the evidence did not suggest that humankind was originally good, or that individual humans are born morally good, but that moral goodness – although possible – is something that has to be achieved. In order to make moral progress we should not look to the past, but to the basic principles that underlie human nature and society.

Notes

1 Sometimes there is a fine line between a 'religion' and 'a great religion'. However, we do not need to study all the primitive forms of religion in order to know that many of them contain large elements of superstition. At the same time it must be stressed that many so-called 'primitive' religions may contain insights into the human condition and also, have a great importance for the social life of a people.

2 Some Christians speculate that if there is intelligent life elsewhere in

the universe, there may be equivalent incarnations on other planets. Further, there is nothing inherently impossible in the notion of Jesus's return to earth. However, if the purpose of the incarnation were a divine identification with humankind, then there is a strong case for claiming that this needs to happen only once (apart from the possibility of a second coming at the end of the age).

3　*Enchiridion* 16.

4　Luke 19, 41.

5　Rom. 12, 15.

6　Mark 12, 30.

7　The eightfold path is one of the four 'Noble Truths' of Buddhism.

8　Hinduism is found in many different forms, and the particular contrast being made would not apply to all of them. For example, some Hindus believe in a personal God and some believe that the individual has an eternal destiny. The term *Advaita* means 'non-dualist', in opposition to the dualism (*Dvaita*) of, for example, Madhva. The term *Vedanta* refers to a system of thought (allegedly) based on the *Vedas* (the most ancient texts of the Hindu tradition).

9　See chapter 5, *Life 'in Christ'*.

10　Theresa of Avila, *The Interior Castle* (1577), London, Fount, 1995, II, 5 (p. 176).

11　See, for example, Ghada Karmi, *Women, Islam and Patriachalism* in *Feminism and Islam*, ed. M. Yamani, Ithaca Press, Reading, 1996, pp. 80–1. The claim that Jesus did not really die on the cross (4, 156–7) is perhaps the most problematic for Christians, because, even if Jesus is not seen as a unique 'Son of God', the suffering and death of the Messiah (a term which the Qur'an ascribes to Jesus eleven times) is integrally related to his mission to identify with humanity, and – like the Good Samaritan – to go where the suffering people are. Risk is an essential element in this kind of life. Moreover, both the suffering and the death were just what prophets like Isaiah predicted for the coming Messiah. However, this is one of many places where we have to be careful not to build up too much of an argument from a single verse. This can be illustrated by the fact that even in the case of the death of Jesus there are some Islamic scholars who do not insist on the denial of the death as an historical event, but interpret the Qur'anic statement as a spiritual reference to the fact that Jesus was always alive in God. This is of a piece with a hadith that goes "Do not regard those who have been killed in the cause of Allah as dead, rather they are alive with their Lord."

12　The basic meaning of 'holy' is simply 'set apart' from the 'ordinary'.

13　See, for example, H. Selsam and H. Martel (eds.), *Reader in Marxist Philosophy*, International Publishers, New York, 1963, pp. 193, 198.

"Now – since the appearance of *Capital* – the materialist conception of history is no longer a hypothesis, but a scientifically demonstrated proposition" (Lenin).

14   Marx's *Economic and Philosophical Manuscripts*, tr. T. B. Bottomore, in Erich Fromm, *Marx's Concept of Man*, Ungar, New York, 1967, p. 103. Emphases in text.

15   On the translation of *jian'ai* see A. C. Graham, *Disputers of the Tao*, Open Court, Illinois, 1989, p. 41. (The *ai* should not be confused with the Japanese *ai*, as in *aikido*.)

16   See *Basic Writings of Mo Tzu, Hsun Tzu, and Han Fei Tzu*, tr. Burton Watson, Columbia University Press, 1967, pp. 110 ff.

14. The Rational Defence of the Christian Faith

Three sorts of argument

The principal aim of this book is to expound the essentials of the Christian faith and, therefore, to say what it *is*, rather than to show that it is true. However, it is impossible to draw a sharp line between describing *what* Christians believe and *why* they believe, so that on several occasions I have had to examine the grounds for Christian faith, for example, in the discussion of the resurrection and of the reliability of scripture. In this chapter, we shall look more directly at the problem of how faith can and should be supported by reason.

When someone argues in defence of a faith, there are three kinds of argument that are relevant. First, there are what I shall call 'positive arguments', in which one seeks to show that a certain belief is true, or at least plausible, from arguments that appeal to general experience rather than to private and personal experience. I shall briefly outline four of these positive arguments in the next four sections. These are not presented as 'proofs', for reasons discussed in the first chapter, but they are offered as providing reasonable grounds for belief in God. None of these four arguments is specifically Christian and they can be used equally by Muslims and other theists. Positive arguments for a more specifically Christian faith have been suggested in chapters 4 to 6 and during the discussion of the resurrection in chapter 12.

Second, there are what I shall refer to as 'negative arguments'. Here one tries to show that alternative philosophies of life are false or inadequate. There have already been some examples of this kind of argument, as in the discussions of Marxism and of determinism, and later in this chapter I shall consider first, modern secular humanism, and second, what is sometimes called 'the new atheism' – namely the aggressive atheism of Richard Dawkins and some other recent writers.

Third, there is the kind of argument that can be drawn from personal experience, either in the form of events in one's own life that one believes to be providential or miraculous, or in the form of inner feelings of joy or of strength that seem to indicate a direct encounter with God. It is hard to formulate arguments on such events or feelings that are likely to convince others, but these things may form a powerful argument for the one who experiences them. I shall briefly consider some of these experiences in the last section.

Creation as an act of will

Since humankind first began to wonder, we have asked how there came to be a world or a universe at all. Some have put the question this way: "Why is there something rather than nothing?" To feel the force of this question, we need to share in the sense of amazement and awe that many people feel when they see the heavens in their glory on a cloudless night, or when, in other contexts, we are overwhelmed by the beauty and wonder of nature. If anything, modern science has sharpened the question, partly by adding to our knowledge of the immense richness of nature and partly by the gathering evidence that the whole universe started with a colossal cosmic explosion some thirteen billion years ago.

In the past, many thinkers have claimed that the very existence of the universe proved that there must be a creative source that is itself outside the spatial and temporal limits of the universe, namely God. More modestly, I suggest that, although it cannot be *proved* that the universe has such a source, the universe suggests a creator and only if it is the result of the will of such a creator can any sort of *explanation* be offered for the universe. This is not a proof because, while it is always reasonable to ask questions about the origin of things within the universe, we cannot prove that it is reasonable to ask questions about the origin of the universe as a *whole*. This issue, in turn, is related to theories of meaning which are themselves hotly disputed among professional philosophers. One consequence of this situation is that many atheists, or logical positivists,[1] have a kind of 'faith' in a disputed theory of meaning that parallels theists' faith in God.

This argument that there must be a source of the universe is sometimes countered as follows: "If you make God the author of the universe and the being who explains its existence, then you simply put the question of why anything exists one step further back, for who made God, or what is the explanation for his existence?" This counter-attack is understandable, but it is based on a mistake. There is nothing in the nature of matter, or of light, or of any other constituent of the physical universe to suggest that they are eternal. Therefore the question "Where does the universe come from?" seems to many people a perfectly reasonable question. In contrast, the very idea of God is of a being who transcends space and time, so that (as discussed in chapter 2) questions such as who made him, or what accounts for his existence, can have no sense. They merely indicate that the questioner has not understood the idea of God.

Order and beauty as the work of Mind

Among the traditional arguments for the existence of God, the argument from design is the most popular. This argument is based not on the existence of the universe as such, but on the order and beauty that it displays. Instead of asking, "Why is there something rather than nothing?" this argument starts with the question, "How is it that nature displays an order that is not only beautiful, but that is so well fitted for the emergence and support of human life?" The force of this question is felt through the same kind of amazement that was referred to in the last section, only with the emphasis on the wonder of each detail and the wonder of the order and harmony of the whole.

As with the first argument, it is important not to overstate it. For example, it cannot provide *proof* for the existence of a designing Mind behind the universe, because it is always possible to insist that what we call the beauty of nature is merely a reflection of the way we are conditioned to see it and that the perfect fitness of the environment for human life can be explained, at least partially, by Darwinian theories. The environment has conditioned what can survive, so of course anything that lives has to fit into the order of nature.

The last point indicates that the way in which the argument from design is put depends a great deal on one's attitude to modern science. In the old days, Christians tended to see the handiwork of God in the *gaps* that science could not explain,[2] but more and more Christians are tending to see this as a mistake. The superficial reason for seeing this as a mistake is the embarrassment felt as science seems to fill in more and more of the gaps, thus leaving the idea of God unnecessary for those who saw God's role in this way. The proper reason for seeing the gap theory as a mistake is that God works typically *in and through* natural processes. From this point of view, neither science in general nor Darwinism in particular poses a threat to the Christian interpretation of the universe. God has chosen to make a universe that makes itself and evolution is yet one more example of the marvellous system that he has created.

As with the first argument, once the claim to a strict proof is abandoned, the argument from design can be, in its own way, a powerful and legitimate form of argument. The more we see the wonder and richness of nature, and the more we become aware of the extraordinary collection of circumstances that have to be in place for the development of human life to be possible,[3] the more the Christian feels that the universe suggests or points to the Mind that lies behind it.

The moral order grounded in God

It is easy to see how, during the evolution of human society, there developed certain taboos and other social restrictions on human action in order to preserve society. For example, unless a particular group had some rules about the use of violence within that group, it would not survive, especially if it were competing with a rival group for a scarce supply of food. However, there is a gulf between the taboos and customs that are necessary for the *survival* of the group and the developed moral law as it is felt by most men and women. It may be true that this law is often honoured in the breach rather than in the observance, as the saying goes, but the point is not how well the moral law is kept, but the fact that it is felt to be there as an ideal which we *ought* to obey.

Attempts to reduce this moral law to the demands of group survival run into many difficulties, for human beings sometimes face moral demands that put their own survival and sometimes even that of their group at risk. One can even imagine cases where people might feel a moral duty to risk the whole human species, for example, if our survival as a human race depended on the pollution of the galaxy and the consequent death of many life forms, some of which might be as intelligent and sensitive as ourselves. Even the possibility of this calls in question the view that morality is only a reflection of group survival. In general, the experience of human love suggests the discovery of a dimension of being that goes beyond the rules for the survival of any species.

Once again, the argument must not be overstated. It is not that a non-religious explanation of morality is simply impossible, it is rather that the sense of *ought* which humankind experiences, and the nature of the call to *love* one another, are utterly congruous with and suggestive of our spiritual nature. If we are children of God and creatures who are emerging from the animal level to the personal or spiritual level, then the moral dimension can be understood as one aspect of this higher level (along with self-consciousness, freedom and creativity, which are all inseparably linked with the capacity to love). Seen in this way, it is no longer surprising that the moral dimension transcends the requirements of survival, for the spiritual life must go beyond the egoism of the animal life, however innocent this may be.

It follows that morality, and especially our awareness of love, can point to a source of this love that lies beyond our humanity, a source which both plants the seed, or potentiality, for the capacity to love within human nature, and which then draws out this potentiality by the power and example of love. In this way a partial *explanation* can be offered for the extraordinary phenomenon of love.

We must note, however, that when Christians suggest that the moral dimension is grounded in God, they do not mean that morality is simply a matter of what God wills.[4] The position is much more interesting than that. God is, in his very nature, the Good, the True and the Beautiful. What he wills is always good, because he wills in accordance with his nature, but it is not his sheer willing that makes something good. It is rather that God's loving nature is the source of all good and his will always reflects this. This is the ground for the comments on the nature of God's sovereignty, made in the context of Islam, in chapter 13.

The common elements in religious experience

The sympathetic study of different world religions has brought into focus the important discovery that the great religions share certain fundamental types of experience, for example, the sense of the numinous, the experience of inner power and grace, the sense of union with the divine and a sense of universal compassion. Even if, as individuals, we never have any of these extraordinary experiences, we can be aware that they occur and aware of the universality of their occurrence. Thus, the argument which I am building up here is not an argument from private experience of the kind to be discussed in the last section, but a *general* argument based on types of experience that are common to many people. Hence, it is a 'positive argument', analogous to others that appeal to evidence that is open to all who care to examine it. The argument itself involves the suggestion that the universality of these experiences points to a spiritual reality that is encountered by men and women in all religions.

Once again, I am not claiming that here is a *proof* for the truth of religion. In the first place, different religions often interpret these experiences somewhat differently and, more importantly, there is always the possibility of non-religious interpretations of all religious experience. From one point of view, all religious experiences are also psychological experiences and all sorts of psychological interpretations have been put forward, such as those of Freud.[5] Christians should not deny that psychology can study these experiences and illuminate them, but they may wonder whether *purely* psychological explanations can ever be adequate. Certainly, some of Freud's suggestions seem naive and far-fetched.[6] At this point, the 'positive argument', based on the suggestion that the religious experience of humankind points towards a spiritual reality, begins to overlap with the 'negative argument' that other interpretations of experience are inadequate.

A final observation on the present line of argument goes as follows: When our knowledge of the religious experience of others is coupled with the observation of outstanding sanctity, as in the case of Francis of Assisi, then the suggestion that there has been an encounter with a spiritual reality has added force.

The negative arguments for faith

Negative arguments by themselves can never be enough to show the truth of a philosophy of life, but they may form an important secondary support when a philosophy is challenged by what is claimed to be a more adequate alternative. I cannot possibly consider in this section all the alternatives that have been put forward, but I shall begin this section with a consideration of one of the most common, that of the secular humanist.

Unfortunately, the word 'humanism' is used to cover several different philosophies of life and, indeed, in its origins it referred to a movement within Christianity that stressed the importance of certain human values, especially some of those associated with the ancient classical world. Here, therefore, I shall only be concerned with one common variant which uses as its maxim the ancient saying "Man is the measure of all things"[7] and which goes by the name of 'secular humanism'. Nor can what I say be applied directly to all humanists who use this slogan, since they embrace such a variety of views.

There are two issues that I want to stress. The first relates to animals. If humanity is the measure of all things, then the only reason why animals should be respected and cared for is on account of their usefulness for us. For example, polar bears should be protected *because* we can enjoy looking at them, or hunting them, or because they are an important part of the ecology on which we depend. I do not deny that these are good reasons for protecting polar bears (although we may worry about hunting when it is for pleasure rather than for need), but I question whether this is an adequate account of why we should respect polar bears, or other animals. In a Christian view of nature, they are part of God's creation and we can give them an importance and dignity that need not be related to the human need of them. In my own view, we should say that wild animals, in particular, have some sort of right to be there and to be protected in the enjoyment of their territory, except when there is some pressing human urgency, for example, when they endanger a human child, or when indigenous people need them for their livelihood. Christians have all too often failed to see this implication of the doctrine of creation and have tended to exploit the animal kingdom as much as any, in part through a doubtful interpretation of Genesis.[8] According to the parable, Adam is to 'tend' the garden, in other words to be a steward of nature, not a despoiler. Unfortunately the human role has often been seen as one of dominion rather than of stewardship. A Christian philosophy allows for, and in my view demands, a positive philosophy of the animal kingdom, whereas a philosophy based on the maxim "Man is the measure of all things" – if this is taken in any literal sense – *cannot in principle.* But if secular humanists abandon this maxim, then it is incumbent on them to state very clearly what they mean by humanism.

The second issue goes even deeper, but is hard to bring out, and I shall only indicate an issue that demands a much fuller treatment. Most humanists wish to produce a philosophy of life in which humanity has a certain dignity and the high calling to realize a potential nobility. However, this can only be done by investing the notion of 'humankind' with some of the metaphysical attributes that Christians give to God. Thus, far from removing the difficulties that follow from introducing any discussion of a 'higher purpose' or a 'spiritual reality', secular humanists tend to reintroduce the same difficulties, but without realizing that they do so. The metaphysical implications are hidden or disguised in all the talk of secularism and the denial of God. Within a theistic philosophy one can begin to explain why human beings can have an *intrinsic* value; outside it, this term is problematic.

I want to follow these general comments on secular humanism with some more specific comments on Richard Dawkins's *The God Delusion* (2006). This author has written some useful and important books exploring themes in science (such as that of the 'selfish gene') and explaining basic scientific ideas to the non-specialist. However, most unfortunately, the book I refer to is a prize example of a common form of irrationality, because it consistently caricatures the position Dawkins wants to attack. From a rational perspective, fundamental criticism of any position has to take it at its best, or what Terry Eagleton, in a review of Dawkins's book, calls 'the toughest case'.[9] While 90 per cent of the book is a praiseworthy attack on various forms of fundamentalism, more rational forms of Christianity are simply lumped in with the rest, and consequently caricatured in what amounts to committing the old fallacy of 'attacking the straw man'.

Here I shall outline four of the more obvious errors.

(i) Dawkins denies that the concept of 'good' is part of the concept of God, calling it an 'add-on' (108). However, in the Christian tradition (rooted in the position of Plato in the *Euthyphro*), God is *identified* with the Good. Accordingly, early apologists such as Origen, in the third century, claimed that Scriptures *must* be interpreted in a way that is 'worthy of God'.

(ii) He treats the concept of God as if it were an *empirical* hypothesis – which it manifestly is not. An empirical hypothesis is one that is verified or falsified by pieces of evidence, whereas a metaphysical[10] hypothesis, like that of theism, is witnessed by the way in which one interprets the *whole* of reality. Here, once again, is a basic misunderstanding of the nature of a metaphysical claim.

(iii) He dismisses Christianity on the grounds that it has produced more evil than good. But logically, even if it were the case that the faith had done more harm than good (which I question) this would not prove that religion is false, only that bad religion is bad – as in the old saying *corruptio optimi pessima* (the corruption of the best is the worst). I share many of Dawkins's strictures on evils done in the name of religion, but this leads me – with far more logic – to prefer atheism to bad religion. The (metaphysical) God hypothesis is left untouched.

(iv) He accuses the church of 'more or less arbitrarily' choosing four gospels out of the many that have been discovered (95). But historically this is absurd. As explored in chapter 12, evidence (such as the Chester Beatty and Martin Bodmer papyri) suggest that three, and possibly all four of the gospels in the Bible date from the first century, while – with the possible exception of the *Gospel of Thomas* – the other gospels (many of which – as already indicated – are full of absurd stories about miracles performed by the infant Jesus) are much later. In other words there was a perfectly rational ground for the choice of gospels, namely that they came from the first generation of Christians, some of whom were eye-witness to the key events.

Overall, my own position is not only more rational than that of Dawkins, it is also more tolerant, for he believes that only atheism is a rational position to hold. In contrast, during the discussion of suffering in chapter 10, I concluded that it is possible for a rational person to be either a believer in God or an atheist (although not an atheist who caricatures Christianity, or other religions). I also believe it is possible to be a rational agnostic or a believer in an Eastern 'monism'. I disagree with atheists, but I do not claim that they are all irrational.

I shall conclude this section on 'negative arguments' by returning to the theme of false or misleading characterizations of Christian teaching. Recently I was a guest at a meeting of Muslims in Cambridge that was addressed by a convert from Christianity to Islam. When the speaker described some of his positive experiences within Islam I had no problem, but when he went on to describe the Christianity he had abandoned, his account of the atonement was a gross caricature of what many Christians believe (as was his account of the doctrine of the Trinity). Not only had he (rightly) rejected this caricature, he gave to the whole audience the impression that a crude substitution theory was an essential part of Christian belief.

Simply put, when it comes to 'theories'[11] of the atonement, there are four main varieties. The two recommended in this book are (i) a variation on Abelard's account of how the life and death of Jesus 'draws' us to an unselfish love of God; and (ii) an exploration of the way in which – in Christ – we can begin to enter a new kind of living, in a community that *participates* in the life and death and resurrection of Jesus. Traditionally the other principal 'theories' are (iii) Anselm's 'substitution theory', according to which Jesus satisfied the demands of divine justice by himself paying the price that we could not pay, and (iv) the 'Christus Victor' theory (found in Luther and elsewhere) in which Christ won redemption by overcoming the power of the devil. I do not object to these third and fourth theories when they are seen as powerful metaphors (and as such they certainly appear in the New Testament, as when the Son of Man came "to give his life as a ransom for many" – Mk 10, 45), but when they are taken as actual accounts of how redemption works, they seriously distort the situation, and raise huge objections, both moral and theological.

Support for the recommended view of atonement theory can be found in the devotional writings of the influential Anglican clergyman and non-jurist, William Law (1686–1761). He expresses horror at the way in which God is so often painted as disagreeable and vengeful, and – in contrast with the substitution theory – he sees the redemptive work of Christ as being the result of a new birth within us, made possible by Jesus's identification with humankind: "... all that he does for us, as buying, ransom, and redeeming us, is done wholly and solely by a birth of his own nature and spirit brought to life in us ... Not a word is there said in the Scriptures of a righteousness or justice, as an attribute in God, that must be satisfied."[12]

The witness of personal experience

When Christians are asked by a friend, "Why do you believe?", many of them are unlikely to give any of the arguments so far discussed, although when pressed they might well use some of them as supporting arguments. One likely reply to the question is to quote personal experiences. As we have seen, these can take many forms; there may have been an experience of the numinous, or of loving support and a sense of inner strength, especially during a time of crisis, or there may have been an overwhelming sense of forgiveness and of a load of sin being taken away. Alternatively, there may have been outward events that have seemed either extraordinarily providential or miraculous, such as a friend's recovery from a serious illness. Any of these experiences or events may lead a person to the belief that they have had an intimation of spiritual reality, as when the poet Francis Thompson writes:

> I dimly guess what Time in mists confounds;
> Yet ever and anon a trumpet sounds
> From the hid battlements of Eternity;
> Those shaken mists a space unsettle, then
> Round the half-glimpsèd turrets slowly wash again.[13]

It is clearly impossible for an outsider to evaluate the inner experiences that seem to provide such intimations and, in most cases, almost impossible for them to evaluate the outside events that strike one person as providential or miraculous, for the force of such events often depends on the significance they have within the life of the person. In other words, we are not here concerned with general arguments, addressed to all men and women, but with inner experiences or outward events that can only have the force of an argument or of a witness to an individual. Among these personal experiences are those of individuals who feel certain that they have encountered the living presence of Jesus, either in his resurrection body (as with 'doubting Thomas', John 20, 24–8) or in some other sense of immediate presence (as with Sadhu Sundar Singh). It is interesting to note that there is no evidence that Thomas needed actually to feel the wounds of Jesus, the encounter was enough to turn doubt into faith.

Provided the individual observes the warnings that I shall mention, I cannot see why experiences such as those described should not be taken seriously as possible indications of contact with a spiritual reality. Whereas in the Middle Ages it was important to warn people against superstition, it is as important now to warn people not only of superstition in its twenty-first-century dress, but equally of the irrational materialism which many people just assume to be a necessary part of scientific and rational thought. There is nothing in the nature of science, nor in the inquiring and critical rational faculty, to indicate that there is *no* spiritual reality behind and beyond the reality that we find through our five senses. Atheism and materialism are just as much interpretations of our experience as is Christianity or some other spiritual view of the universe. Reason, in itself, should not start with a presumption either way, but as soon as it begins a critical reflection, then it seems to me that the indications that support a spiritual interpretation of the universe have at least as great a force.

If we seek an unblind faith, there are three warnings that should be heeded when we consider personal experience. First, we must be aware that there are several possible interpretations of any experience and, therefore, that we must not simply jump for the one that suits us or attracts us, without a consideration of the alternatives. Second, what appears to be a private revelation of some kind must be tested to see if it is *contrary* to rational judgment or to our basic moral convictions,[14] remembering Jesus's warning "You will know them by their fruits."[15] The point here – as already stressed – is that it is one thing for a personal revelation to show us something that *goes beyond* our present understanding and that demands that we enlarge our vision; it is quite another thing for an (apparent) revelation to *go against* the rational or the good. We have to assume that if the Christian God is a reality, he is a God of truth and of justice and, if we allow our experience to be interpreted in a way that does violence to truth or goodness, then we are heading for a blind faith and the possibility of the horrors of Jonestown or of the killing of innocents by suicide bombers. The third warning takes up a theme from chapter 6, when we took note of the overwhelming religious experiences of those referred to as the 'once-born'. For example, I recall a teenage boy who was so moved by a sudden sense of forgiveness and acceptance by God that he wept. I cannot see any grounds for criticizing such a reaction to a religious experience, but there is the danger that the person who is so moved might expect all others – who truly seek to be disciples of Jesus – to be moved in the same way. Our individual stories are often very different.

Having noted these warnings that should be observed by anyone who has personal experiences of a dramatic kind, we may then see them as an important and legitimate part of the life of faith. Without them life would be duller, many of our insights would remain undiscovered and, above all, many people would lack that sense of personal warmth which fills out our understanding of God's love. For too many, the notion of God's love is confined to an intellectual idea. It should also become a living and warming experience and such it is in the daily life of many ordinary Christians.

I want to close this chapter with a reflection on the relation of arguments from personal experience to arguments based on an appeal to reason. What is often called 'natural theology' – that is the attempt to inquire into the existence and nature of God with the help of reason – has been a major concern of many philosophers at least from the time of Plato. However, the whole enterprise is viewed with suspicion, not only by those atheists and agnostics who think that reason has made no progress in this field of inquiry, but also by a number of profoundly religious thinkers. Probably the most powerful contemporary exponents of this view are followers of Karl Barth, who maintain that the word of God speaks to us, uniquely, in Jesus Christ, and his voice cannot be subjected to any form of human judgement. As it is often put, God's word comes to us vertically, from on high, and not horizontally, as mediated through human sources. Only in Jesus Christ is the divine activity revealed to us. Hence Barth's dismissal of the ancient tradition according to which human reason can begin to grapple with some divine matters, even if it only aspires to see "dim reflections, as in a mirror" (1 Cor. 13, 12). For those Christians who take this position, arguments from personal experience, especially when it is believed that God's word is heard in the heart, take on an added importance.

As will be clear from the earlier sections of this chapter, I do not myself adopt the negative view of human reason taken by Barth and his followers.[16] The basis of my response is to be found in Aquinas's refrain that the order of divine grace does not destroy nature but rather fulfils or completes it.[17] The gospel message, when this position is emphasized, is not so much a divine 'No' to human strivings, as a 'Yes' to all those strivings that reflect a (God-given) awareness of what is good or true or beautiful. In the light of this claim, a Christian can view other religious traditions and, indeed, certain aspects of secular humanism, as positive attempts to respond to the divine logos. Christianity still has something unique to say, but it is a message that completes and fulfils human endeavours, taken at their best, rather than a denial of them.

Key to this response to Barthianism is the way in which the words recorded in St John's gospel – "No-one comes to the Father except through me" (14, 6) – are interpreted. We have seen in earlier chapters that it is perfectly possible to interpret these words in a liberal rather than a Barthian way. The 'me', on the former view, is the eternal logos, God's 'word' to human beings as it comes to them within their own language and culture. What is unique about Christianity is the belief that this word was also incarnate in a particular, historical human life. Many insights follow from this belief, but they do not have to include a negative assessment of all human attempts to employ their rational faculties in a search for ultimate truth.

Similar remarks apply to the notion of divine transcendence. Barth, like many others, is rightly anxious to preserve an understanding of the nature of God that does not diminish his stature by framing him in purely human terms. I hold that divine transcendence is not under threat from the more traditional approach – when that is properly presented – and only appears to be so for two reasons. First, some of those *called* liberals have departed from the kind of mainstream Christianity that is defended in this book. Second, the claim that human thought – at its best – can attain some glimmerings of real understanding of the divine (a kind of limited natural theology) is properly rooted, not in a denial of transcendence, but in an alternative, Christian account of creation. In this account, – as stressed in several places in this book – the Creator has chosen to leave a kind of stamp or image of himself within humankind: a kind of 'candle of the Lord' within us,[18] that enables us, within certain limits, to transcend the purely natural order. This view has at least two important consequences. First, it means that some analogies for the nature of God can be found in human experience, because this is how the transcendent has chosen to make us. Second, it means that the human capacity to reason is itself a kind of divine gift in which, in the language of Aquinas, we can begin to 'participate' in the eternal law of God.[19]

Notes

1   There is an interesting difference between the position of a logical positivist, such as A. J. Ayer, and traditional atheism. Ayer denied that he was an atheist, because he claimed that the denial of the existence of God itself implied that the term 'God' was meaningful. He preferred to say that the issue of the existence of God did not arise, because the term had no 'literal meaning'. Many contemporary atheists have, in fact, a position that is similar to that of Ayer, so that 'atheism' has become a somewhat unclear term, used – popularly – both for those who think that God does not exist, and for those who think that the concept of God is incoherent.

2   See C. A. Coulson, *Science and Christian Belief*, Oxford University Press, 1955, p. 22.

3   The requirement for the universe to have this collection of features is sometimes called 'the anthropic principle'.

4   See chapter 12, note 5 and Michael Langford, *Providence*, p. 178, note 27.

5   See his *Totem and Taboo* (1913) and *The Future of an Illusion* (1927).

6   I shall give two illustrations of this inadequacy. First his view that religious faith is basically wish-fulfilment neglects many examples of faiths that have believed in no personal after-life, but which have still made exacting demands on their followers. Also, when there is a belief in personal survival, Freud does not appreciate the difference between survival *as a result of*, and *as a motive for*, faith. Second, his explanation of Jewish monotheism (in *Moses and Monotheism*, 1939) depends on an anthropological 'horde-theory' that is now generally discredited, and a belief in biologically-inherited memories that is problematical. (Some psychologists, especially those who follow Jung's theory of the collective unconscious, do make allowance for the possibility of inherited memories. The topic is discussed under the heading of 'epigenetics'.)

7   Protagoras, born about 490 BCE.

8   Gen. 1, 28–30; 2, 19–20. I suggest that the proper interpretation of these passages indicates human responsibility, not a right of exploitation.

9   Terry Eagleton, *Lunging, Flailing, Mispunching*, in the *London Review of Books*, 19 October 2006, 32–34.

10   The definition of 'metaphysics' is difficult, because the word originally referred to a book by Aristotle given that name (literally 'after the physics') by others. (Aristotle called the subject of this book 'first philosophy'.) Subsequently the term has been used to cover a range of issues that are claimed to be ultimate or fundamental. Metaphysical issues are open to a kind of rational examination, but not empirical, scientific testing.

11   *Theories* of the atonement should not be confused with the 'fact', or better, 'experiential claim' that Christians find atonement through the life and work of Jesus.

12   William Law, '*The Spirit of Love*', in *Works*, London, 1762 (reprinted 1893), VIII, 74-5.

13   From *The Hound of Heaven*.

14   On rare occasions we may be called upon to re-evaluate our moral convictions, but we must be careful not to be swayed by an overpowering emotion to set aside a considered moral judgement.

15   Matt. 7, 16.

16   In his later writings Barth's strictures on the inadequacy of all human reason are to some extent modified, and he does make some attempt to enter into a dialogue with others. See, for example, his positive assessment of the Enlightenment thinker, Beccaria, in *Church Dogmatics*, Vol. III, Part 4, Par. 52, p. 438.

17   Aquinas, *Summa Theologiae*, 1a Q1 A8 ad 2; *gratia non tollat naturam*

sed perficiat. Similar expressions occur elsewhere.

18   The expression 'the candle of the Lord' was used by some of the Cambridge Platonists, Nathaniel Culverwell in particular, to refer to the kind of rational capacity with which humans have been endowed by the Creator.

19   One powerful example of this is Aquinas's definition of natural law, *participatio legis aeternae in rationali creatura 'lex naturae' dicitur.* S.T. 1a 2ae Q. 91 A. 2.

15. Prayer and Work

Theory and practice

An adequate account of any religion ought to look at it from several viewpoints. In this book, I have been primarily concerned with what might be called the theoretical aspect of Christianity, namely the fundamentals of what Christians believe. However, I want to acknowledge the equal importance of what might be called the practical aspect of Christianity, that is its spiritual life, its rituals, its moral code and so on. This practical side of Christianity might also be described as the *activity* of the Christian faith, at church, at home, at work and at prayer.

Although the distinction that I have just made is real, it is important to see that it is impossible to draw a sharp line between the theory and the practice of Christianity, for what is truly believed is bound to affect what kinds of persons we are and how we act. Also, what we do is bound up with how we understand what we are doing. For example, if I have a sense of vocation, this is likely to affect both what activities I devote myself to and the manner in which I do them. The result of this is that a book on the fundamentals of Christian belief needs to say something about the more practical side of Christianity, especially in respect to the nature of prayer and of work, both of which raise certain problems for the thoughtful Christian.

Prayer and magic

In the following sections, I am not concerned with practical instruction on how to pray, for which the reader should look elsewhere,[1] but with an understanding of what prayer is and what it is not.

In the first place, prayer is not an attempt to change God's mind.

This can be seen by stressing the important distinction between religion and magic that goes back to the work of Frazer[2] and other anthropologists who have studied both. Religion and magic are often found intermingled in our actual experience, including that of the Christian churches, but in principle they are very different. In magic, the aim is to control, or to manipulate for one's own purpose, God or gods or spiritual forces of an ill-defined sort. Magic is believed to work by a sort of lever principle that is almost mechanical, provided that one accepts the 'solidarity' between things that is part of the mentality of many primitive people. Rain, for example, is literally interconnected with the secret name for rain, or with the god of rain, or with a ritual dance that is symbolic of rain. Thus, by invoking the name of rain or of the rain-god, or by acting out a rain dance, it is believed that one can actually produce rain by operating the appropriate lever. Similarly, by invoking the name of God or of a god, especially a secret and 'real' name, then one somehow 'conjures' the deity and forces it to respond. More generally, any imagined use of spiritual force for one's own ends is suggestive of this ancient magical outlook and it is for this reason that it is easy to think of examples within the practice of many religious people.

By contrast with religion in its pure form, instead of making spiritual forces work for us, we put ourselves at the service of God. Indirectly, there may be some benefit for us, such as the joy of communion with God, but this is not the purpose of true worship, as we have seen elsewhere. In a mature Christianity, we love because he first loved us[3] and consequently heaven may be the *result* of the good life, but it cannot be its *motive*, for otherwise we can have only a shallow copy of the good life.

The rejection of magical attitudes to religion should begin to make clear why true prayer is not the attempt to change God's mind. This conclusion is strengthened by the realization that there is something ludicrous in the very idea of God changing his mind, once we have grasped what the Christian idea of God is (with a certain reservation that I shall make later in this chapter). God already loves what he has made and no request of ours can make him love his creatures more, or give special preference to one as we might to a favourite child or friend. God has no favourites in this sense, although in another way we are all God's favourites. In a paradoxical way, no one is especially important and yet everyone is infinitely important.

Three stages of growth

The true meaning of prayer may be understood more fully if we take note of three stages in the spiritual life through which Christians pass.

The first stage is proper and appropriate for the religion of a young child. Here God is highly personal and modelled on the kindest and worthiest adults that the child knows. As we have seen, some Christians never grow beyond this stage and the result is either a quite inadequate religion, or, more often, a rejection of God – although strictly speaking this is not a rejection of God himself, but of an inadequate picture of God.

The second stage develops through a reaction against the childish anthropomorphism of the first stage. The stress now is on the spiritual and moral laws that govern all things. Much or all of the talk about God is seen as symbolic and, in the anxiety to avoid false or infantile beliefs, the personal nature of God is played down, sometimes to vanishing point. Congruously, the emphasis on personal reward, or on an afterlife with God, is put aside. We have already noted the apparently surprising fact that surveys of opinion among church members show that many of them believe in no personal survival. What matters is to live the life of love, following the example of Jesus as nearly as we are able.

The third stage, which I believe represents that of the mature Christian, involves a return to the idea that God is personal, but not in the simple-minded way that was appropriate to the first stage. The thing that allows for a return to the view that God is indeed personal, without relapsing into a childish faith, is the realization that what we mean by 'person', in relation to every person, needs to develop. The selfish ego, to which we all naturally wish to cling, is an inheritance from our animal nature. It is not in itself evil, but it is something which we have to learn to transcend as we die to the old self, otherwise it can become a source of evil. Moreover, it is not as if we could have become true persons directly, without going through the stage of having an animal ego. This is something I tried to bring out in the discussion of evolution. Full human 'personhood', like human goodness, is an *achievement* that has to be reached by a process of growth as we emerge from one level of living to another. Thus the childish ego and the childish faith in a personal God of stage one are not wrong for that stage; what is wrong is to stay at that stage. It is often a realization of this that leads to stage two, but this reaction is too negative. The Christian synthesis builds both on the

simple faith of the child and on the insights of stage two and returns
to a belief in a personal God, but with a more mature idea if what
'personal' means. There is the dying of an old idea and an old ego,
but the birth of something new. "Unless a grain of wheat falls into
the earth and dies, it remains alone ... "[4]

With the arrival of the third stage, the whole nature of petitionary
prayer (that in which we ask for things) takes on a new appearance.
There is something absurd in asking for personal favours, but nothing
at all absurd in asking for what we need in order to fulfil our lives as
Christians. As Augustine puts it, "God does not ask us to tell him
our needs in order that he may learn about them, but in order that
we may be made capable of receiving his gifts."[5] Hence the prayer
"Give us this day our daily bread" is absolutely appropriate once we
realize the symbolic meaning of bread; and likewise the prayer for
forgiveness and for strength. Also, since we are meant to retain some
personal relationship with God, analogous to the relationship of child
to parent, there is no reason why we should not ask God about other
things that are in our hearts, whether in relation to ourselves or to
other people, provided that (i) we believe that these things are good
(i.e. they are not just for our selfish satisfaction); and (ii) we pray
'in his name', which means within the context of a relationship 'in
Christ' in which we only expect to be granted what is for the good. It
is in this context that Jesus promised that prayer would be answered[6]
and we should note that this promise was made in the overall context
of Jesus's saying, "I am the vine, you are the branches."[7] The fact that
prayer within this relationship does not rule out asking for specific
things that are in our hearts is proved by Jesus's own prayer at the
garden of Gethsemane: "My Father, if it be possible, let this cup pass
from me." But we note that Jesus then continued: "Yet not what
I want but what you want."[8] We may also recall how Paul prayed
three times that what he called his "thorn in the flesh" – probably
some kind of physical ailment – might be taken away, and how he
eventually realized that sometimes a weakness can be a source of
strength. God's answer to Paul was: "My grace is sufficient for you,
for my strength is made perfect in weakness."[9]

Can prayer make a difference?

The question still remains: "Can petitionary prayer actually make
a difference?" We have seen that God's mind will not be changed

by prayer, but at the same time we are told to pray for the sick and suffering. Is this kind of prayer *only* meant to change our attitudes so that we will do something that we would not otherwise have done?

I believe that there is more to prayer than changing our attitude, or even stirring us to action, hence the reservation made in *Prayer and Magic*. The basis for this is our understanding of God's creation, which I have claimed to be an order, or inter-related system, which has its own laws. One consequence of this emphasis is that, unless God is to resort to miracles at every moment, there are many things that God can only work through us, as a part of the created order. This means more than God working through our hands, although this is indeed one way in which prayer may be answered, as when doctors pray for the suffering in a poor country and then feel moved to go and work there themselves. There is also the strange way in which we are interconnected with the whole created order, and especially with the rest of humankind, at the spiritual level. Part of this interconnection may be indicated by telepathy, another part by what Jung called the 'collective unconscious'. Whatever the mechanisms involved, about which we may be agnostic, it could be that my very concern for someone or something, and my mental reflection or my loving concern, may in itself alter the balance of forces that are at work and which together cause change. Thus what God may wish to do, he may now be more able to do, just because this balance of spiritual forces is different.

If not pushed too far, the following analogy may be helpful for the situation that arises when one person prays for another, or even if they simply have a loving concern for them. We can think of God as a great radio transmitter and each person as a small receiver with a small transmitter attached to it. Let us suppose that for some reason A's receiver cannot hear God's transmission because of some fault, but that B, who is a friend of A, manages to act as a relay station, passing on God's message or God's power through his own small transmitter. A may be open to B and then, through B, receive some of God's power indirectly.

On the basis of this analogy and making use of the principle that God not only chooses to work through people but in many cases has set up an order that demands that he work through people, it is not hard to see how prayer might really make a difference, without having to assume that God somehow changes his mind.

Prayer and petitionary prayer

In the previous sections, we have thought of prayer primarily in terms of petitionary prayer, that is of asking for something. However, in order to see the problem of the answer to prayer in proper perspective, we have to remember that petitionary prayer is only a small part of prayer, except perhaps at the first of the three stages. Prayer is equally a listening or waiting upon God, often in silence, sometimes with just a few words indicating adoration, thanksgiving, or penitence. If we ask: "Does prayer make a difference?" when we are thinking of prayer in these forms, the question seems out of place. There may indeed be a difference made to ourselves, but this is not the purpose of such prayers. As we have seen earlier,[10] worship is to be understood in terms of a response and recognition of what is due to God, not in terms of what we can gain.

It does not follow that problems about the effect of petitionary prayer are unimportant, for even at the third stage it is a legitimate part of prayer, as we have seen from the practice of Jesus; but in the context of the wider meaning of prayer the problem looks very different. The chief emphasis in an understanding of prayer should be its role as an expression of our relationship with God and, through God, with our neighbours and the whole of God's creation.

Work and prayer

For Christians who have come to see the whole of life as a response to God's love, there cannot be a fundamental distinction between work and prayer. Our response includes thought, word and action and each of these affects, and is affected by, the others. There is a splendid passage in the book of *Ecclesiasticus* that reminds us of this. It describes the various occupations of humankind and their role in the life of a nation, with the strong implication that the intellectual should in no way look down on the person who works with their hands, for "without these shall not a city be inhabited". After stressing the fact that those who work with their hands will not understand things that concern the wise, the passage concludes: "But they will maintain the fabric of the world; and in the handywork of their craft is their prayer."[11]

It is a mistake to interpret this passage to mean that only in the case of artisans is work an extension of prayer. It applies equally to the occupation of anyone who realizes what work is really about. The root of this realization goes back to our philosophy of humanity, which recognizes that not only are we a species struggling to emerge from the animal to the spiritual level, but we are also necessarily a social species whose true nature is bound up with inter-personal relationships. Our work is part of the way in which we contribute to the social order, or the way in which we 'tend' it, given our particular gifts and opportunities, just as Adam in the parable tended the garden in which he was placed.

Unfortunately, we have created a world where it is impossible, or almost impossible, for some men and women to find work at all, or any work that has the dignity of helping to run the social order and contribute to the legitimate wants and needs of human beings. Since useful occupation is such an important element in our response to God and in achieving human dignity, it is vital that Christians concern themselves with this problem of unemployment. The implications of this for the spiritual richness or poverty of humanity are enormous. This is one of the reasons why I stressed the importance of Marx's thought at the end of chapter 13, including his insight that we need to pay attention to the *structures* in society that tend to exploit or alienate or impoverish people.

Another question that is affected by a proper understanding of work is: "What kinds of work can a Christian properly undertake?" Part of the answer must be that any job that is important for the human social order, however menial it may be, is a legitimate and potentially dignified form of work. A Christian may have the conviction that they have a particular talent that ought to be used in one of the more classical professions, but this is absolutely no grounds for any feeling of superiority.

However, there is an aspect of the question "What kinds of work can a Christian properly undertake?" which is much harder to answer. Should Christians accept a job seen as socially parasitic and useless, such as – arguably at least – being a clerk in a gambling club, if this is the only kind of job they can find in order to maintain their family? I can see no easy answer to this, but as the occupation gets further and further from social usefulness, then one would need increasingly strong grounds for accepting it, until with occupations that one considers intrinsically wrong (such as that of an interrogator who is expected to use torture), it is hard to see any possible grounds for taking them on. A similar problem arises when the acceptance of a job helps to maintain part of a social system that the Christian feels ought not to exist, or ought at least to be drastically reformed. In this case, a crucial question for the Christian to consider is this: "If I accept this job will I simply be helping to maintain a system that I believe ought to be changed, or will I have some opportunity for working towards a change in the system from within?"

Two senses of 'vocation'

The discussion of the kinds of occupation that are suitable for the Christian leads naturally into the question of Christian vocation. Many people are confused about this because the word 'vocation' is used in two somewhat different senses within the context of the Christian faith. In one sense, which I call the primary sense, every Christian has a vocation. 'Vocation' literally means 'calling' and St Paul speaks of the calling of his readers when he says, "Lead a life worthy of the calling to which you have been called."[12] This is a reference to the way in which we are all called to respond to God's love and to show this response in the way in which we live. Within this primary sense of vocation, all Christians should be concerned with what work they do, for example by thinking about its social usefulness, and with the manner in which the work is done in terms of the energy and cheerfulness that are shown.

Christians also use the word 'vocation' in a secondary or derivative sense, although it may be the more familiar to some. This is when a Christian believes that he or she has a specific call to a particular task or profession, most traditionally as a nurse or priest or doctor or teacher, but in principle to any worthwhile occupation. In such cases, Christians may not have worked out that this is the task or the role that their talents suggest: instead they may have had what seemed to be a 'call' in the form of a private religious experience. Sometimes it is as if a voice had actually spoken, sometimes it is more a growing conviction that is felt to come from God.

Naturally enough, when we are dealing with private religious experiences such as these, the same warnings apply as those discussed in chapter 14. If an apparent call conflicts with common sense, then we must suspect that we have misinterpreted our experience. However, there are limits to rational tests for a divine call, as the examples of Abraham and of Moses illustrate.[13] There are also many recent examples of Christians who have responded to calls that seemed crazy to their friends, but who achieve a success which was thought to be impossible.

Both of these senses of vocation should be put in the broader context of the relationship of Christian ethics to the universal ethical standards that govern most people in most cultures – the general, or 'natural' moral law that St Paul described as written in the hearts of all people (Romans 2, 14–15). On most issues, the *content* of ethics is the same for, say, a secular humanist and a Christian, although there are some issues where belief in grace, or a specific teaching, may make a difference.[14] Frequently, religious traditions have 'blazed a trail' with respect to a moral value, for example, Jesus's regard for children, but once the trail is blazed, then many secular people will follow it. Sometimes too, secular people 'blaze a trail' which religious people come to follow, as in the pioneering work of some secular utilitarians in prison reform, or some of the early proponents of the liberation of women. Similarly, the atheist Charles Bradlaugh[15] is one of my personal, though purely secular, heroes. Much of the time, the difference between Christian and secular ethics is not a matter of *content*, but a matter of the *status* of the principles involved. For a Christian, the principle that we should respect persons is rooted, at least in part, in the belief that every person has an intrinsic value that results from being a unique individual whose very existence reflects a divine purpose. Each person is an integral part of the great tapestry that God is weaving. The result is that – with respect to the value of the individual person – although there is common ground with the secular humanist – Christians are able to provide a deeper and more adequate account of why persons have intrinsic worth.

A range of acceptable lifestyles

Although this book does not intend to survey the whole field of practical Christian ethics, some issues concerning human sexuality are integrally related to the holding of an unblind faith.

In chapter 3 we noticed that in the early church there was a tendency to believe that although the married life was acceptable, the celibate state was intrinsically more noble. Many Christians are highly suspicious of this elevation of one kind of calling above another, although most accept that celibacy is a genuine spiritual call for some men and women. However, there is nothing 'lower' about the expression of human sexuality, provided that, like everything else, it is in accordance with love and responsibility.

In recent decades, a more relaxed approach to a range of legitimate lifestyles has taken on a new prominence because of the discussion of homosexuality. It is important to appreciate that new features of this debate are the well-founded claims (i) that homosexual activity is very common in the animal world, (ii) that this activity may be 'natural' in having a Darwinian explanation in terms of behaviour that helps a species to survive (for example, by reducing tension among males excluded from the herd), and (iii) a significant minority of adult human beings find that their sexual inclinations are exclusively homosexual.[16]

In the case of human beings, the extent to which homosexual orientation is biologically programmed is controversial. There is no evidence for a single 'gay gene', but some studies, especially those of twins reared apart (whose early environments are different), may indicate that there are genetic factors in homosexuality. However, because of scientific controversies concerning how to interpret these studies, I am leaving *open* the possibility of genetic factors in homosexual orientation.[17] Nevertheless, the new evidence concerning orientation (either because of biology or early environment or a combination of the two) is important. In the past it was understandable that people could think that all sexual preferences were matters of *choice*, and this encouraged the view that there could be universal rules about appropriate sexual behaviour that applied to all people. Perhaps, even in the past, sexual rules were unnecessarily rigid, but my point is that new knowledge has forced all rational and kindly people to reassess what these rules should be – whether one is Christian or not. In particular, we have to ask whether traditionalists are justified in demanding that those who, as adults, find that they have only homosexual orientations, are morally bound to be celibate.

It is very important to be careful about the implications of biological factors, if they are established. If it is the case that – for some people – a homosexual orientation is wholly or partly the result of biology (or of early environmental factors), this does not immediately lead to the conclusion that it is permissible to follow it. Many 'natural' inclinations, such as anger, have to be tempered or managed by the virtuous person. Nevertheless, the fact (whether or not the cause is biological) that some people – as adults – find that they have exclusively homosexual orientations has important consequences. Some traditionalists have argued that 'nature' gives us *the* purpose of sexuality, namely procreation, and have then gone on to claim that any sexual activity that knowingly frustrates this overarching purpose must be wrong. In contrast, I am suggesting that – quite apart from theological considerations – 'nature' seems to endow sexuality with at least two purposes, namely procreation and the cementing of relationships that are expressions of genuine love, that make life happier, and that – as a result – reduce tensions (which, in turn, may help to promote procreation). Even the ordinary observation of those birds who mate for life (watching how they respond to each other), suggests that there is more to the bond than a striving for reproduction.

Prior to adulthood there is a strong case for a conservative approach in both heterosexual and homosexual sexual relations, in part because of the danger of sexually transmitted diseases, in part because of the likelihood that some actions may trivialize (and thus reduce the potency of) an activity that can have the power to symbolize and cement seriously committed relationships and, perhaps, most importantly, because there is unlikely to be the wisdom to know when there is a real danger of causing hurt to another person. In the case of homosexuality, there is also the problem that young people cannot be certain of their eventual orientation, and what is done at an early age can impact on this.

With respect to adults, not all reflective Christians agree about what the appropriate moral rules on this matter should now be, nor on how to interpret Biblical references to homosexuality,[18] and in this short discussion I do not propose to settle the issues but only to show how and why an increasing number of Christians tend to favour the moral legitimacy of a wider range of lifestyles than in the past. One of the reasons for change is a realization of the importance of listening to different voices (even if one does not always agree with them). Formerly it was often a case of men laying down the law about how women should behave, without listening to the voices of women,[19] and similarly, I am nervous about married people, such as myself, laying down the law about how those with gay or Lesbian orientations should live, without listening to their voices.[20]

However, in my view, there is one moral principle in the area of sexual relations that should be treated as absolute, namely that we should always treat all persons as ends in themselves, and not merely as means. This principle – I would argue – is an example of one of those universal parts of the moral law, referred to by St Paul in Romans 2, 14–15, that should be seen as binding on all people, be they Christians or members of another faith or secular humanists. Moreover, this principle, which is often seen as an implication of the Golden Rule, has huge practical implications for sexual and all other inter-personal relationships. For example, it is hard to see how casual or promiscuous relationships can possibly accord with this demand, because outside a relationship in which the other person is both known and valued, how can one be sure that the other is not being 'used' – as a kind of 'commodity'? The use of another person for our own gratification, without taking into account their long-term interests, is wrong. 'Respect for persons' lies at the heart of morality, and the Christian doctrine of love, based on both the example and the teaching of Jesus, far from rejecting this principle, gives it an even higher status.

The challenge and excitement of a Christian life

When I was a small boy, I used to wish that I lived in an age or place of real adventure. I wanted to have fought in the Wars of the Roses, or to have taken part in some of the adventures recounted by Tolkien. I think that I am now more realistic. One reason is that I have some idea what it would actually have been like to have fought in the Wars of the Roses which, for those taking part, was anything but romantic. However, the most substantial reason is that every human life has all the drama and excitement it needs, if only we pay sufficient attention to the significance of what is going on within us and around us. Let me try to describe this in terms of three concentric circles.

First, and most immediately, there is the battle within the inner circle of our own selves. I have argued that becoming a person is a process of emergence which involves a spiritual struggle that is every bit as dramatic and significant as the battles we read about in history. Moreover, this is the one battle in which *we* are always able to play a decisive role. If the Christian faith is true, then, with the help of God, here is a battle that we *can* win, but which we may easily not win. Sometimes the battle seems like a boring grind, but it can hardly be more of a boring grind than the actual historical campaigns that we tend to romanticize. The proper way to see these periods of tedium is as challenges of a special sort, for the painful side of the struggle against evil within us is only sometimes manifested in an obvious crisis of conscience, as when we face a dramatic temptation. Equally important is the challenge to accept the periods of growth in which nothing seems to be happening and when boredom itself is part of the temptation.

Within the spiritual life this acceptance of periods of time in which nothing spectacular seems to be happening, and a strong personal discipline is needed in order to keep going, is especially true in the practice of prayer. As one poet has put it, "Prayer is like watching for the kingfisher ... but sometimes, when you've almost stopped expecting it, a flash of brightness gives encouragement".[21]

At the opposite extreme to boredom, or to what theologians used to call 'accidie' (a kind of spiritual sloth or sense of being fed up) is the experience of really strong temptation. For many this takes a sexual form – not because sexual passion is wrong in itself – but because so often it carries a powerful temptation to do things that we believe to be wrong. Looking back on his youth, Sophocles described having a sexual drive as like being a slave to a madman (or being 'chained to a madman'), and was glad to be rid of it![22] For others the most powerful impulses that need control may concern anger, ambition, pride, envy, avarice, laziness, etc. In one form or another, almost everybody faces battles in these arenas, and it may be helpful to realize that despite the pain, these battles are often the contexts in which personal and spiritual growth takes place.

Second, there is the circle of our friends and others with whom we are in immediate contact. Although each person has his or her own private story, we can profoundly influence other people through the way in which we represent the good, or fail to represent it. My friend or neighbour's fall or despair is, in part, my fault, for we are 'our brother's keeper'. If I take a bribe, or get involved in a shady business deal, or fail to do my best to make my marriage a success, or fail in one of the countless other situations that I face, I contribute to the decay of society and the injustices of the world. It is amazing how many outwardly respectable people are involved in one kind of misdeed or another, or are failing to fulfil some basic duty towards others and, because the effects on other people are not always obvious, such actions or lack of actions tend to be condoned by the conscience. "Anyway, everybody's doing it," we tend to say. But in what we do and in what we do not do, we help to create the quality of life around us. If people matter, can one ask for something more significant than this?

Third, there is the level of the world order, about which we so often feel helpless. What can I do about the torture of political prisoners, or starving children, or the pollution of the atmosphere, and so on? But of course, it is precisely because most people take the attitude that they can do nothing about such things that these problems exist. We can make a small difference, through the way we wage our personal battle and the battle at the level of the second circle, and it is only by everyone taking these battles seriously that the global battle can be fought. Moreover, in some cases we can have a direct input in the global battle, albeit – for most of us – a very small one: for example, by supporting an organization that works for political prisoners or starving children, or by working for them. Further, we can never rule out the possibility that an apparently small act of goodness may have momentous consequences. (Further still, organizations such as Avaaz.org have recently enabled ordinary people, via the internet, to have a direct input into some events that are of world-wide concern, such as the stoning to death of people in Iran.)

All told, there is no lack of exciting and meaningful adventure in this world; the problem is our blindness to the significance of what is right in front of us.

Finally, let me attempt to link the foregoing remarks to the theme of love and that first commandment without which everything else is wasted. Love is the theme that binds together the theoretical understanding of the Christian faith, with which I have been primarily concerned throughout this book, and the practical side of the Christian faith.

Let us suppose we are looking back over our lives a few hours before death, say from a known disease or from execution. What is it that we shall most regret? Surely, with the sense of perspective that this situation would give us, many of the things that we have cherished would seem futile. What does it really matter that I landed that job or had that reputation or made that money? Soon I shall be dead and then all these things will mean nothing. But there are some things that we shall look back on with a sense of real satisfaction. "Well, whatever happens, that was good!" If we have any sense of real values, these things will involve the awareness of something beautiful, especially in the form of some good relationship with other people. "That was a real friendship"; "Mary and I really had something going together"; "that was a great time when we were all together as a family"; "that musical performance in which I shared (as a performer or listener) had a never-to-be forgotten quality", and so on. Such memories, and the events which lie behind them, including all those in which there was special courage or kindness – or special moments of pleasure in the attention paid to what is good or true or beautiful – have a kind of *intrinsic* value, that may, as it were, resonate through the rest of time.

Similarly, the things that we shall most regret will often be failures in matters that concern those close to us. "If only ... ." Perhaps the greatest pains of the next life, for the good and for the bad, will be the sense of having missed this or that opportunity to show love to someone, an opportunity that can never be repeated. Think of the potential pain of truly evil people if ever they grow enough to realize the vastness of the opportunities for love that have been missed. Perhaps this is the real meaning of hell.

But the last note must be of hope. Christians believe that love is not only the highest value, in terms of which life must be measured, it is also the name for that ultimate reality that has created this whole order and governs it in his own mysterious way, using earthen vessels like ourselves. So although what has not been done in the name of love represents a tragic loss, there is the future and the prospect of creative action to come, both in the rest of this life and for all eternity.

Notes

1   Among many books giving good practical guidance on prayer see Mark Gibbard, *Why Pray*, SCM Press, 1970, and other books by this author.

2   J. G. Frazer, *The Golden Bough*, vol. 1 (of 12, 1907–15), pp. 220 ff. *Cf.* B. Malinowski, *Magic, Science an Religion*, Anchor, 1954, pp. 87ff.

3   1 John, 4, 19.

4   John, 12, 12.

5   Ep. 130 (*To Proba*), VIII, 17, PL 33.500 quoted in P. Baelz, *Prayer and Providence*, SCM Press, 1968, p. 112.

6   John 15, 7.

7   John 15, 5.

8   Matt. 26, 39.

9   II Cor. 12, 9 (AV, reading 'you' for 'thee').

10   See chapter 2, *Faith and the idea of God*.

11   Ecclus. (Also known as 'The Wisdom of Ben Sirach') 38, 24–34 (RV).

12   Eph. 4, 1.

13   Gen. 12, 1–4; Ex. 3, 10–11.

14   An interesting example is provided by the ethics of starting a nuclear war in which the whole of humanity might be exterminated. A secular case can be made for the claim that in some circumstances such extermination might be a lesser evil than millennia of cruel

dictatorship. For a strict utilitarian, zero pleasure and pain is better than any overall negative number. A Christian – I would argue – could never take such a position, because belief in grace would liken the terrible scenario to the exile in Babylon, and would conclude that God would eventually bring good out of the evil. Of course, many secularists would concur, but their reasoning could not be based on this belief in grace.

15   Charles Bradlaugh, 1833–1891, was a radical politician who fought for a series of of reforms regarding freedom of speech and the right to affirm (as an alternative to swearing on the Bible).

16   For scientific data on these topics one could begin with A. F. Dixson, *Primate Sexuality*, Oxford, OUP, 1998; F. de Waal, *Peacemaking Among Primates*, Harvard UP, 1989; and the scientific journal, *Animal Behaviour Abstracts*, Maryland. Surveys of adults suggest that somewhere around 2% of people have exclusively homosexual orientations.

17   Among important studies is T. J. Bouchard et al., *Psychological Differences: The Minnesota Study of Twins Reared Apart*, in *Science*, 1990, 250: 223–8, published by the American Association for the Advancement of Science.

18   References in the Old Testament (mostly in Leviticus) run into the difficulty that many injunctions are generally thought to be obsolete or reflective of a primitive outlook (such as the demand that those who curse their father or mother should be put to death – Lev. 20, 9). The gospels make no direct reference to the topic and St Paul, especially in Romans 1, is thought by some commentators to be condemning (rightly) a range of Roman practices such as the sexual exploitation of children. The application to (say) two forty-year-olds in a life-long, same-sex, committed relationship, is highly controversial. (Personally, because he came from an orthodox Jewish background, I suspect that Paul did intend to condemn all homosexual practices, and not only exploitative ones, but the question remains concerning how far Paul's views on this matter are definitive for contemporary Christians.) For a well-reasoned reading of these texts (with generally conservative conclusions), see Richard B. Hays, *The Moral Vision of the New Testament*, T and T Clark, Edinburgh, 1996, ch. 16. One problem with Hays' position is that if his argument is to support a universal moral teaching (corresponding to the universal morality of Romans 2, 14–15), rather than a matter of a specially Christian vocation (corresponding to a 'positive Divine Law'), then his conclusions need to be backed with some kind of non-Biblical argument that has some force for non-Christians.

19   See Carol Gilligan, *In a Different Voice*, Harvard University Press, 1982.

in this book, an interesting distinction is made between the ethics of justice and the ethics of care, a distinction that highlights (although it does not exactly mirror) the difference between male and female voices.

20   Stanley Hauerwas is an example of a theologian who seeks to listen to the voice of gay and Lesbian Christians, for example in his *Sanctify Them in the Truth*, T and T Clark, Edinburgh, 1998, ch. 6.

21   Ann Lewin, 'Disclosure', in *The Lion Book of Christian Poetry*, compiled by Mary Batchelor, Lion Hudson, Oxford, 2005.

22   Plato, *Republic*, 329c.

Epilogue

1. Re Chapter 1. Ideally, more should be said on the nature of 'rationality'. I have expanded on this topic in my *A Liberal Theology for the Twenty-first Century* (Ashgate, 2001, pp. 13–22).

2. Re p. 158. Nanak, the first guru in Sikhism, advocated equality for men and women, but there are serious questions (e.g. in Sikh women's websites) concerning whether this has been achieved in the practice of Sikhism. A similar caveat should be added concerning some early Quaker practice, for example when the men and women met separately (which they did in some meetings) there were occasional complaints that the men had taken over the business affairs.

3. Re p. 173. Some scientific hypotheses, notably in cosmology, do relate to the universe as a whole. However, when these are not open to particular, empirical evidence many physicists think that there has occurred a blurring of the distinction between science and metaphysics. Similar remarks should be made concerning the suggestion, by some eminent scientists, that we can explain the extraordinary suitability of the universe, as a whole, for the production of human life by positing a multitude (perhaps infinitude) of universes. This is at least as controversial as the suggestion that there is an intelligent Mind that created the universe and is also – arguably – less 'economical' in terms of Ockam's razor.

4. A general comment on John Calvin is in order. My criticisms relate to his doctrines of divine sovereignty, and the related issues of predestination and free will. I also have serious problems with his account of the fall (allegedly leading to our total depravity), of the sacraments, and his approach to those he deemed to be heretics. However, I should put on record that when I read his famous Institutes, much of the time I sense that I am dealing with a great theologian, many of whose teachings I share.